Getting Started with Google Kubernetes Engine

Deploying scalable applications with Google Kubernetes Engine (GKE) cluster configuration and advanced networking

Nilanjana Saha

Nishanta Banik

www.bpbonline.com

First Edition 2025

ISBN: 978-93-6589-713-5

LIMITS OF LIABILITY AND DISCLAIMER OF WARRANTY

To View Complete BPB Publications Catalogue Scan the QR Code:

www.bpbonline.com

Dedicated to

Our beloved daughter:

Niharika

who reminds us every day that learning never stops

About the Authors

- **Nilanjana Saha** is a skilled Cloud DevOps Engineer with over 16 years of experience in cloud technologies. She is currently employed at RTL Germany as a platform engineer and product owner where she works on designing, automation, and deployment of highly scalable and reliable applications using cloud services and DevOps tools across multiple cloud environments. She has worked across various industries for global MNCs as well as start-ups in a fast-paced and agile environment, where she demonstrated her passion for building products to solve business problems. She holds a Google Cloud Certified - Professional Cloud Architect (2023) certification and values knowledge sharing and collaboration at work.

- **Nishanta Banik** is a seasoned IT professional with over 18 years of IT experience in cloud architecture, DevOps, automation, and infrastructure management. He is currently working as a freelancer as a Senior Cloud DevOps Consultant. He is based out of Germany. He has worked with clients in various industry verticals, including finance, insurance, healthcare, and manufacturing. He is passionate about mentoring and guiding IT professionals to upskill themselves and achieve their career goals. He holds several IT Certifications including Google Cloud Certified - Professional Cloud Architect (2023).

About the Reviewers

- Boasting over more than fifteen years of dynamic experience in the Information technology sector, **Thiago** specialized in designing, architecting, and automating mission-critical deployments across expansive infrastructures. His expertise lies in crafting robust CI/CD pipelines and configuring management tools with a strong focus on infra as code principles. Proficient in fostering seamless communication, fostering collaborative environments, and excelling in both team settings and independent projects, Thiago brings to the table advanced English proficiency and a hands-on approach, driven by a passion for problem-solving and delivering results. Renowned for his analytical acumen, Thiago consistently drives innovation by envisioning and implementing strategies and solutions.

- **Vaibhav Tupe** is a distinguished Technology Advisory Board Member and Engineering leader specializing in cybersecurity, cloud, and AI-ready data center infrastructure. With over 13 years of experience, he currently serves as a Technology Leader at Equinix USA, where he drives high-performance cloud interconnection, enabling private, secure hybrid and multi-cloud connectivity to accelerate digital transformation and AI adoption.

  As a trusted advisor to startups, Vaibhav provides insightful guidance on cybersecurity, cloud innovations, and emerging technologies, shaping scalable and secure enterprise solutions. As a senior IEEE member, he has published research papers and organized IEEE conferences, contributing to advancements in AI, cloud, security, and digital infrastructure. He is recognized for his thought leadership, mentoring high-performing teams, and driving transformative initiatives that improve efficiency and customer success.

  Beyond his professional contributions, Vaibhav is deeply committed to AI and technology literacy in rural areas. He actively develops digital curricula for rural colleges, organizes career mentorship programs, and speaks at technology conferences to promote inclusive innovation. His expertise at the intersection of cloud, security, and next-generation digital infrastructure drives his passion for building resilient, future-ready systems that advance global innovation.

Acknowledgements

This book was almost waiting to happen in our home. As a couple working mostly from home for the past few years, our evenings often revolve around technology—discussing ideas over our favorite tea, exchanging thoughts on the latest trends, and facing challenges together. Writing this book felt like a natural extension of those conversations, a way to capture and share what we have learned.

A huge thank you to our family and friends for their support, especially our daughter Niharika. Her curiosity, patience, and love have been a constant source of motivation for us. She has been part of this journey in her own way, often watching us work together.

We are deeply grateful to BPB Publications for their guidance in bringing this book to life. We would also like to thank our passionate colleagues we've met in Germany, who inspired us even more to share our knowledge.

Moving to Germany from India, was a decision driven by our thirst for deeper expertise and learning in the IT industry, and we've been fortunate to work alongside some of the brightest minds. Their insights, feedback, and shared experiences have shaped our understanding and, ultimately, this book.

Finally, to our readers—thank you for your interest and support. We hope this book makes your GKE journey smoother and maybe even sparks some of those tech discussions of your own.

Happy learning!

Preface

The only way to make sense out of change is to plunge into it,
move with it, and join the dance.

– Alan Watts

In a world of constant change, especially in the field of cloud computing, adaptability is key. This book is not a traditional textbook—it is a hands-on guide, written by engineers, for engineers. Over the years of working with **Google Kubernetes Engine** (**GKE**), we have gathered insights and practical knowledge that we wish we had when starting out. This book is our way of sharing that knowledge with you, in the hope that it will simplify your journey and make GKE more accessible, whether you are a beginner or an experienced IT professional.

GKE has rapidly become one of the most powerful platforms for managing containerized applications. As businesses increasingly rely on cloud computing, GKE stands out for its scalability, flexibility, and efficiency. With all its power, it can also be complex. That is where this book comes in. We have designed it to be a practical, hands-on resource that simplifies GKE, helping you get started quickly and build the skills you need to deploy and manage containerized applications confidently.

In the early chapters, we will start with the basics—introducing you to containerization and Kubernetes, setting the stage for your GKE experience. From there, we will guide you through the process of creating and configuring GKE clusters, deploying applications, and troubleshooting common issues. Each chapter is carefully crafted to focus on real-world scenarios, with step-by-step tutorials that give you hands-on experience with the platform. As you progress, you will explore advanced features like network policies, workload identity, and integration with tools like Helm and Argo CD.

By the time you reach the end of the book, you will be ready to architect, deploy, and maintain containerized applications on Google Cloud with confidence. Whether you are a student eager to learn, a developer looking to expand your skills, or an IT professional seeking to refine your expertise, this book will equip you with the knowledge to leverage the full power of GKE.

Our goal is simple: Make cloud-native application management easier and more approachable for everyone. We hope this book helps you take that first step into the world of GKE and empowers you to tackle complex cloud challenges with clarity and confidence.

Welcome to your journey with GKE!

Chapter 1: Introduction to Kubernetes and Containerization - This chapter begins by looking at why traditional applications struggle in today's fast-paced world and how containerization solves those problems. You will learn what containers are, why they are so useful, and how Kubernetes helps manage them efficiently. Think of this as your foundation for everything that follows in the book.

Chapter 2: Overview of Google Cloud Platform - Before diving into GKE, it is important to understand the basics of **Google Cloud Platform** (**GCP**). This chapter introduces you to GCP's key services and how they provide the backbone for running Kubernetes. We then explore GKE and how it makes Kubernetes easier to manage in the cloud.

Chapter 3: Creating and Configuring a GKE Cluster - Here is where things get hands-on! We walk you through setting up your first GKE cluster, configuring essential components, and making sure everything is running smoothly. By the end of this chapter, you will have a working cluster and the confidence to explore further.

Chapter 4: Setting Up Your GKE Environment - Setting up your environment properly is key to a smooth GKE experience. In this chapter, we cover the must-have tools and configurations to ensure you are ready to work with GKE efficiently. Think of this as setting up your workspace before getting started with real-world projects.

Chapter 5: Deploying Applications on GKE - Now comes the exciting part—getting your applications up and running on GKE. We cover everything from basic deployments to advanced tools like Helm and ArgoCD, helping you deploy, manage, and scale applications efficiently.

Chapter 6: Networking in GKE - Networking is crucial for making your applications work seamlessly. In this chapter, we break down GKE networking concepts in a simple way—how services communicate, how traffic flows, and how to optimize performance.

Chapter 7: Monitoring and Logging - Keeping an eye on your applications and infrastructure is vital. This chapter shows you how to use monitoring and logging tools to track performance, detect issues early, and keep everything running smoothly.

Chapter 8: Security in GKE - Security is not just an add-on—it is a necessity. Here, we cover how to protect your clusters, secure secrets, and follow best practices to ensure your applications remain safe from threats.

Chapter 9: Troubleshooting and Best Practices - Things do not always go as planned, so knowing how to troubleshoot is a must. We walk through common GKE issues, debugging techniques, and best practices to keep your clusters stable and efficient.

Chapter 10: Advanced Topics in GKE - In this final chapter, we will level up and explore advanced GKE features like workload identity, network policies, and managing complex applications. By the end, you will have a solid grasp of GKE's full potential.

Code Bundle and Coloured Images

Please follow the link to download the
Code Bundle and the ***Coloured Images*** of the book:

https://rebrand.ly/lfem7do

The code bundle for the book is also hosted on GitHub at **https://github.com/bpbpublications/Getting-Started-with-Google-Kubernetes-Engine**. In case there's an update to the code, it will be updated on the existing GitHub repository.

We have code bundles from our rich catalogue of books and videos available at **https://github.com/bpbpublications**. Check them out!

Errata

We take immense pride in our work at BPB Publications and follow best practices to ensure the accuracy of our content to provide with an indulging reading experience to our subscribers. Our readers are our mirrors, and we use their inputs to reflect and improve upon human errors, if any, that may have occurred during the publishing processes involved. To let us maintain the quality and help us reach out to any readers who might be having difficulties due to any unforeseen errors, please write to us at :

errata@bpbonline.com

Your support, suggestions and feedbacks are highly appreciated by the BPB Publications' Family.

Did you know that BPB offers eBook versions of every book published, with PDF and ePub files available? You can upgrade to the eBook version at www.bpbonline.com and as a print book customer, you are entitled to a discount on the eBook copy. Get in touch with us at :

business@bpbonline.com for more details.

At **www.bpbonline.com**, you can also read a collection of free technical articles, sign up for a range of free newsletters, and receive exclusive discounts and offers on BPB books and eBooks.

Piracy

If you come across any illegal copies of our works in any form on the internet, we would be grateful if you would provide us with the location address or website name. Please contact us at **business@bpbonline.com** with a link to the material.

If you are interested in becoming an author

If there is a topic that you have expertise in, and you are interested in either writing or contributing to a book, please visit **www.bpbonline.com**. We have worked with thousands of developers and tech professionals, just like you, to help them share their insights with the global tech community. You can make a general application, apply for a specific hot topic that we are recruiting an author for, or submit your own idea.

Reviews

Please leave a review. Once you have read and used this book, why not leave a review on the site that you purchased it from? Potential readers can then see and use your unbiased opinion to make purchase decisions. We at BPB can understand what you think about our products, and our authors can see your feedback on their book. Thank you!

For more information about BPB, please visit **www.bpbonline.com**.

Join our book's Discord space

Join the book's Discord Workspace for Latest updates, Offers, Tech happenings around the world, New Release and Sessions with the Authors:

https://discord.bpbonline.com

Table of Contents

CHAPTER 1
Introduction to Kubernetes and Containerization

Introduction

In this opening chapter, we explore the core principles of Kubernetes and containerization, the most integral concepts that one needs to understand before diving into **Google Kubernetes Engine** (**GKE**). The chapter begins with the difficulties faced while hosting traditional monolithic applications in dynamic and scalable settings. It subsequently introduces containerization, shedding light on the origins of containers and their role in encapsulating applications and their dependencies, ensuring uniformity across diverse environments. Following this, we delve into the foundational concepts of Kubernetes, which serves the primary function of orchestrating these containers.

Structure

The chapter covers the following topics:

- Evolution of infrastructure
- Need for containerization
- Docker
- Container orchestration
- Kubernetes

Objectives

By the end of this chapter, you will be able to understand why containers and Kubernetes came into existence and the basic concepts around container orchestration. You will also learn key differences between traditional virtual hypervisors and container engine. To get the foundation strong, you will learn about Docker, the purpose of container orchestration and basics of Kubernetes.

Evolution of infrastructure

Let us imagine that you need to set up a physical server which will host several applications, and the server has physical hardware on which operating system is installed. For simplicity, let us assume that we have hosted three applications A, B and C on our server.

Now, each of the applications needs different set of software like libraries and dependencies to function properly.

Generally, when we download the application installation package, and try to install it, we can see a message saying, **`Installing libraries and dependencies`**.

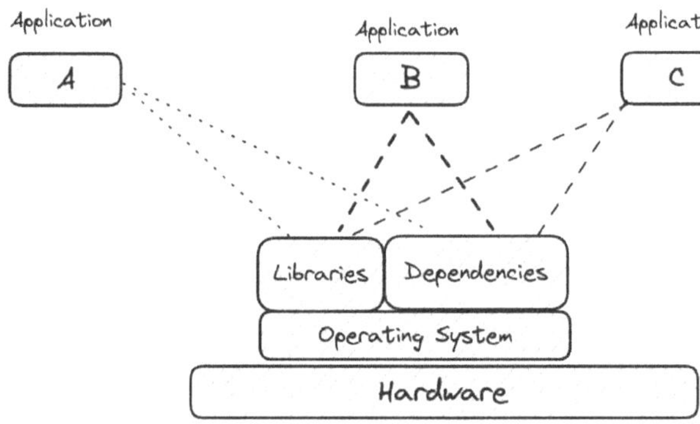

Figure 1.1*: Monolithic software architecture*

Now, let us say, application A needs a version 1 of some software and application B needs version 2 of the same software. If you install application A with its version 1 dependency, application B will not run. If we do the opposite, then application A will not run. Also, you need to keep a check on the compatibility of one application with another, every time you want to host a new application on the server or want to upgrade an existing application.

This situation has quite an appropriate name called **Matrix from Hell**.

For every additional application that you need to host on the same server, you will need to navigate through an endless number of software libraries and their dependencies which adds up to the confusion. It was very common a few years ago, that developers spent days or weeks configuring their system or server before they could actually start working in a new environment.

This complexity was fairly resolved with the advent of **virtual servers**. We now had a solution that on the same physical server, we could create partitions using the **virtual server hypervisor**. The hypervisor was layer between the hardware and the operating system which helped to create a logical separation. So instead of a common operating system, for every application we could create a logical box. In each of the box, we could now host its own operating system on which we could now install our application along with its packages.

So, every application could reside in one of its own virtual servers with its own version of operating system, libraries and dependencies. Hence, resolving the above-mentioned Matrix from Hell situation.

In the following figure, you can see the software architecture using virtual machines:

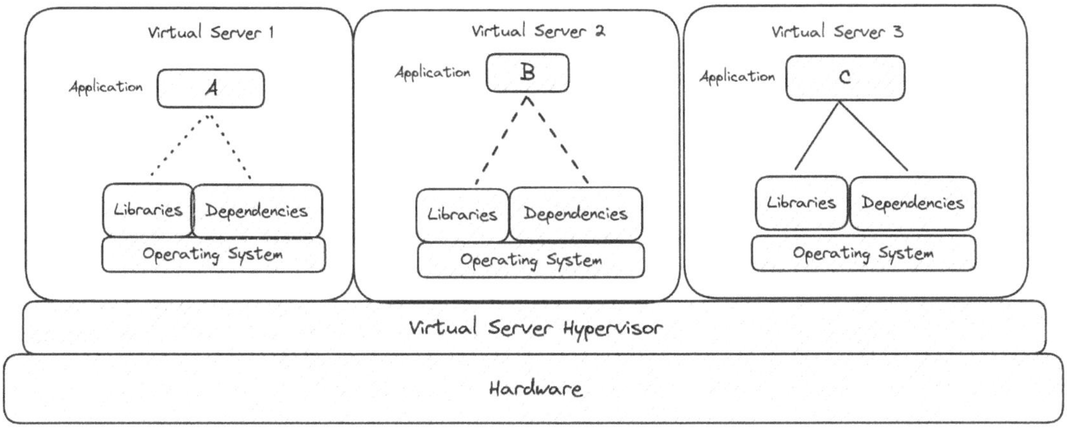

***Figure 1.2**: Software architecture using virtual machines*

Need for containerization

The concept of virtual servers is a great innovation in infrastructure setup and mostly in any standard enterprise environment. One of the drawbacks of using virtual servers is the number of resources and time required to build and run the system. Even in a minimal setup, you would need a good CPU, memory and disk space, and hence, over a period of time it can become quite expensive to use and maintain.

Now, let us look at the world of containers. Imagine that on the hardware and operating system, there is a logical layer which has the capability to share the bulkiest part of the operating system. So, every application still gets its own box with its own wrapper of libraries and dependencies, but it becomes light weight as it does not need to contain the entire operating system within itself. Specifically, the containers will share the operating system kernel, and it is able to function in isolation without interfering with another containers.

This logical unit is called **container engine** which runs on top of the operating system layer. In the following figure, you can see software architecture using container engine:

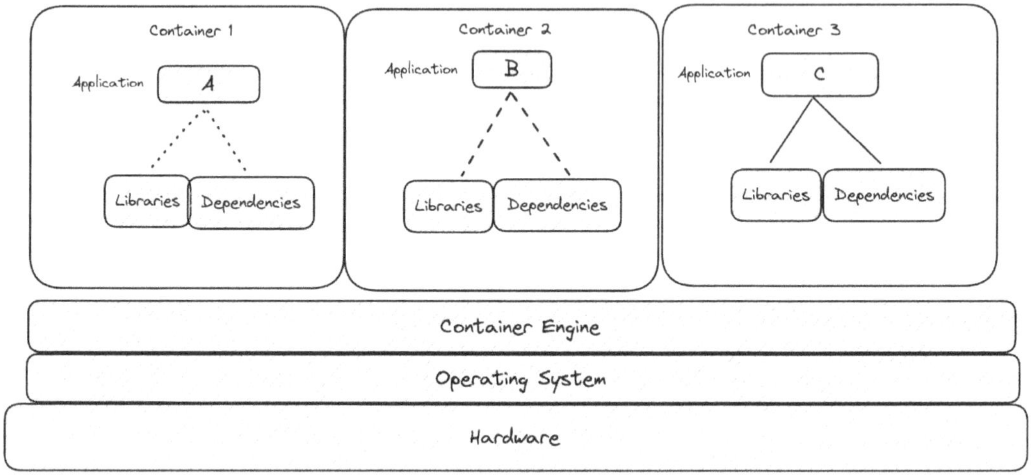

***Figure 1.3**: Software architecture using container engine*

While hosting the application, you no longer need to install any software, libraries or dependencies. You can simply choose to run the container on your existing system, and it will no longer ask you to install any prerequisite before accessing the application. Every container is a self-sustainable unit and if you get more users, you just need to get more number of containers via which you can scale your application quite easily.

To get accustomed to the world of containers, let us explore the basic understanding of common terms you will come across. This is shown in the following figure:

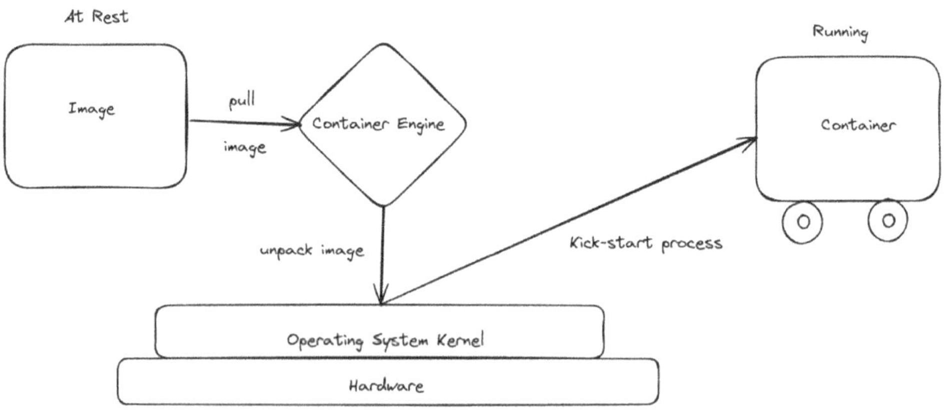

***Figure 1.4**: Image vs. container*

Just like any other program, there are two states of the container — at rest and running.

When it is at rest, it is typically a set of files and is called **image**.

When we type in the command to run the image, the container engine pulls a copy from a repository, unpacks its files and submits it to the operating system kernel. The kernel is the core of the operating system. It provides most of the critical services like starting, terminating, and scheduling of processes.

This running version of the image is called **container,** and it is just similar to running a process on the operating system kernel.

There are several container images formats, but the most standard and governed format is called **Open Container Initiative** (**OCI**). Since a similar format is used to build all images, they behave in the same manner as in any given system.

There are several container engines, for example, Docker, **Container Runtime Interface - Open Container Initiative** (**CRI-O**), RailCar, **Rocket** (**RKT**), and **Linux Containers** (**LXC**) etc.

Most popular container engine is Docker.

Docker

Docker is a containerization platform that allows you to package an application and its dependencies together in a standardized unit called a **container**. Understanding Docker helps you grasp the fundamental concepts of containerization, including how to create, deploy, and manage containers.

To get started with Docker, the easiest way is to get Docker Desktop.

You can follow the instructions in the link **https://docs.docker.com/get-docker/** to get Docker Desktop.

Important commands in Docker

We will quickly get acquainted with the common commands that you need to know to use Docker. These commands are as follows:

- **Docker run**: To create a container from an image:
  ```
  docker run nginx
  ```
- **Docker ps**: Gives a list of all running containers:
  ```
  docker ps -all
  ```
- **Docker stop**: This command is used to stop a running container:
  ```
  docker stop contaniner_id
  ```
- **Docker rm**: This command is used to remove a Docker container:
  ```
  docker rm my_container
  ```

- **Docker pull**: This command is used to download a Docker image from a registry:

  ```
  docker pull nginx
  ```

- **Docker network ls**: This command is used to know the details of the list of networks in the cluster:

  ```
  Docker network ls
  ```

- **Docker logs**: This command is used to check the logs of all the Docker containers:

  ```
  docker logs container_id
  ```

- **Docker exec**: This command is used to execute a command in a running container:

  ```
  docker exec -it container_id
  ```

- **Docker compose**: This command is used to manage multi-container Docker applications. You define the configuration of your application's services, networks, and volumes in a file called **`docker-compose.yml`**, and then use the **`docker-compose`** command to start and stop your application:

  ```
  docker-compose up
  docker-compose down
  ```

Container orchestration

In the last section, we have seen that containers can help us bundle up the applications and run them very quickly without the hassles of configuring the system.

Now imagine, we have some containers running on our system. For some reason, if one of the container fails, we need to manually start a new container again to take its place, or, if we suddenly get some new users accessing our application, *how do we scale up the containers on the go?* Would it not be better if we have a system to do this type of management automatically for us?

This is where container orchestration comes into the picture. As the name suggests, it helps us to orchestrate the containers. Container orchestration tools help automate the deployment, scaling, and management of containerized applications in a distributed computing environment.

The key aspects of container orchestration are as follows:

- **Deployment automation**: Orchestration tools facilitate the automated deployment of containerized applications. They define how containers should be created, deployed, and interconnected.
- **Scaling**: Container orchestration enables automatic scaling of applications based on demand. It can add or remove containers to ensure that the application can handle varying workloads efficiently.

- **Load balancing**: Orchestration tools often include load balancing mechanisms to distribute incoming traffic across multiple containers, ensuring optimal performance and resource utilization.
- **Service discovery**: Container orchestration helps in service discovery, allowing containers to find and communicate with each other within the same application or service.
- **Rolling updates and rollbacks**: Orchestration tools support rolling updates, enabling the seamless deployment of new versions of an application without downtime. If issues arise, they also facilitate easy rollbacks to previous versions.
- **Resource management**: Orchestration tools manage the allocation and utilization of computing resources (CPU, memory, storage) across containers and nodes in a cluster.
- **High availability**: Container orchestration ensures high availability by distributing containers across multiple nodes, making applications resilient to node failures.

Popular container orchestration tools are as follows:

- **Kubernetes**: One of the most widely adopted container orchestration platforms, Kubernetes provides a robust set of features for deploying, scaling, and managing containerized applications.
- **Docker Swarm**: Docker's native orchestration tool is simpler than Kubernetes and is suitable for smaller-scale deployments.
- **Apache Mesos**: A general-purpose cluster manager that can orchestrate both containers and other types of workloads.

Kubernetes

Kubernetes is an open-source platform for managing containers. The name Kubernetes originates from Greek, meaning helmsman or pilot. K8s as an abbreviation result from counting the eight letters between the *K* and the *s*. It was originally founded by *Google* and open-sourced in the year 2014. Since then, it has been rapidly growing and evolved as its own ecosystem.

When you deploy Kubernetes, you get a cluster, which mainly has mainly two components: The control plane which is the master, and the worker machines called as the **node**.

A Kubernetes cluster consists of a set of worker nodes that run containerized applications. Every cluster has at least one worker node. The worker node(s) host the **Pods** that are the components of the application workload. Container is encapsulated within a Pod and Pod is smallest unit that can exist in the cluster. The control plane manages the worker nodes and the Pods in the cluster. In production environments, the control plane usually runs across multiple computers and a cluster usually runs multiple nodes, providing fault-tolerance and high availability.

The following figure outlines the various components you need to have for a complete and working Kubernetes cluster:

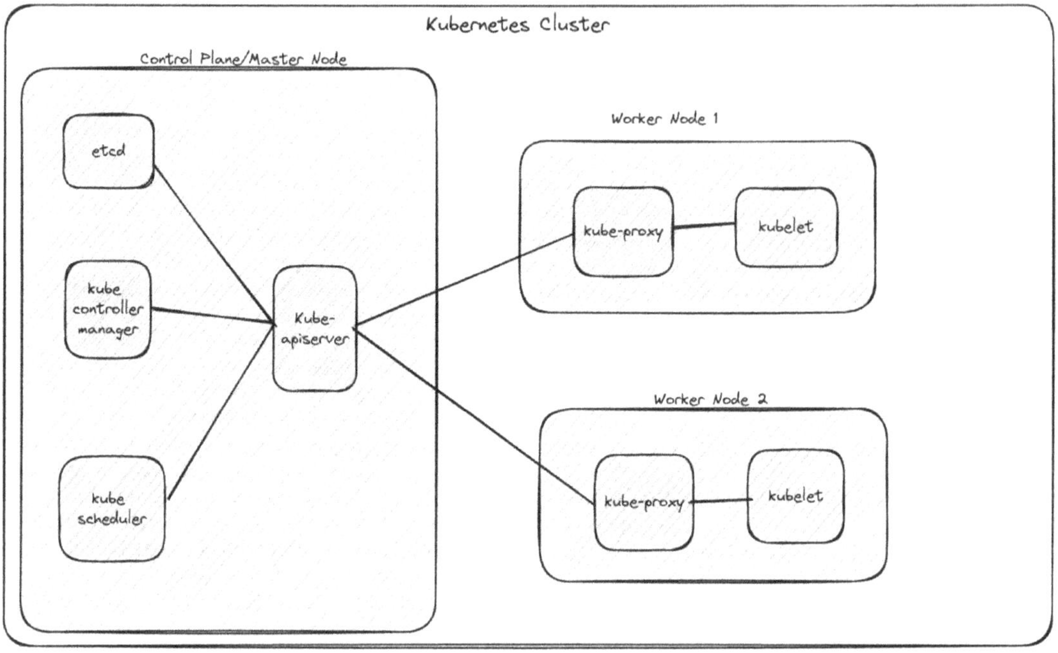

***Figure 1.5**: Kubernetes architecture*

Control plane components

The control plane is the brain of the Kubernetes cluster, managing and coordinating all activities.

It is the central management entity responsible for regulating and controlling the state of the entire system. It consists of a set of components that make global decisions about the cluster (for example, scheduling), as well as detecting and responding to cluster events (like starting up a new Pod when a deployment's replicas field is unsatisfied).

The main components of the control plane include:

- **Kube-apiserver**: The API server is the front end for the Kubernetes control plane and communicates with all other components across the Kubernetes cluster.
- **etcd**: A distributed key-value store that stores the cluster's configuration data. This data represents the state of the cluster at any given time.
- **Kube-controller-manager**: Runs controller processes, which are responsible for observing the state of the cluster and making necessary changes to achieve the

desired state. Examples of controllers include the ReplicationController, Node controller, and Endpoint controller.

- **Kube-scheduler**: Assigns Pods to nodes based on resource requirements, constraints, and other policies. It is responsible for distributing workloads across the cluster.

Node components

In Kubernetes, the node components are responsible for running and managing containers on each node in the cluster. These components work together to ensure that containers are scheduled, started, and run as expected. Here are the main node components in Kubernetes:

- **Kubelet**: The Kubelet is an agent that runs on each node in the cluster. It is responsible for making sure that containers are running in a Pod. It communicates with the control plane to receive instructions in the form of **Pod specifications** (**PodSpec**) and ensures that the containers described in those PodSpecs are running and healthy.
- **Kube-proxy**: Kube-proxy is a network proxy that runs on each node in the cluster. It maintains network rules on the nodes to allow communication to the Pods from network sessions inside or outside the cluster. It also provides a simple round robin load balancing of service connections.
- **Container runtime:** The container runtime is the software responsible for running containers. Kubernetes supports multiple container runtimes, with Docker being a popular choice. Other container runtimes include containerd, CRI-O, and others. The container runtime interacts with the underlying system to start, stop, and manage containers.

These node components work together to ensure the proper execution and networking of containers on each node:

- The Kubelet communicates with the control plane to receive PodSpecs and starts and stops containers accordingly.
- The Kube-proxy maintains network rules to enable communication between Pods and external entities.
- The container runtime runs and manages the containers, interacting with the operating system's kernel to isolate and manage the container processes.

Each node in the cluster has its own set of these components, and they collaborate to maintain the desired state of the containers and Pods on that node. The node components, along with the control plane components, collectively form the foundation of a Kubernetes cluster, enabling the orchestration of containerized applications at scale.

Common terms in Kubernetes ecosystem

Kubernetes comes with a set of specific terms and concepts that are essential to understanding how the platform works. Here is a summary of some common terms used in Kubernetes:

- **Cluster**: A collection of nodes that work together to run containerized applications. The cluster consists of a master node (control plane) and worker nodes.
- **Node**: A physical or virtual machine in the Kubernetes cluster where containers are deployed. Nodes are responsible for running Pods.
- **Pod**: The smallest deployable unit in Kubernetes. A Pod represents a single instance of a running process and can contain one or more containers that share the same network and storage.
- **Container**: A lightweight, standalone, and executable software package that includes everything needed to run a piece of software, including the code, runtime, libraries, and system tools.
- **Container runtime**: The software responsible for running containers. Docker, containerd, and CRI-O are examples of container runtimes.
- **Control plane**: The set of components that manage the overall state of the cluster. It includes the master node components like the API server, etcd, controller manager, and scheduler.
- **Master node**: The node that hosts the control plane components, including the API server, etcd, controller manager, and scheduler.

These terms provide a foundational understanding of Kubernetes and are essential for anyone working with container orchestration and application deployment using Kubernetes.

Now, let us look at some additional concepts which are also very important to understand Kubernetes:

- **Workloads**:
    - **Definition**: A workload is an application running on Kubernetes. Whether your workload is a single component or several that work together, on Kubernetes you run it inside a set of Pods.
- **Pod**:
    - **Definition**: As mentioned earlier, a Pod is the smallest deployable unit in Kubernetes. It represents a single instance of a running process in a cluster and can consist of one or more containers that share the same network namespace, storage, and specifications.

- **Use case**: Pods are used to deploy and manage containers in Kubernetes. They encapsulate one or more tightly coupled containers, such as those that need to share data volumes or network resources.

- **ReplicaSet**:
  - **Definition**: A ReplicaSet is a controller in Kubernetes that ensures a specified number of identical replicas (instances) of a Pod are running at all times. If the actual number of replicas deviates from the desired state, the ReplicaSet automatically adjusts by creating or deleting Pods.
  - **Use case**: ReplicaSets are useful for ensuring high availability and scalability of applications. They are often used in conjunction with Pods to maintain a desired number of running instances.
- **Deployment**:
  - **Definition**: A deployment is a higher-level abstraction that manages ReplicaSets. It allows you to declare the desired state for your application and handles the deployment, scaling, and updating of ReplicaSets accordingly. Deployments support rolling updates and rollbacks.
  - **Use case**: Deployments are commonly used to define and manage the lifecycle of applications. They abstract away the complexities of managing ReplicaSets and make it easier to roll out changes to your application.
- **Service**:
  - **Definition**: A service is an abstraction that defines a logical set of Pods and a policy by which to access them. It provides a stable endpoint (IP address and port) that other applications or services can use to communicate with the Pods.
  - **Use case**: Services enable communication between different Pods or external entities. They abstract away the details of Pod IP addresses and provide a reliable way to expose and consume application services within a Kubernetes cluster.

The following figure shows the hierarchy and interdependence of Kubernetes components:

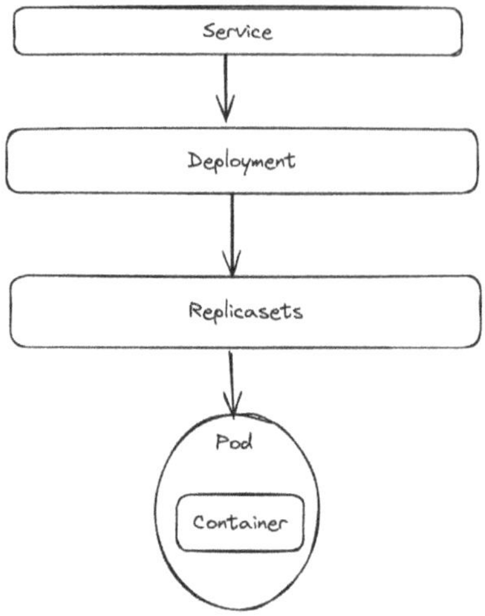

***Figure 1.6**: Hierarchy and interdependency of Kubernetes components*

Some more important terms are as follows:

- **Namespace:**
  - **Definition**: A namespace in Kubernetes is a way to divide cluster resources into multiple virtual clusters. It provides scope for names, and each namespace can have its own set of resources, such as Pods, services, and storage, without interfering with resources in other namespaces.
  - **Use case**: Namespaces are used to organize and isolate workloads, especially in multi-tenant environments or when different teams or projects share a Kubernetes cluster. They help prevent naming conflicts and provide a level of resource separation.
- **Ingress:**
  - **Definition**: Ingress is an API object in Kubernetes that provides HTTP and HTTPS routing to services based on rules. It acts as an entry point to the cluster and allows external access to services by exposing them to the external world.
  - **Use case**: Ingress is commonly used to enable external access to services within a Kubernetes cluster. It allows you to define rules for routing requests to different services based on paths, hostnames, or other criteria.
- **ConfigMap:**
  - **Definition**: A ConfigMap is a Kubernetes object used to store configuration data in key-value pairs. It allows you to decouple configuration from

application code and provides a way to configure applications or containers dynamically.

- **Use case**: ConfigMaps are used to store non-sensitive configuration data, such as environment variables, command line arguments, or configuration files. Applications can then read this configuration data at runtime, making it easier to manage and update configurations without modifying the application code.

- **Secret:**
  - **Definition**: A Secret is a Kubernetes object used to store sensitive information, such as passwords, API keys, and tokens. Secrets provide a secure way to handle confidential data and ensure it is not exposed in plaintext.
  - **Use case**: Secrets are used to manage and protect sensitive information required by applications, such as database passwords or API tokens. They are encoded and can be mounted into Pods as files or used as environment variables, allowing applications to access the secret data securely.
- **StatefulSets:**
  - **Definition**: StatefulSet is a controller in Kubernetes that allows you to run one or more related Pods that do track state somehow. It is often used for stateful applications where each Pod has a unique identity and persistent storage. StatefulSets are designed to maintain a consistent and unique network identity for each Pod.
  - **Use case**: StatefulSets are suitable for applications that require stable network identities, ordered Pod deployment, and persistent storage. Examples include databases like MySQL or stateful applications where the order of Pod creation and identity matter.
- **Persistent Volumes (PVs):**
  - **Definition**: PVs are a Kubernetes abstraction for storage resources in a cluster. They represent physical storage provisioned by an administrator and can be dynamically or statically provisioned.
  - **Use case**: PVs provide a way for applications to access persistent storage in a cluster. They are used to store data that should persist beyond the lifespan of individual Pods, ensuring data durability and persistence for stateful applications like databases, file systems, or any workload requiring long-term storage. PVs abstract the details of underlying storage technologies, allowing Pods to claim and use storage resources without being tied to the specifics of the storage implementation.

- **DaemonSet:**
  - **Definition**: DaemonSet is a controller in Kubernetes that defines Pods providing facilities local to nodes. It ensures that a copy of a Pod runs on every node in the cluster, allowing for local, node-specific operations. DaemonSets are often used for cluster-wide tasks or node-level services.
  - **Use case**: DaemonSets are useful for running node-level agents or services, such as monitoring agents, log collectors, or network plugins. They ensure that a specific Pod runs on each node, providing node-local functionality.
- **Job:**
  - **Definition**: A Job in Kubernetes defines a task that runs to completion just once. It creates one or more Pods to perform a particular job, and once the job is done, the Pods terminate.
  - **Use case**: Jobs are suitable for tasks that run to completion, such as batch processing, data backup, or any task that needs to be executed once.
- **CronJob:**
  - **Definition**: A CronJob in Kubernetes is similar to a Job but allows you to run the same Job multiple times according to a specified schedule, similar to a cron job in Unix-like systems.
  - **Use case**: CronJobs are useful for recurring tasks that need to be executed at specified intervals, such as periodic data processing, cleanup, or regular maintenance tasks.
- **Persistent Volume Claims (PVCs):**
  - **Definition**: PVCs are a Kubernetes abstraction used by applications to request storage resources from PVs. A PVC specifies the desired storage size, access mode, and other attributes required by the application, and Kubernetes will find a matching PV or dynamically provision one to satisfy the claim.
  - **Use case**: PVCs allow applications to request and use persistent storage without needing to manage the underlying infrastructure. They are used in scenarios where the application requires persistent data, such as in databases or other stateful applications. PVCs decouple the application from the underlying storage, providing flexibility in managing storage resources. By using PVCs, users can request storage dynamically and ensure that data survives Pod restarts or rescheduling across different nodes in the cluster.

These Kubernetes objects contribute to the overall flexibility, security, and manageability of containerized applications in a Kubernetes environment.

Conclusion

To sum it up, in this chapter, we explored how technology infrastructure has evolved over time. We talked about the basics of containerization, which is like packing applications in containers for easy management. Containers offer many benefits, and we discussed the importance of orchestrating them effectively.

We have explored Docker, a tool that helps with container management, and learned some key commands. Then, we focused on Kubernetes, a powerful platform for orchestrating containers at scale. We covered its essential components of Kubernetes and got an overview of most commonly used terms in Kubernetes world.

As you continue reading, in the next chapter, you will gain a deeper understanding of Google Cloud Platform. With that we build a solid foundation which will be valuable in navigating the GKE. So, get ready to explore more and be well-prepared for the exciting challenges ahead!

Multiple choice questions

1. **What is the primary purpose of containerization in modern IT infrastructure?**
    a. Enhancing network security
    b. Efficiently managing and deploying applications
    c. Optimizing database performance
    d. Minimizing server hardware costs
2. **Which of the following best describes Docker?**
    a. An operating system
    b. A container orchestration platform
    c. A programming language
    d. A containerization tool
3. **What role does Kubernetes play in container orchestration?**
    a. Managing network security
    b. Scaling server hardware
    c. Orchestrating and automating containerized applications
    d. Optimizing database queries
4. **Which components are part of the control plane in Kubernetes?**
    a. Pods and nodes
    b. Containers and images

c. API server and controller manager

d. Load balancer and Ingress

5. **Why is understanding container orchestration important in modern IT?**

    a. It reduces electricity consumption in data centers

    b. It enables efficient management and scaling of containerized applications

    c. It enhances the graphics rendering capabilities of applications

    d. It automates software development processes

Answers

1	b
2	d
3	c
4	c
5	b

Join our book's Discord space

Join the book's Discord Workspace for Latest updates, Offers, Tech happenings around the world, New Release and Sessions with the Authors:

https://discord.bpbonline.com

CHAPTER 2
Overview of Google Cloud Platform

Introduction

In this chapter, we begin by establishing a foundation in **Google Cloud Platform** (**GCP**) fundamentals, ensuring that readers have a solid understanding of the cloud infrastructure that underpins GKE. We look at key components and processes involved in Google Cloud. Then, we transition into the basics of GKE.

Structure

The chapter covers the following topics:

- Introduction to Google Cloud platform
- Overview of GCP's global infrastructure
- GCP resource hierarchy
- GCP compute products
- Exploring GCP with Google Cloud
- GCP networking for GKE
- Introduction to Google Kubernetes Engine

Objectives

By the end of this chapter, you will gain a comprehensive understanding of GCP and GKE, the synergy between them, and get a grip of the core fundamentals in GCP.

Introduction to Google Cloud Platform

Google Cloud Platform, in a general sense, is like a super convenient and flexible way to use infrastructure, without having to worry about the technical setup of the hardware. Hence, the cloud products are called managed services. It is like renting a ready-to-go setup for whatever you need. The key benefits that a Google Cloud Platform provides us are as follows:

- **Save money**: Instead of buying lots of expensive computer hardware, you can rent it as you need it. This means you only pay for what you use.
- **Global footprint**: You can access your files and programs from anywhere with the internet. It is like having your applications easily accessible wherever you go.
- **Scalability**: If you need more computer power, you can get it really quickly. In case you do not need it, you can easily give it back. It is like having a computer that can get bigger or smaller whenever you want. This feature is called scalability.
- **Low latency**: It is easier for people to work on projects together globally. They can all use the same computer programs and share information more easily and quickly.
- **Security**: The companies that provide cloud services work hard to keep your information safe. They have special ways of protecting your applications.
- **High availability**: Your applications are almost always available. Even if something goes wrong, there are backup plans to make sure you can still get to your files and programs. Every cloud service provider ensures to maintain high availability of the underlying infrastructure and its services.
- **Fault tolerance**: You do not have to worry about fixing and updating your infrastructure or computer hardware. The cloud service provider will take care of all that for you.
- **Sustainability**: Using the cloud can be good for the environment. It is similar to using energy more efficiently, which helps save the planet.

GCP is a suite of cloud computing products provided by *Google*, offering a wide range of infrastructure and services. It enables businesses to build, deploy, and scale applications efficiently. GCP provides a comprehensive set of tools and services for computing, storage, databases, data analytics, machine learning, and more facilitating the development of innovative and scalable solutions. Each service plays a crucial role in supporting different aspects of application development, data management, and infrastructure operations.

Overview of GCP's global infrastructure

Google Cloud operates an extensive global network of data centers, strategically distributed around the world. This infrastructure ensures low-latency access to GCP services from virtually any location. The key elements of GCP's global infrastructure include:

- **Regions and zones**: GCP is organized into regions, each containing multiple zones. Regions are geographically separate areas, and zones are data centers within those regions. This structure enhances redundancy and fault tolerance. For example, the us-west1 region denotes a region on the west coast of the *United States* that has three zones: us-west1-a, us-west1-b, and us-west1-c. Refer to *Figure 2.1.*
- **Global load balancing**: GCP's global load balancers distribute traffic across multiple regions, ensuring high availability and reliability.
- **Interconnected network**: GCP's high-performance network backbone connects its global data centers, facilitating fast and secure data transfer.

This global infrastructure forms the foundation for scalable, reliable, and performant cloud services on GCP. The following figure shows an example region and its zones in Google's Cloud infrastructure:

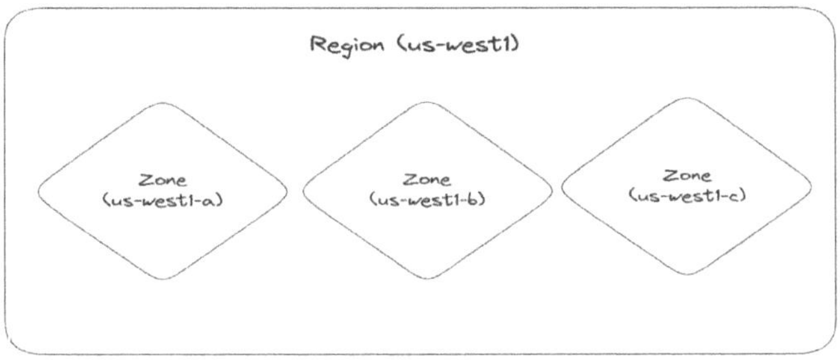

***Figure 2.1**: GCP global scope*

GCP resource hierarchy

In GCP, the hierarchical structure helps in organizing, managing, and securing GCP resources effectively based on organizational needs and requirements. Some of them are as follows:

- **Organization**: Top-level billing entity typically associated with the company. An organization contains folders.
- **Folder**: Useful for organizing resources based on departments, teams, or projects. Folders contain projects.
- **Project**: Projects contain resources which are deployed to specific regions and zones. All resources within a project share the same project ID and project number.

The following figure shows the resource hierarchy:

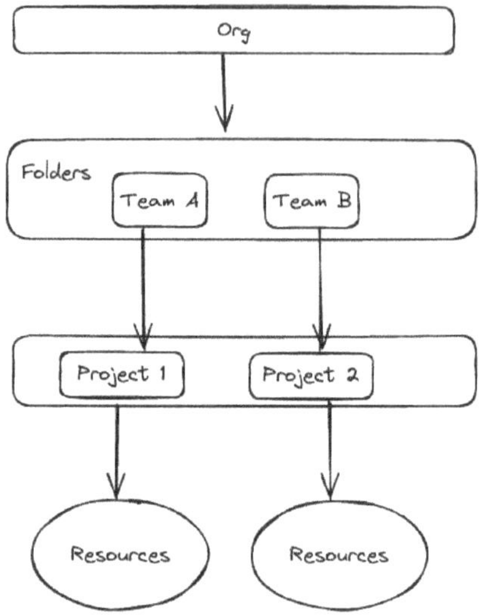

***Figure 2.2**: Resource hierarchy*

GCP compute products

In terms of resources, GCP offers a variety of infrastructure or compute products, that cater to different use cases and preferences. When it comes to building things in the cloud, it depends on two main factors: independence and control. When you want to be more independent (which means less responsibilities to manage infrastructure), you lose the control of infrastructure. If you want more control, then you must also take more responsibility to manage the infrastructure.

The following are the key examples of GCP compute products and how they can fit different use cases:

- **Full independence with Google App Engine (PaaS)**: Imagine you want to focus only on your code, and you do not want to bother with servers or infrastructure. That is where Google App Engine comes in. It is like having your own space to deploy applications. You give it your code, and it takes care of everything else be it scaling, balancing, or maintenance. You have the freedom to create without worrying about the nitty-gritty details of infrastructure or hardware. This is called **platform as a service** (**PaaS**) and the GCP compute product is known as Google App Engine.
- **Balanced independence and automation with Google Cloud Functions (FaaS)**: Imagine you have little tasks that should happen by themselves, or you need something specific to occur when an event takes place. However, most of the time, you do not want anything running. Enter Google Cloud Functions, your

own digital genie for these tasks. Just let it know what you want, and it handles everything. It is perfect for fast tasks without dealing with all the infrastructure details. This is known as **function as a service** (**FaaS**), and Google Cloud's version is called **Google Cloud Functions**.

- **Control over VMs with Google Compute Engine (IaaS)**: Maybe you want control over the **virtual machines** (**VMs**) and the whole setup. Google Compute Engine lets you have that control. It is like having your own workshop with all the tools and materials. You decide how your VMs are set up, what software to install, and how to manage them. This falls under the category of **infrastructure as a service** (**IaaS**), and in the world of Google Cloud, it is known as **Google Compute Engine**.
- **Container control with GKE (CaaS)**: For those who want control but also love using containers (little packages for your applications), there is GKE. It is like having your own container orchestra. You decide how to organize and manage your containers, but you do not have to worry about the heavy lifting of orchestration. GKE takes care of that for you. This falls under the umbrella of container as a service, and in the Google Cloud universe, it is known as **GKE**.

There is another product called **Google Cloud Run**. It is a fully managed, serverless compute platform that enables developers to deploy and run containerized applications effortlessly. With Cloud Run, you focus on writing code, package it into a container, and Cloud Run takes care of the rest: handling scaling, managing infrastructure, and charging you only for the actual resources used. It is perfect for developers who want simplicity without sacrificing flexibility, making deployment, and scaling as easy as clicking a button.

In a nutshell, GCP gives you choices. Whether you want the freedom to create without worrying about infrastructure (App Engine), quick automation without managing servers (Cloud Functions), full control over VMs (Compute Engine), or container control without the orchestration hassle (Kubernetes Engine), or a fully managed, serverless option (Cloud Run), GCP has the right tools to match your style of building in the cloud.

The following figure illustrates the range of GCP compute products, showing how they balance independence and control based on different use cases:

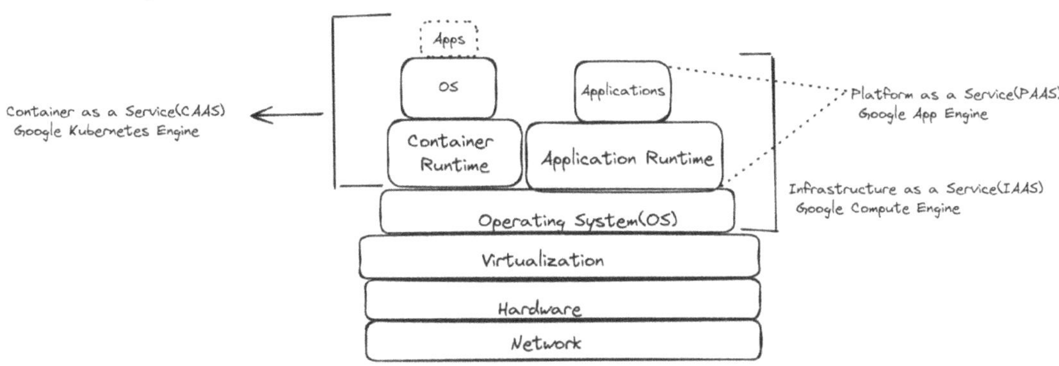

Figure 2.3: GCP compute products (independence vs. control)

Creating a GCP account is a straightforward process. The following is a step-by-step guide:

1. **Visit the GCP Console**: Go to the GCP Console at **https://console.cloud.google.com/** as shown in the following figure:

Figure 2.4: GCP login page

2. **Sign in or create a Google account**: If you already have a Google account, sign in with your existing credentials. If not, click on **Create account** to set up a new Google account.
3. **Fill in your information**: Follow the prompts to provide the necessary information, including your first and last name, desired email address (which will be your GCP username), and a secure password.
4. **Accept the terms and conditions**: Read through Google's terms of service and privacy policy. If you agree, check the box indicating that you accept the terms.
5. **Set up a billing account**: To use GCP services, you need to set up a billing account. You will be prompted to enter your billing information, including credit card details. Google Cloud often provides a free trial with a certain amount of credits, allowing you to explore GCP services without immediate charges.
6. **Verify your account**: Google may ask you to verify your account through a verification code sent to your provided email or phone number. Follow the verification steps to confirm your identity.

7. **Access the GCP Console**: Once your account is set up and verified, you can access the GCP Console. This is the central hub for managing your GCP resources, projects, and services. You can now create your own project by first selecting **NEW PROJECT** option as shown in the following figure:

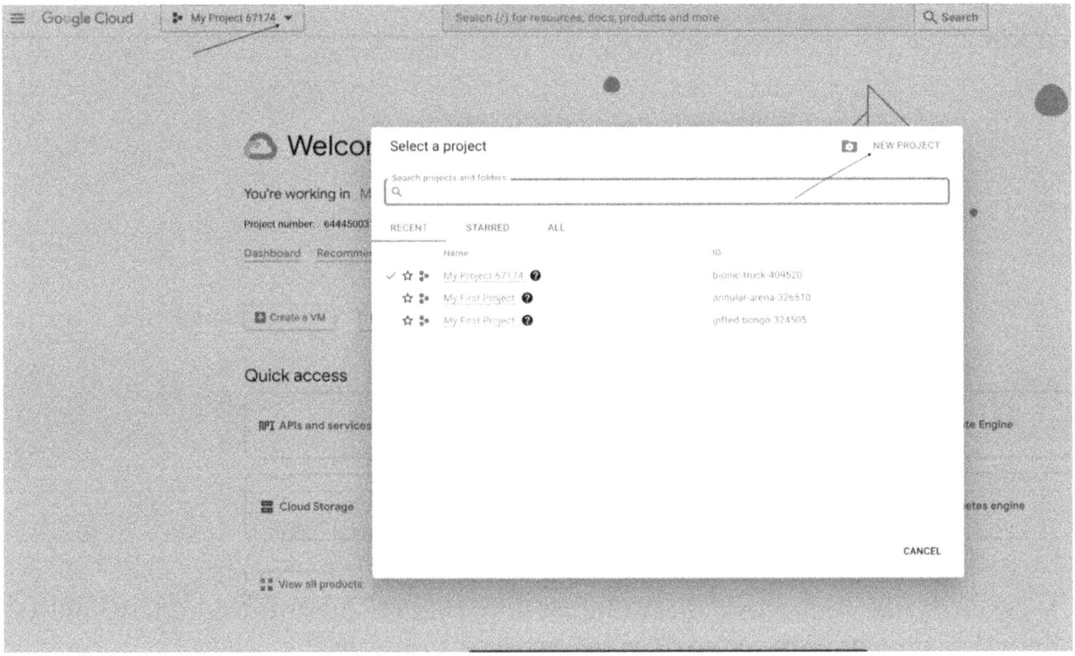

Figure 2.5: GCP: Create new project

Then provide the **New Project** name as shown in the following figure:

Figure 2.6: GCP fill up new project name

Once the project is created, you will see the following homepage:

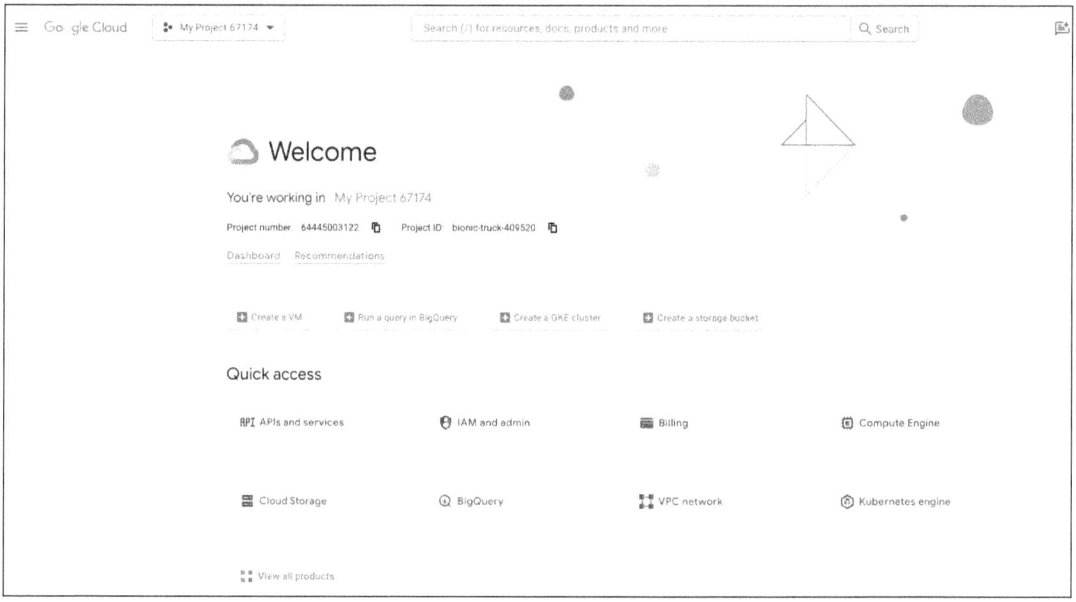

Figure 2.7: GCP home page after creating new project

Note: GCP may update its onboarding process, so it is advisable to check the official documentation or website for the most current instructions.

After completing these steps, you will have a GCP account ready to explore the vast array of cloud services offered by GCP.

Exploring GCP with Google Cloud

Google Cloud, your go-to buddy for navigating GCP from the command line. It is like having a magic wand to interact with all things Google Cloud.

The following are the steps to activate and use Cloud Shell:

1. **Open the Google Cloud Console**: Go to the Google Cloud Console.
2. **Activate Cloud Shell**: In the top right corner of the console, click on the Cloud Shell icon. It looks like a small shell icon and is located near the top right corner of the console as shown in the following figure:

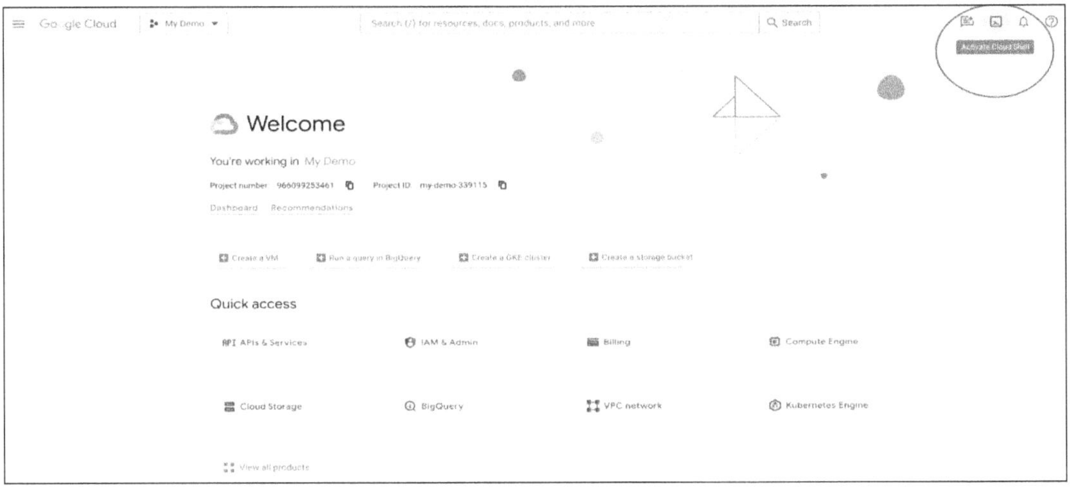

Figure 2.8: Activate Cloud Shell on top right corner

3. **Launch Cloud Shell**: If it is your first time using Cloud Shell, it might take a moment to set up.

   Once ready, you will see a command line interface at the bottom of the console, indicating that Cloud Shell is ready for use as shown in the following figure:

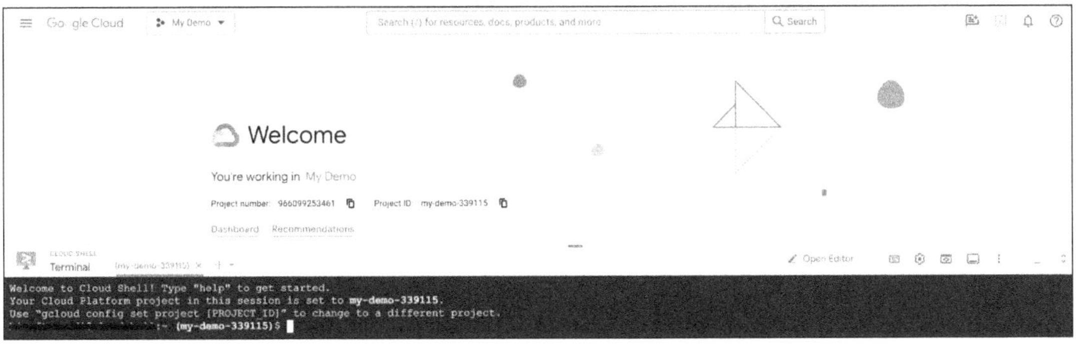

Figure 2.9: GCP integrated Gcloud Terminal

4. **Use gcloud commands**: You can now use **`gcloud`** commands directly within Cloud Shell. The Cloud Shell environment comes pre-configured with the necessary tools, including the **`gcloud`** command line tool.

Here are some example commands:

- To check the **`version`** of **`gcloud`**, you can use the following command:

  `gcloud version`

- To list your GCP **`projects`**, you can use:

  `gcloud projects list`

- To set the default **project** for your session, use:
  `gcloud config set project YOUR_PROJECT_ID`

Here are some basic **gcloud** command syntax examples for common tasks in GCP:

- **Logging in**:
  - **Syntax**: `gcloud auth login`
  - **Example**: `gcloud auth login`
- **Setting a project**:
  - **Syntax**: `gcloud config set project PROJECT_ID`
  - **Example**: `gcloud config set project my-awesome-project`
- **Listing Compute Engine instances**:
  - **Syntax**: `gcloud compute instances list`
  - **Example**: `gcloud compute instances list`

GCP networking for GKE

GCP provides a robust set of networking services that enable users to build, manage, and optimize their network infrastructure. Here is a simplified overview of key concepts related to GCP networking which is required for GKE:

- **Virtual Private Cloud (VPC) networks**: VPC is like having your own private digital space in the cloud. It allows you to create a logically isolated network to deploy your resources, such as VMs or databases. A GCP project can have multiple VPCs networks, and these are global resources which means they are not associated with a particular region or zone.
- **Subnet**: Subnet is like dividing your digital space into neighborhoods. It is a smaller section of a VPC with its own IP range, providing organization and segmentation. Scope of subnet is regional.
- **Firewall rules**: Firewall rules are like setting security gates for your digital neighborhood. They control the traffic allowed in and out of your VMs and resources.
- **Cloud DNS**: Cloud DNS is like having a smart address book for your digital world. It translates human-readable domain names to IP addresses, directing traffic to the correct destination.
- **Shared VPC**: Shared VPC is like having a joint community center for multiple projects. It allows resources from different projects to share a common network.

In summary, GCP networking involves creating private spaces (VPC), organizing them into sections (subnets), securing them with gates (firewall rules) and ensuring efficient address resolution (Cloud DNS). Shared VPC provides a collaborative environment for multiple projects.

The following is an example of a standalone project and how VPC and subnets can be organized for enabling or restricting communication between VMs:

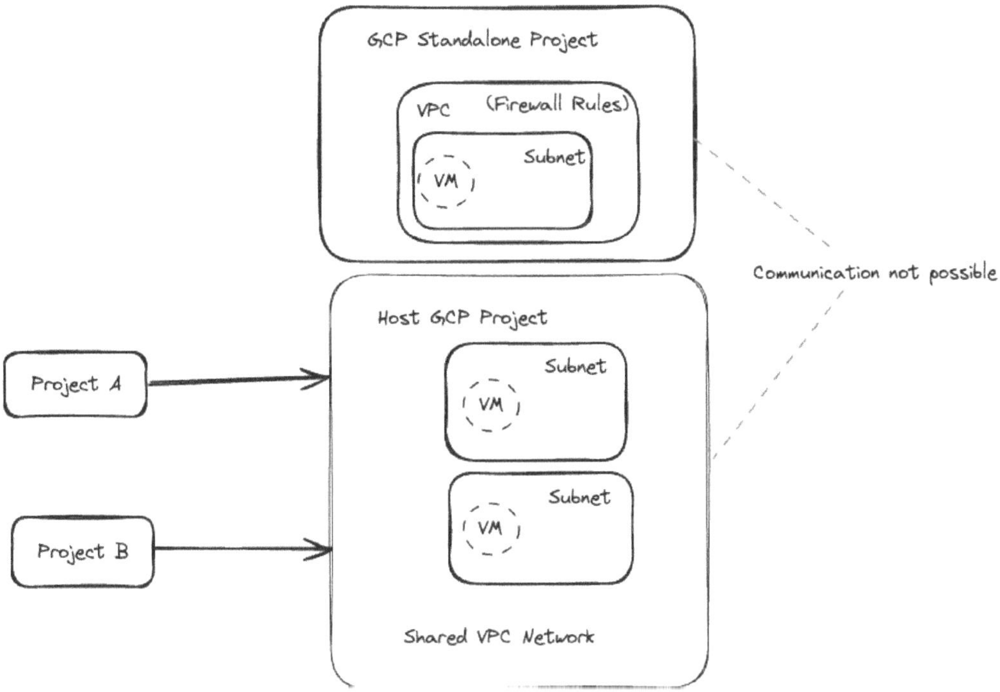

***Figure 2.10**: GCP networking services*

Setting up networking for GKE

A VPC and subnet are created to isolate GKE networking resources.

The following **gcloud** command demonstrates how to create a VPC and a subnet in Google Cloud:

```
# Create a VPC
gcloud compute networks create my-gke-vpc --subnet-mode=auto
# Create a subnet within the VPC
gcloud compute networks subnets create my-gke-subnet \
    --network=my-gke-vpc \
    --region=us-central1 \
    --range=192.168.0.0/24
```

GCP storage and database products

Apart from compute and network, another building block of cloud infrastructure is about storing the data.

GCP offers a variety of storage and database solutions to meet different needs. First, let us analyze the basic difference between storage and database:

Key questions	Storage	Database
What does it mean?	Storage systems manage raw, unstructured data, treating it as a series of bytes or blocks. It does not impose any structure on the data.	Databases deal with structured data, where information is organized in tables with predefined schemas. It supports relational or non-relational data models.
How is it organized?	Data is typically organized in a straightforward manner, without any inherent relationships or dependencies. It is like having a large, flexible container to store files, documents, images, or any other digital content.	Data is organized into tables, rows, and columns, with defined relationships between tables. It is like having a highly organized filing system with specific categories and relationships between different pieces of information.
How to use it?	Storage is generally used for storing and retrieving data. It provides a place to keep files and resources, but it does not inherently understand the content or relationships between pieces of data.	Databases not only store data but also provide sophisticated operations such as querying, updating, and deleting data. They are designed for efficient retrieval and management of structured information.

***Table 2.1**: Storage vs database*

Types of storage in GCP

Google Cloud offers various storage options to meet different needs. The following table shows the main types of storage available in GCP:

Category	GCP product
Block storage It manages data as raw, unstructured blocks.	**Persistent Disks**: Reliable, durable storage for VMs instances for GCE and GKE. **Local SSD**: Ephemeral locally attached storage for VMs and containers. **Hyperdisk**: Next generation of block storage delivering higher scale and best in class price/performance.

Category	GCP product
File storage File storage is like a shared digital folder for collaborative file access. It organizes data in a hierarchical structure with directories and files.	**Filestore**: Fully managed service for file migration and storage. Easily mount file shares on Compute Engine VMs. **Parallelstore**: High bandwidth, high IOPS, ultra-low latency, managed parallel file service. **Google Cloud NetApp Volumes**: NetApp's best-in-class file storage service, in Google Cloud.
Object storage Store any type of data, any amount of data, and retrieve it as often as you had like.	**Cloud storage**: When you use Cloud storage, you create one or more storage buckets, and within these buckets, you can store, organize, and manage your objects (files or data). Each bucket has a globally unique name, and you can configure access control, versioning, and other settings at the bucket level. **It has four types**: **Standard storage**: Storage for data that is frequently accessed (hot data) and/or stored for only brief periods of time. **Nearline storage**: Low cost, highly durable storage service for storing infrequently accessed data (stored for 30 days). **Coldline storage**: A very low cost, highly durable storage service for storing infrequently accessed data (stored for 90 days). **Archival storage**: The lowest cost, highly durable storage service for data archiving, online backup, and disaster recovery (stored for 365 days).
Mobile app services Specialized storage solution designed for mobile and web applications integrated with Firebase. It provides secure and scalable storage for user-generated content like images, videos, and app data.	**Cloud storage for Firebase**: Scalable storage for user-generated content from your app.

Table 2.2: Types of storage

To transfer or migrate data, we can use any of the following services:

- **Online transfer**: Online transfer is like sending your digital items over the internet. It is the process of moving your files or data directly from one place to another using online connectivity.
- **Storage transfer service**: Storage transfer service is like a digital moving service provided by Google Cloud. It helps you transfer large amounts of data from other cloud storage or on-premises locations to Google Cloud storage. It is like a reliable digital mover for your files.

- **gsutil**: It is a command line tool that allows you to interact with Google Cloud storage, letting you upload, download, and manage your files and buckets with simple commands.

  Syntax: `gsutil cp your-local-file.txt gs://your-bucket-name/`

- **Transfer appliance**: The transfer appliance is like a super-fast, secure courier for your massive digital data. It is a physical device provided by Google Cloud that you can use to transfer large volumes of data from your on-premises environment to Google Cloud. It is a bit like shipping your data on a secure digital hard drive instead of over the internet.

Types of databases in GCP

Google Cloud offers various database options to meet different needs. Here are the main types of databases available in GCP:

<table>
<tr><th>Database type</th><th>Cloud service</th></tr>
<tr><td>Relational

Organized tables with rows and columns, and these tables can relate to each other.

Online transaction processing (OLTP) – Predefined schema, atomic

Online analytical processing (OLAP) – Columnar storage, distribute data and useful for large queries</td><td>OLTP:

• Cloud SQL: Fully managed MySQL, PostgreSQL, and SQL Server.

o Use cases: Suitable for applications requiring a traditional relational database model, such as web applications, content management systems, and business applications.

• Cloud Spanner: Cloud-native with unlimited scale, global consistency, and up to 99.999% availability.

Processes more than 3 billion requests per second at peak.

o Use cases: Ideal for globally distributed applications with high scalability requirements, such as global e-commerce platforms and financial services.

OLAP:

• Bigquery: Serverless, highly scalable, and cost-effective multi-cloud data warehouse designed for business agility and offers up to 99.99% availability.</td></tr>
</table>

<table>
<tr><th>Database type</th><th>Cloud service</th></tr>
<tr><td>Non-relational

Flexible schema, data stored like collection of documents making it easier to adapt to different data types like text, images, or JSON.</td><td>• Cloud Firestore: NoSQL document database that supports flexible data models, real-time updates, and seamless integration with mobile and web applications.
  o Use cases: Suitable for applications where flexible and scalable document-based data storage is needed, such as mobile app backends, real-time collaboration, and user profiles.
• Cloud Bigtable: Scalable NoSQL database service designed for large-scale analytics and operational workloads, offering low-latency access to massive amounts of data.
  o Use cases: Commonly used for time-series data, IoT data, and analytics platforms requiring fast and efficient data access.</td></tr>
<tr><td>In memory store

It is like having a super-fast, temporary brain for your computer. It stores data in the computer's memory (RAM), making it lightning-fast to access and process.</td><td>• Cloud memory store: Fully managed in-memory data store service that is compatible with Redis. It provides a high-performance, in-memory caching solution for improving application response times.
  o Use cases: Ideal for applications that require fast and low-latency access to frequently accessed data, such as caching frequently read database queries or storing session data.</td></tr>
</table>

Table 2.3: Types of databases

Cloud Identity and Access Management

Cloud **Identity and Access Management** (**IAM**) is a critical component of GCP that helps you manage user access and permissions across your cloud resources. With IAM, you can define who has access to specific resources and what actions they are allowed to perform. This enables you to control and secure your cloud environment by granting the right permissions to the right users and services, ensuring that only authorized individuals can access or modify your resources. IAM simplifies the process of managing user roles, maintaining security, and enforcing compliance within your GCP environment.

The following are some use cases to understand how IAM works.

Use case 1

To create a user account in IAM, follow the given steps:

1. Authenticate with GCP

   ```
   gcloud auth login
   ```

2. Create a new user account (**John Doe**)

```
gcloud iam service-accounts create john-doe \
    --description="User account for John Doe" \
    --display-name="John Doe"
```

3. Grant IAM roles to the user

```
gcloud projects add-iam-policy-binding your-project-id \
    --member="serviceAccount:john-doe@your-project-id.iam.
gserviceaccount.com" \
    --role="roles/viewer"
```

4. Generate key for authentication (optional)

```
gcloud iam service-accounts keys create ~/john-doe-key.json \
    --iam-account= john-doe@your-project-id.iam.gserviceaccount.com
```

Explanation:

- **gcloud iam service-accounts create**: Creates a new service account (user account) named *John Doe*. You can add a description and display name to provide more information about the account.
- **gcloud projects add-iam-policy-binding**: Grants IAM roles to the user account. In this example, *John Doe* is granted the viewer role.
- **gcloud iam service-accounts keys create**: Generates a private key for the service account. This step is optional and is typically done if the service account needs to authenticate programmatically.

Use case 2

To manage access to a Cloud Storage bucket, follow the given steps:

1. Create a new GCP project:

```
gcloud projects create my-awesome-project
gcloud config set project my-awesome-project
```

2. Create a Cloud Storage bucket:

```
gsutil mb -p my-awesome-project gs://my-awesome-bucket
```

3. Using `gcloud`:

```
gcloud storage buckets create gs://my-awesome-bucket \
  --project=my-awesome-project \
  --location=us-central1 \
  --storage-class=STANDARD
```

4. Assign IAM roles to users:

   i. Granting a user the storage object viewer role:

   ```
   gcloud projects add-iam-policy-binding my-awesome-project \
   --member=user:jane.doe@example.com \
   --role=roles/storage.objectViewer
   ```

   ii. Verify IAM permissions:

   ```
   gcloud projects get-iam-policy my-awesome-project \
   --flatten="bindings[].members" \
   --format="table(bindings.role, bindings.members)" \
   --filter="bindings.members:user:jane.doe@example.com"
   ```

5. Cloud monitoring and logging:

   Note: Monitors and logs activities in your GCP environment, aiding in security analysis, detection, and incident response. We will discuss monitoring and logging for GKE in later chapters.

   i. Enable monitoring and logging API:

   ```
   gcloud services enablemonitoring.googleapis.com logging.
   googleapis.com
   ```

Introduction to Google Kubernetes Engine

Let us understand GKE, your guide to managing containers effortlessly in the cloud:

- **Understanding GKE**: GKE is a fully managed Kubernetes service provided by GCP. In simple terms, GKE is like having a skilled team of experts who take care of all the complexities involved in setting up, managing, and scaling your applications using Kubernetes.
- **Functions of GKE**: GKE takes care of the heavy lifting. You tell it what applications you want, and GKE ensures they run smoothly, no matter how many or how few. It is like having a reliable assistant to handle all the technical details.
- **Where to start**: Start by creating a Kubernetes cluster with GKE. It is like setting up your own playground for containers. GKE takes care of the infrastructure, and you get to focus on your awesome applications. We will discuss the steps in details in *Chapter 3, Creating and Configuring a GKE Cluster.*

In a nutshell, GKE is your go-to companion for exploring the world of containers in the cloud. It is easy to use, scalable, and takes the hassle out of managing your applications. With GKE, you are in control of a powerful, yet user-friendly, container management experience.

GKE and Kubernetes are related, but there are some key differences between the two. Let us break down these differences in simple terms:

- **Managed service vs. open-source project**:
  - **GKE**: It is a managed service provided by Google Cloud. It is like having a fully equipped kitchen where you can cook without worrying about shopping for ingredients or cleaning up afterward. GKE takes care of the underlying infrastructure, making it easier for you to deploy and manage containerized applications.
  - **Kubernetes:** Kubernetes, often referred to as K8s, is an open-source container orchestration platform. You must set up and manage the environment yourself, if it is on-premises and in case it is hosted on a cloud provider like Google Cloud, Amazon, or Microsoft, we can use it as a managed service.
- **Ease of use**:
  - **GKE:** GKE is designed to be user-friendly. It abstracts much of the complexity associated with setting up and managing a Kubernetes cluster. With GKE, you can get started quickly and focus more on deploying and scaling your applications.
  - **Kubernetes:** Setting up a Kubernetes cluster manually requires more effort and knowledge. While there are tools to assist with installation (e.g., kubeadm), it generally involves more configuration and management tasks compared to a managed service like GKE.
- **Automatic upgrades and patches**:
  - **GKE:** GKE automatically handles upgrades and patches for the Kubernetes master and nodes. It is like having a chef who keeps your kitchen equipment up to date without you having to worry about it.
  - **Kubernetes:** With Kubernetes, you are responsible for managing upgrades and patches yourself. While there are tools and guides to assist, it requires more hands-on effort.
- **Integrated monitoring and logging**:
  - **GKE:** GKE provides integrated monitoring and logging tools, making it easier to track the performance and health of your applications. It is like having built-in sensors that keep you informed about what is happening in your kitchen.
  - **Kubernetes:** For Kubernetes, you might need to set up additional monitoring and logging solutions or integrate with third-party tools to achieve similar visibility.

- **Billing and pricing:**
  - **GKE:** GKE has its own pricing model based on the resources used by your cluster. You pay for the managed service and resources allocated to your applications.
  - **Kubernetes:** While Kubernetes itself is free and open-source, you pay for the underlying infrastructure of on-premise or if you are using a cloud provider, the costs are associated with VMs, storage, and other resources.

In essence, GKE is a managed service that simplifies the deployment and management of Kubernetes clusters, while Kubernetes is the open-source platform that can be deployed and managed on various environments, including GCP. The choice between them often depends on factors such as ease of use, management overhead, and specific requirements for control and customization.

GKE pricing and billing considerations

GKE offers the following three main editions:

- **Standard edition**: Includes fully automated cluster lifecycle management, autoscaling, cost visibility and automated infrastructure cost optimization. Priced at $0.10 per cluster per hour.
- **Enterprise edition**: Includes standard edition features and multi-team, multi-cluster, self-service operations, advanced security, service mesh, configuration, system logs and metrics, and a unified console experience. Priced at $0.00822 per vCPU per hour.
- **Autopilot mode**: Accrue a flat fee of $0.10/hour for each cluster after the free tier, plus the CPU, memory, and ephemeral storage resources.

When considering GKE pricing and billing, several factors come into play such as:

- **Node pricing:**
  - GKE uses Compute Engine VM instances as nodes to run the Kubernetes cluster.
  - You are billed for the resources (CPU and memory) allocated to these nodes.
  - Pricing varies based on the machine type, location, and any sustained use discounts.
- **Node pools:**
  - GKE allows you to create node pools with different machine types or configurations.
  - You can have multiple node pools within a cluster, each with its own pricing.

- **Autoscaling:**
  - GKE supports autoscaling, allowing the cluster to dynamically adjust the number of nodes based on demand.
  - Autoscaling helps optimize costs by adjusting resources based on the actual workload.
- **Node upgrades:**
  - GKE provides regular updates for Kubernetes and the underlying node OS.
  - Upgrading nodes may incur additional costs, as new machine types or resources could be used.
- **Node locations:**
  - The location (region or zone) where your nodes are deployed affects pricing.
  - Some regions may have different pricing for resources, and cross-region traffic may incur additional costs.
- **Cluster management fee:**
  - GKE has a cluster management fee, which is a flat fee for the control plane (Kubernetes master) management.
  - The fee is per cluster, irrespective of the number of nodes or node pools.
- **Additional features:**
  - Features like private clusters, regional clusters and advanced networking options may have associated costs. Also, backup for GKE is a separate service that can be used to protect and manage GKE data and this also has additional costs.
- **Usage monitoring:**
  - Regularly monitor your GKE usage and billing details in the GCP Console or through the Billing API.
  - Set up budget alerts to receive notifications if costs exceed a predefined threshold.
- **Persistent storage:**
  - Costs associated with persistent storage volumes (such as Google Cloud Persistent Disks) used by your cluster.
- **Data transfer:**
  - Consider data transfer costs, especially if your GKE cluster communicates with resources outside the GCP network.

Conclusion

In this exploration of GCP and GKE, we have uncovered how the cloud offers a flexible and powerful environment for building and scaling applications. GCP provides a vast digital playground where developers can innovate while relying on managed services that handle infrastructure and operational tasks. With Kubernetes as the core orchestrator, GKE elevates container management by offering a fully managed, scalable, and secure platform. This combination of GCP's robust infrastructure and Kubernetes' container orchestration creates a seamless experience for deploying and managing cloud-native applications. Whether it is automating workloads, managing clusters, or enhancing security, GCP and GKE empower developers to focus on what matters most—delivering innovative solutions.

As we move forward, the next chapter will focus on creating and configuring a GKE cluster, guiding you through the steps to get your Kubernetes environment up and running in Google Cloud.

Multiple choice questions

1. **What is GCP known for?**
   a. Gaming platform
   b. Generalized programming compiler
   c. Google Cloud Platform
   d. Generalized Cloud provider
2. **What is the primary role of Kubernetes in GCP?**
   a. Managing VMs
   b. Orchestrating containers
   c. Hosting databases
   d. Handling networking
3. **What does GKE stand for?**
   a. Google Kubernetes environment
   b. Global Kubernetes Engine
   c. Google Kubernetes Engine
   d. General Kubernetes extension

4. **What GCP service allows users to run VMs on demand?**
   a. Google Cloud storage
   b. Google Compute Engine
   c. Google Kubernetes Engine
   d. Google Cloud functions
5. **Which GCP database service is a fully managed, globally distributed, and scalable NoSQL database?**
   a. Google Cloud SQL
   b. Google Cloud Bigtable
   c. Google Cloud Firestore
   d. Google Cloud Spanner

Answer key

1.	c
2.	b
3.	c
4.	b
5.	c

Join our book's Discord space

Join the book's Discord Workspace for Latest updates, Offers, Tech happenings around the world, New Release and Sessions with the Authors:

https://discord.bpbonline.com

CHAPTER 3

Creating and Configuring a GKE Cluster

Introduction

In this chapter, we will work to establish and set up a GKE cluster. Here, we will lead you through the foundational steps of creating your initial GKE cluster, along with providing guidance on configuring crucial elements while creating the GKE clusters.

Structure

The chapter covers the following topics:

- Creating your first GKE cluster
- Customizing cluster configuration
- Enabling and configuring GKE advanced configuration

Objectives

By the end of this chapter, you will acquire proficiency in the fundamental procedures involved in establishing and configuring a GKE cluster. You will be able to tailor cluster configuration to specific requirements and have understanding into the options available within the GKE environment.

Creating your first GKE cluster

In this section we will learn how to set up your first GKE cluster step by step.

Prerequisites

Before we understand creating the GKE cluster, ensure you have the following prerequisites in place:

- **GCP account**: You need an active GCP account. If you do not have one, you can sign up for a free trial as explained in *Chapter 2, Overview of Google Cloud Platform*.
    - **Accessing the Google Cloud Console**:
        1. Open your web browser and navigate to the Google Cloud Console.
        2. Sign in with your GCP account credentials.

GCP Console walkthrough for cluster creation

Creating a GKE cluster via the Google Cloud Console is a straightforward process. Here is a step-by-step guide:

1. Open the Google Cloud Console.
2. Navigate to Google Cloud Console.
3. Select your project.
4. On the GCP Console, select your project at the top, and you will see a screen similar to this one. Select the appropriate project from there, as shown in the following figure:

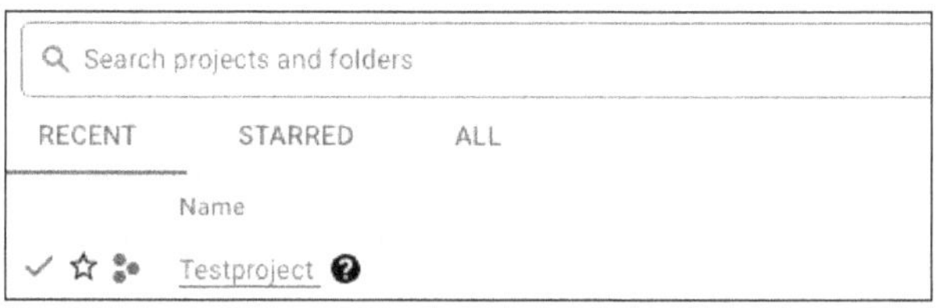

Figure 3.1: Select the GCP project

Before creating a GKE cluster on GCP, you primarily need to enable the Kubernetes Engine API. This API is crucial for managing and interacting with GKE clusters.

The following are the steps to enable the Kubernetes Engine APIs:

1. **Console**: Go to the **APIs & Services** from the left menu or just search **`API & services`** on the top search bar and then search for the required API, as shown in the following figure:

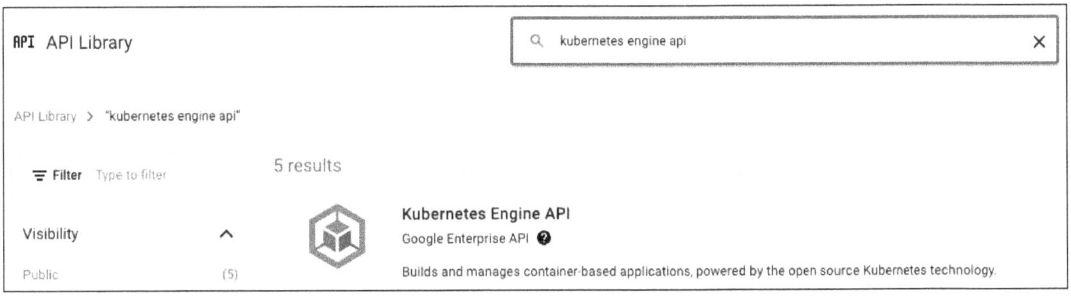

Figure 3.2: *Select the API and services*

2. Click on the **ENABLE APIS AND SERVICES** button.
3. Search for **`Compute Engine API`** and **`Kubernetes Engine API`** and enable each one of them.
4. You can also enable them by using the following commands:

```
gcloud services enable compute.googleapis.com
gcloud services enable container.googleapis.com
```

Note: For details on running these commands with Google Cloud Shell, see Chapter 2, Overview of Google Cloud Platform, section Exploring GCP with gcloud. We will cover running them locally with the gcloud SDK in Chapter 4, Setting Up Your GKE Environment.

5. Navigate to **Kubernetes Engine**.
6. In the left-hand navigation menu, click on **Kubernetes Engine** as shown in the following figure.

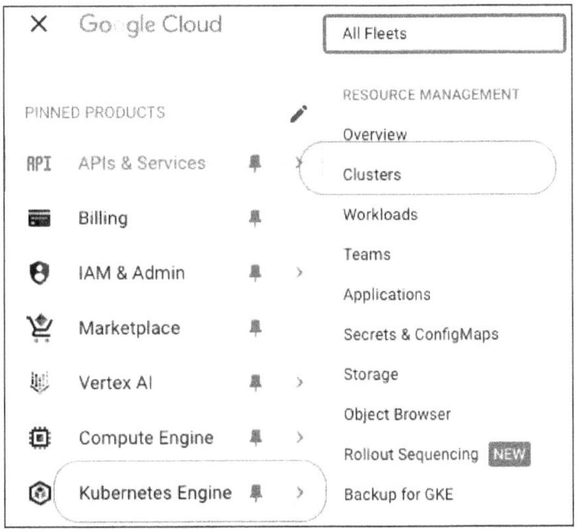

Figure 3.3: *Kubernetes Engine menu*

7. Once inside the **Kubernetes Engine** section, click on the **Clusters** tab.
8. Click on the **CREATE** cluster button as shown in the following figure:

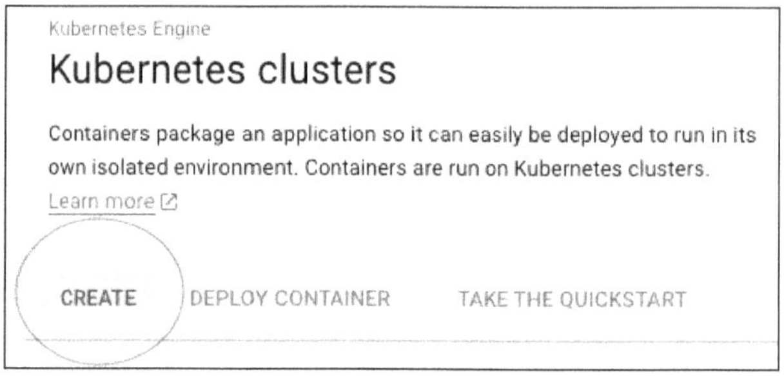

***Figure 3.4**: Create cluster option*

9. **Configure your cluster**: Fill in the necessary information for your GKE cluster.

   You can either choose to create a cluster in Autopilot or **SWITCH TO STANDARD CLUSTER** (switch option: you can find on the top right corner as shown in the following figure):

***Figure 3.5**: Switch to Standard mode option will be on top right corner*

   a. **Cluster name**: Give your cluster a unique name.
   b. **Location**: Select the region and zone where you want your cluster to be located as shown in the following figure:

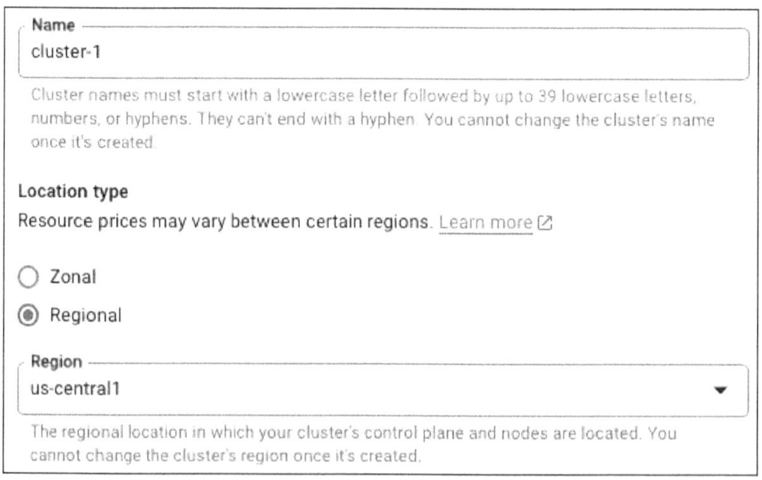

***Figure 3.6**: Create Standard cluster*

Additional settings:

Advanced options: Expand each section to customize additional settings like autoscaling, auto-repair, and disk size. We will cover the advanced configuration and settings in the upcoming section, enabling and configuring GKE advanced configuration.

The following figure shows the configuration that we need to verify before creating the cluster:

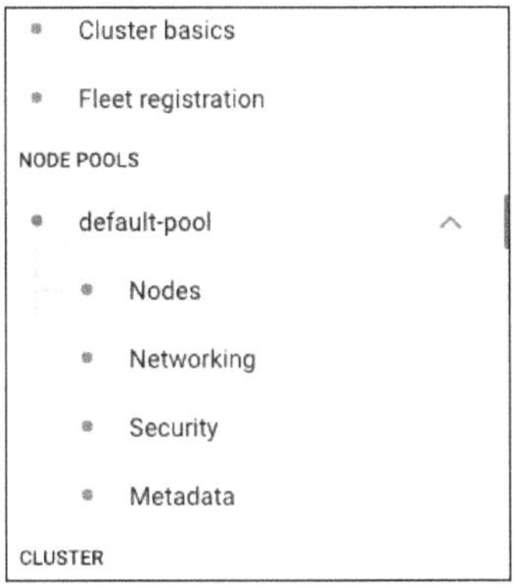

***Figure 3.7**: Configure Standard cluster during creation*

Follow these steps to create and verify your GKE cluster:

1. **Create the cluster**: Click on the Create button at the bottom of the page to initiate the creation of your GKE cluster.
2. **Wait for cluster creation**: The cluster creation process may take a few minutes. You can monitor the progress on the Clusters page.
3. **Verify your cluster**: Open Google Cloud Shell and verify that you can connect to your GKE cluster.

   To connect to your GKE cluster and verify its status, run the following command:

   ```
   gcloud container clusters get-credentials YOUR_CLUSTER_NAME --zone YOUR_CLUSTER_ZONE
   ```

   Replace `YOUR_CLUSTER_NAME` and `YOUR_CLUSTER_ZONE` with the appropriate values.

   You should see a list of nodes in your GKE cluster, indicating that it is up and running using the following command:

   ```
   kubectl get nodes
   ```

Create GCP cluster via command line

The following are the steps to create a GKE cluster (via command line):

1. Open a Terminal window.

2. Run the following command to create a GKE cluster:
   ```
   gcloud container clusters create YOUR_CLUSTER_NAME \
     --region YOUR_CLUSTER_REGION \
     --num-nodes=1 \
     --machine-type=n1-standard-2
   ```
3. Replace **YOUR_CLUSTER_NAME** with the desired name for your GKE cluster and set **YOUR_CLUSTER_REGION** to your preferred GCP region (e.g., **us-central1**).
4. Adjust the **--num-nodes** and **--machine-type** flags according to your requirements.
5. Wait for the cluster creation process to complete. This may take a few minutes.
6. After the cluster is created, configure **kubectl** to use the new cluster:
   ```
   gcloud container clusters get-credentials YOUR_CLUSTER_NAME --region
   YOUR_CLUSTER_REGION
   ```
7. Ensure to replace **YOUR_CLUSTER_NAME** and **YOUR_CLUSTER_REGION** with your actual cluster name and region.
8. Verify that your nodes are ready:
   ```
   kubectl get nodes
   ```

Create GCP cluster using Terraform

If you want to create and manage your infrastructure using Terraform, then the following is an example of Terraform code to create a simple GKE cluster. Before using this code, ensure you have Terraform installed and configured on your machine. You will also need a GCP account, and a project set up, shown as follows:

```
# main.tf

provider "google" {
  credentials = file("<PATH_TO_YOUR_GCP_SERVICE_ACCOUNT_KEY>")
  project     = "<YOUR_GCP_PROJECT_ID>"
  region      = "us-central1"
}

resource "google_container_cluster" "my_cluster" {
  name     = "my-gke-cluster"
  location = "us-central1"

  node_pool {
    name         = "default-pool"
    machine_type = "n1-standard-2"
    disk_size_gb = 100
```

```
    disk_type     = "pd-standard"
    min_count     = 1
    max_count     = 3
  }

  master_auth {
    username = ""
    password = ""

    client_certificate_config {
      issue_client_certificate = false
    }
  }
}
```

Remember to replace **<PATH_TO_YOUR_GCP_SERVICE_ACCOUNT_KEY>** and **<YOUR_GCP_PROJECT_ID>** with the actual path to your GCP service account key file and your GCP project ID, respectively.

To initialize and apply the Terraform configuration, follow these steps:

1. Navigate to the directory containing your Terraform files.
2. Run **terraform init** to initialize the working directory.
3. Run **terraform plan** to preview the changes.
4. Run **terraform apply** and confirm with **yes** when prompted to create the GKE cluster.

This Terraform code creates a GKE cluster with a single node pool. You can customize the configuration based on your requirements, adjusting parameters such as machine type, disk size, and node count.

Keep in mind that managing GKE clusters involves costs, so ensure that you understand the pricing details and clean up resources when they are no longer needed.

Customizing cluster configuration

GKE offers the following modes of operation for clusters:

- **Autopilot mode**: Autopilot is like having a self-driving car for your Kubernetes clusters. With Autopilot mode in GKE, Google Cloud takes care of many of the operational tasks, making it easier for you to manage your applications. GKE manages the underlying infrastructure such as node configuration, autoscaling, auto-upgrades, baseline security configurations, and baseline networking configuration.

- **Standard mode**: Standard mode in GKE provides you with more control over your Kubernetes environment. It gives you the flexibility to manage aspects like node pools and node upgrades according to your preferences.

The following table is a basic comparison between Autopilot and Standard mode:

Key points	Autopilot	Standard
Availability	Regional	Regional or zonal
Billing	Simplified based on resources the applications use.	Based on nodes. Pay for unused resources in nodes.
Upgrades	Automated upgrades	You can configure auto-upgrades and GKE versions when you create or update the cluster.
Security	Many GKE security settings and Kubernetes best practices are enabled by default.	Many GKE security features are not enabled by default. You can enable the features manually and configure the settings.
Node management	**Pre-configured**: Autopilot manages scaling and node resource management.	By default, manually provision new nodes and specify node resources.

Table 3.1: Comparison between Autopilot and Standard mode

Note: While creating the cluster, `enable-autopilot` flag specifies that you want to create an Autopilot cluster. By default, without the flag, cluster is created in Standard mode.

Use the following command to create a GKE cluster with Autopilot mode enabled:

```
gcloud container clusters create [CLUSTER_NAME] --region [REGION] --enable-autopilot
```

Configuration for Autopilot mode

Proceed with the following command to create your cluster:

- **Cluster basics**: Specify the name and region for your cluster.

  The following figure shows the initial page of basic cluster configuration:

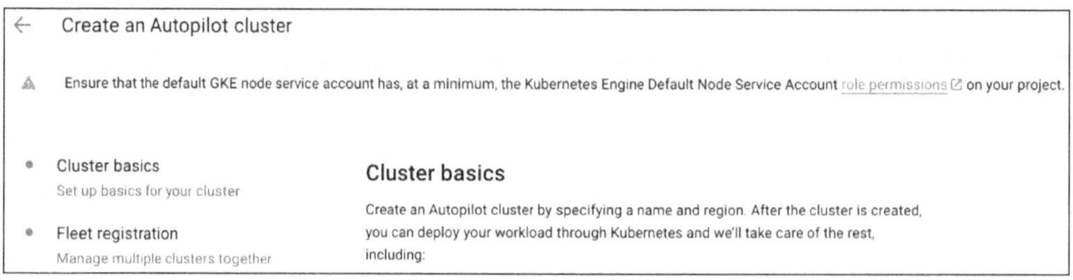

Figure 3.8: Select the cluster basics

- **Networking**: You can keep this as is with the default values or specify values as per your organization requirements as given in the following figure:

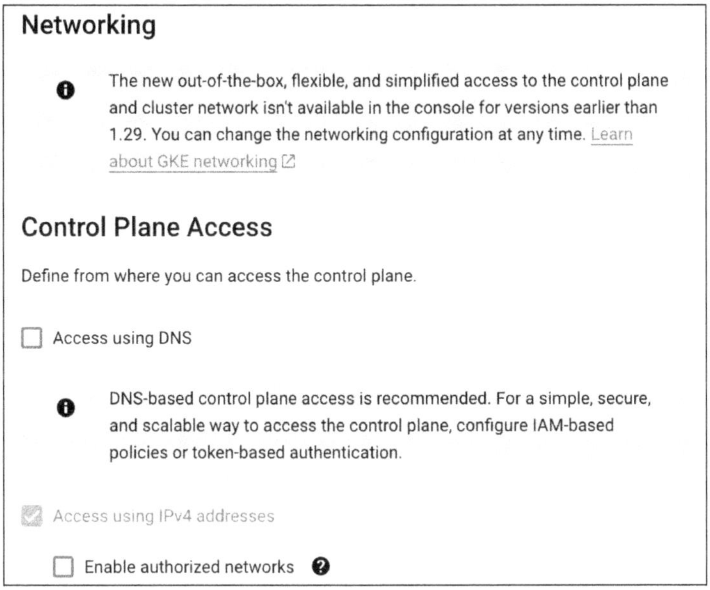

Figure 3.9: Networking section in Autopilot mode

- **Advanced settings and fleet**: We will cover the advanced configuration in the next section, *Enabling and configuring GKE advanced configuration.*

  As given in the following figure, keep the default values as is:

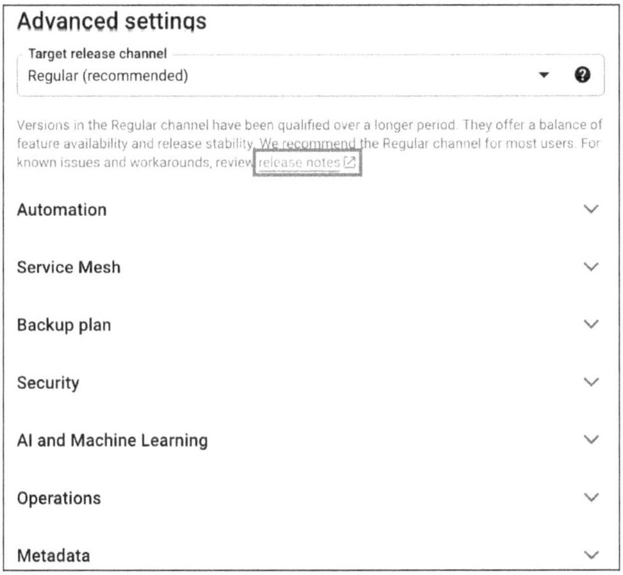

Figure 3.10: Advanced settings in Autopilot mode

- **Review and create**: You can now review the configuration and click on create as given in the following figure:

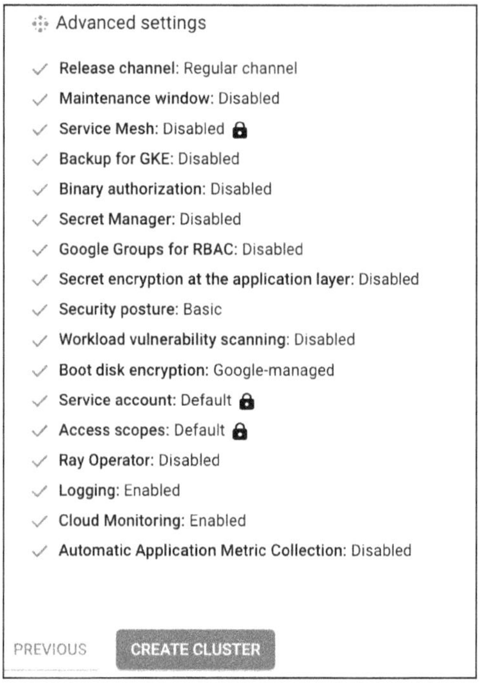

***Figure 3.11**: Review and create cluster in Autopilot mode*

Enabling and configuring GKE advanced configuration

If you are creating the GKE cluster especially in Standard mode, there are lot additional configurations that you must keep in mind.

Cluster basics

In the following table, we will now explain each section for Standard mode:

Settings	Choices
Cluster name	Specify a cluster name.
Zonal or regional cluster	Decide between setting up a zonal or regional cluster. This choice determines if your cluster stays in one zone or spans across multiple zones in a region. Go for a regional cluster only if you really need high availability, as it comes with higher costs.
Control plane version	You can either set it as no channel (formerly static), which means a fixed version, or choose from different release channels. The release channels provide you with a selection of software versions for the Kubernetes control plane, allowing you to align with your preferences regarding stability and feature updates.

***Table 3.2:** Standard mode cluster creation settings*

The following figure shows the basic details of the cluster to be completed before creation:

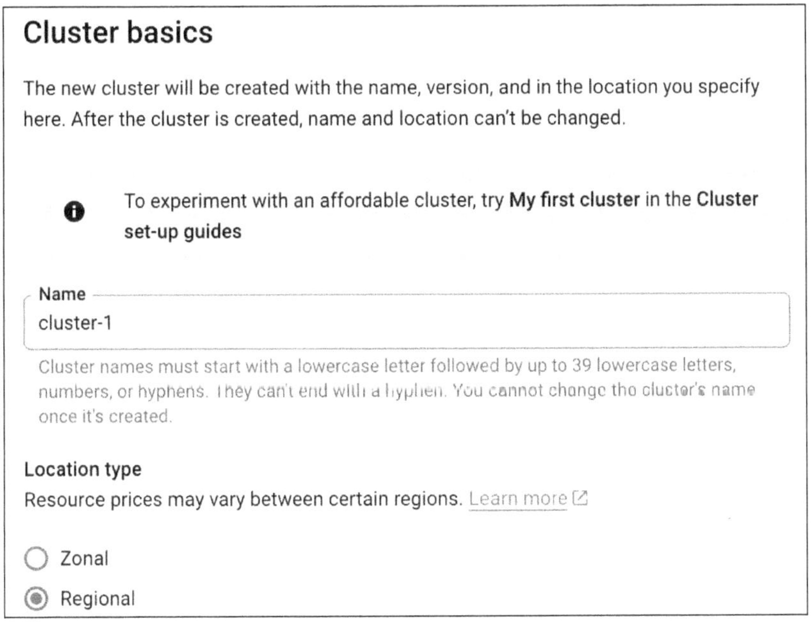

***Figure 3.12:** Cluster basics in Standard mode*

Node pool section

A node pool is a template for groups of nodes created in this cluster. The new cluster will be created with at least one node pool. More node pools can be added and removed after cluster creation.

The following table shows the node pool details:

Settings	Choices
Node pool name	Specify a name for your node pool, providing a clear identifier for the group of nodes in this pool.
Number of nodes	Define the desired quantity of nodes in the pool based on your application's resource requirements and expected workload.
Cluster auto-scaler	Enable cluster auto-scaler to dynamically adjust the number of nodes in response to varying workloads. This helps optimize resource utilization and ensures your applications have the necessary resources during peak demand.
Automatic node repair	Activate automatic node repair to automatically replace malfunctioning nodes, enhancing the resilience of your cluster against potential hardware failures.
Node pool upgrade strategy	**Surge upgrade**: **Best use case**: Suitable for stable workloads where faster upgrades are preferred. It upgrades nodes one at a time in place, creating a temporary additional node during each upgrade. If cost is a significant consideration, you can reduce disruption risk by setting max surge to 0 and max unavailable to 1.
	Blue-green upgrade: **Best use case**: Ideal for workloads sensitive to disruptions. This strategy creates a new node pool alongside the existing one, allowing for a smooth transition. It provides flexible upgrade pacing through batch requests and supports simple rollbacks. However, it is generally higher in cost compared to surge upgrades.

Table 3.3: Node pool creation details

The following figure shows the details to be completed for node pool creation:

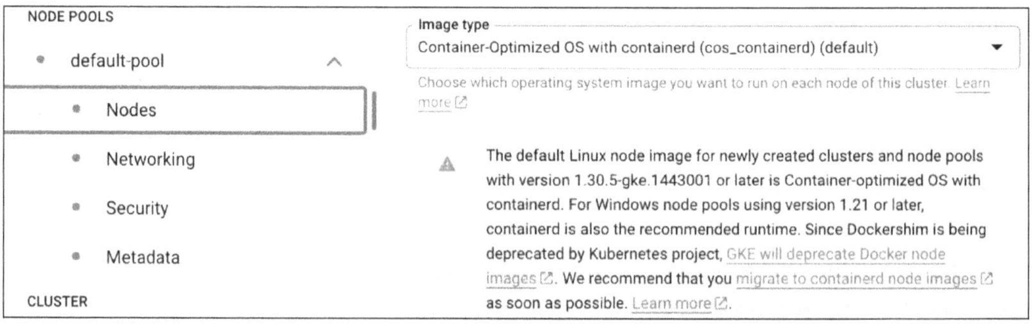

Figure 3.13: Node pool configuration in Standard mode

Configure node settings

The following table gives the details of node settings:

Settings	Choices
Image type	Choose the operating system image for your nodes, such as Container-Optimized OS or Ubuntu. Container-Optimized OS is tailored for running Docker containers, providing a lightweight and optimized environment.
Machine configuration	**General purpose**: Balanced CPU and memory for versatile workloads. It can be used for general tasks like working on documents and running various applications simultaneously. **Compute optimized**: Emphasizes CPU power for compute-intensive tasks that can be used in scientific research for tasks like simulating climate models, predicting protein structures, or processing large datasets in fields such as finance or genomics. **Memory optimized**: Offers high RAM for memory-intensive applications that require extensive data processing and storage in memory, for instance, a server running a large-scale e-commerce website. **Graphics processing unit (GPU)**: Includes specialized processor for parallel processing tasks. designed for parallel processing tasks, like those used in gaming or AI and can be most expensive.
Machine type	Select the specific type of **virtual machine** (**VM**) for your nodes, considering different CPU and memory configurations available in Google Cloud's offerings
Boot disk type and size	**Standard Persistent Disk (PD)**: Balanced performance for everyday tasks. • **Example**: Great for running standard applications and services. Cost effective. **Solid State Drive (SSD) PD**: High-performance, ideal for demanding and I/O-intensive apps. Expensive. • **Example**: Best suited for databases or applications requiring fast data access. **Balanced PD**: Mix of performance and cost efficiency for diverse workloads. • **Example**: Well-suited for workloads that need a good balance between performance and cost. **Size consideration**: • **Tip**: Choose the size of the boot disk based on your specific storage needs. • **Example**: If your applications require more storage space, opt for a larger boot disk size to ensure smooth operation.
Boot disk encryption	Decide whether to enable encryption for the boot disk. Enabling boot disk encryption enhances security by encrypting data at rest on the boot disk, adding an extra layer of protection.

Settings	Choices
Local SSD	Choose whether to use Local SSD for each node. Local SSD offers fast, temporary storage directly connected to the node. It's perfect for tasks that need quick and responsive storage. Keep in mind that any data stored on Local SSDs would not persist if the node is restarted or preempted. **Example scenario**: **Consideration**: Enabling Local SSD is like having a super-fast, but temporary, storage boost for your tasks. **Use case**: If you are running a high-performance computing job that needs speedy access to data but does not require long-term storage, Local SSD could be a game-changer. Just be aware that it is a short-term storage solution.
Enable spot VM option	**Regular option (Standard VM)**: You pay a stable, higher price for a server that you can use continuously. This is suitable for tasks that need a constant and uninterrupted server, like a critical business application. **Spot option (Spot VM):** If you enable this option, you pay a much lower price for a server, but it could be taken away (preempted) with minimal warning time. This is good for tasks that can tolerate interruptions, like large-scale data processing or scientific simulations, where you can pause and resume without much trouble.

Table 3.4: Node setting details

Choose the appropriate **Machine configuration** for your nodes as shown in the following figure:

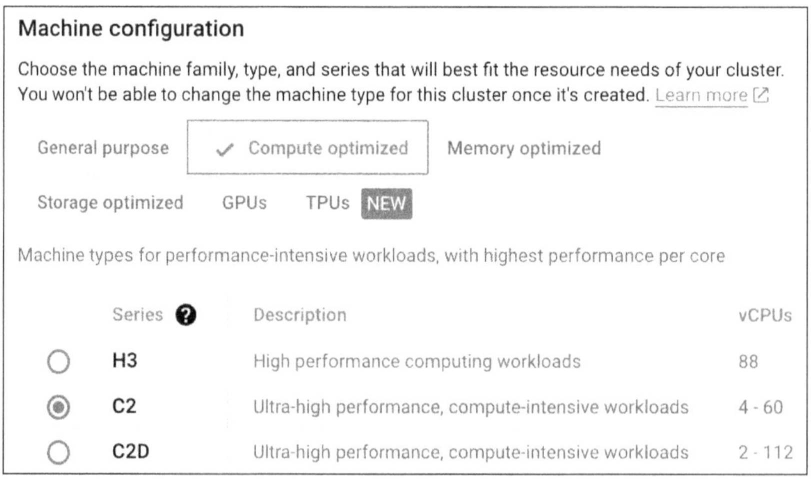

Figure 3.14: Node pool machine configuration in Standard mode

Node networking

You can find the networking details in the node configuration section in the following table:

Settings	Choices
Maximum Pods per node	Decides how many applications (Pods) can run on each server. **Use case**: Choose based on how many tasks your server should handle simultaneously.
Network tags	Labels for sorting and controlling how servers communicate. **Use case**: Helps in organizing and allocating IP addresses for each group of servers. For example, you may have a web network tag for nodes hosting web services and a database network tag for nodes hosting database services.
Node pool address range	Defines the IP address range for nodes within a node pool **Use case**: Helps in organizing and allocating IP addresses for each group of servers.

Table 3.5: Node networking configuration

Please select appropriate networking settings for your node as given below:

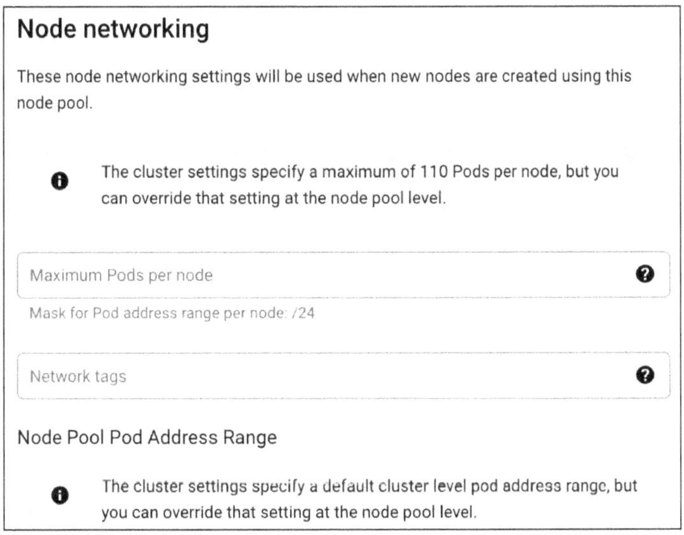

Figure 3.15: Node pool networking in Standard mode

Node security

The following table shows the node security configuration option for nodes:

Settings	Choices
Service account	A service account provides an identity for nodes to interact with other Google Cloud services and resources securely. **Use case**: Compute Engine default service account in GKE. When you create a GKE cluster, the nodes in the cluster require an identity to interact with other Google Cloud services like Cloud Storage, BigQuery, or other GCP APIs. The compute engine default service account serves as the identity for the nodes in GKE clusters, allowing them to authenticate and access various Google Cloud services.
Access scopes	**Allow full access to all Cloud APIs (default)**: Provides broad access to Google Cloud services. **Allow default access**: Grants access to a set of common Google Cloud services. **Use IAM roles**: Allows you to manually specify IAM roles for fine-grained control over access. Changes to access scopes take effect on new nodes that are added to the node pool. Existing nodes are not automatically updated. If you need the changes to apply to existing nodes, you may need to recreate the node pool or update the existing nodes manually.
Shielded options	**Explanation**: Shielded options enhance the security of nodes by providing features such as integrity monitoring, secure boot, and, in the case of confidential GKE nodes, additional confidentiality measures. • **Use case**: Improve the overall security posture of nodes by ensuring their integrity, preventing unauthorized modifications during runtime, and, in confidential node scenarios, protecting against data disclosure. **Enable integrity monitoring**: • **Use case**: Regularly checks and reports on the integrity of the node's firmware and software. Detects unauthorized changes that may indicate a security threat. **Secure boot**: • **Use case**: Ensures that the boot process of the node only uses signed and trusted bootloaders and firmware. Prevents the loading of unauthorized or tampered code during boot-up. **Confidential GKE nodes**: • **Use case**: Provides a secure environment for running workloads that require additional data confidentiality. It leverages technologies like AMD **Secure Encrypted Virtualization** (**SEV**) to protect sensitive data in memory.

Table 3.6: Node security configuration

Please select the appropriate security configuration as shown in the following figure:

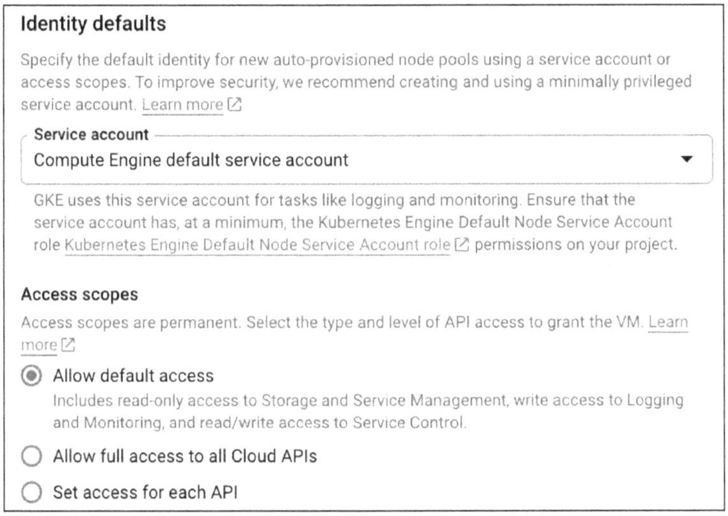

***Figure 3.16**: Node pool security in Standard mode*

Node metadata

Please select the appropriate metadata configuration given below:

Settings	Choices
Kubernetes labels	Labels are key-value pairs attached to nodes, providing metadata for identification and categorization. **Use case**: Helps organize and filter nodes based on characteristics like environment, role, or application.
Node taints	**No execute taint**: Prevents new Pods from being scheduled to a node and removes existing Pods that do not tolerate the taint. • **Use case**: Useful for marking nodes unsuitable for new workloads or evacuating existing workloads during maintenance. **No schedule taint**: Prevents new Pods from being scheduled to a node but does not evict existing Pods. • **Use case**: Useful for marking nodes temporarily unsuitable for new workloads without disrupting existing Pods. **Prefer no schedule taint**: Indicates a preference for not scheduling new Pods to a node but does not prevent it if no other options are available. • **Use case**: Suggests a preference against scheduling but allows flexibility, when necessary, suitable for scenarios where avoidance is preferred but not mandatory.

Settings	Choices
GCE instance metadata (or additional metadata)	GCE instance metadata allows you to provide custom key-value pairs with additional information for nodes. **Use case**: Useful for attaching project-specific metadata to nodes, enhancing customization and integration with external systems.
Additional metadata	Beyond default metadata, you can add custom metadata specific to your application or infrastructure needs. **Use case**: Ideal for attaching information such as configuration details, version numbers, or any custom data needed for applications running on nodes.

***Table 3.7**: Metadata configuration for nodes*

The following figure shows the settings for node metadata:

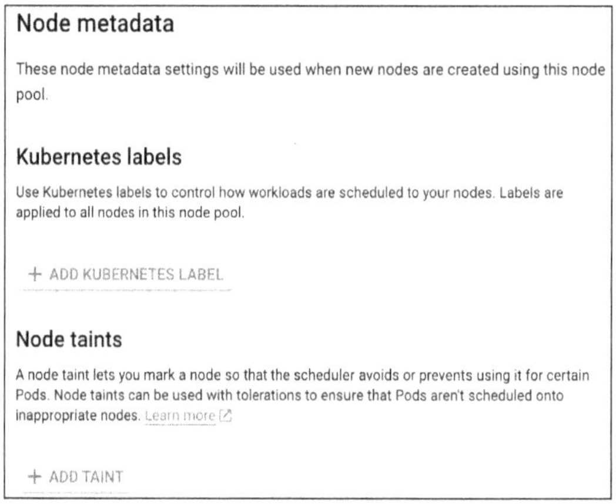

***Figure 3.17**: Node pool metadata in Standard mode*

Automation

You can select the appropriate automation configuration given below:

Settings	Choices
Maintenance policy	Maintenance policy allows you to control when automatic node upgrades occur, providing flexibility for planned maintenance windows. **Use case**: Useful for minimizing disruptions to your workloads by specifying preferred time windows for node upgrades.
Maintenance exclusions	Maintenance exclusions allow you to specify time periods when automatic node upgrades should not occur. **Use case**: Helpful for avoiding upgrades during critical business hours or times of increased system activity.

Settings	Choices
Notifications	Notifications provide alerts about upcoming or ongoing maintenance events and node upgrades. **Use case**: Ensures that administrators and teams are informed in advance, allowing for proactive management and planning during maintenance.
Autoscaling — **Vertical Pod Autoscaling (VPA)**	VPA adjusts the resource requests of containers dynamically based on observed usage, optimizing resource allocation. **Use case**: Ensures that containers get the right number of resources, improving performance and resource utilization.
Auto node provisioning	Auto node provisioning automatically adds nodes to a node pool based on resource requirements. **Use case**: Scales the cluster dynamically to accommodate increasing workload demands, enhancing scalability and resource efficiency.
Autoscaling profile	**Balanced (default) autoscaling profile**: Dynamically adjusts the number of nodes based on a balance between resource utilization and cluster stability. **Optimized utilization autoscaling profile**: Emphasizes maximizing resource utilization, potentially leading to more aggressive scaling actions based on actual demand.

Table 3.8: Automation settings

The following are the settings for automation:

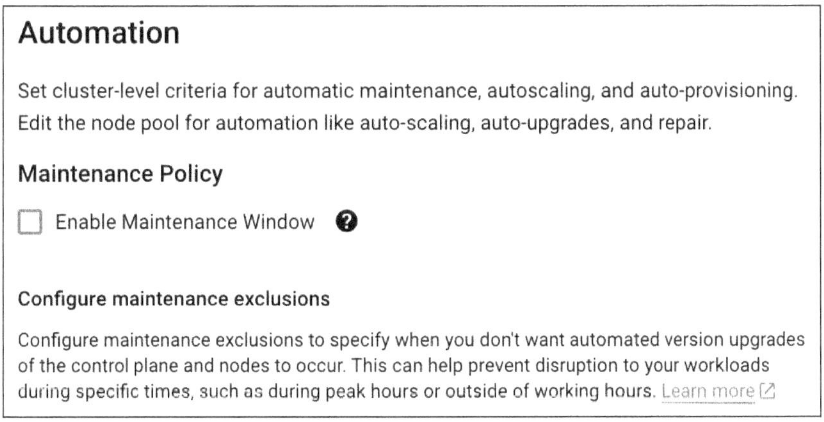

Figure 3.18: Cluster automation in Standard mode

Networking

You can select the appropriate networking configuration, as shown in the following table:

Settings	Choices
Network	A virtual network that connects GKE clusters, providing isolation and controlling communication between resources. **Use case**: Enables secure and controlled network traffic flow between GKE clusters and other Google Cloud resources.
Node subnet	Defines the IP address range for GKE node instances within the virtual network. **Use case**: Allows customization of IP addressing for nodes, helping with network organization and IP space management.
Public vs private cluster	Public clusters have publicly accessible control planes, while private clusters have control planes with private IP addresses. **Use case**: Private clusters enhance security by restricting external access to the control plane, suitable for sensitive workloads.
Advanced networking options	Provides additional network configuration settings, including alias IP ranges, multiple node pools, and subnetworks. **Use case**: Offers flexibility for complex networking requirements, such as multiple node pools with distinct IP addressing.
DNS provider	Provides additional network configuration settings, including alias IP ranges, multiple node pools, and subnetworks. **Use case**: Offers flexibility for complex networking requirements, such as multiple node pools with distinct IP addressing.
Enable node local DNS cache	Enables a DNS caching agent on each node, improving DNS resolution performance. **Use case**: Accelerates DNS resolution by caching responses locally on nodes, reducing latency for DNS queries.

Table 3.9: *Networking configuration*

The following figure shows the networking settings:

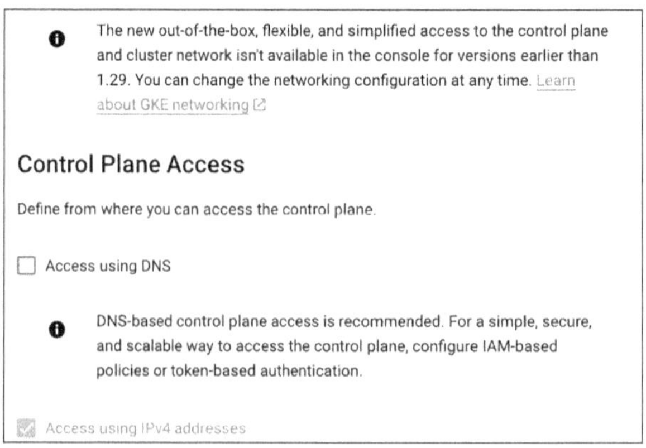

Figure 3.19: *Cluster networking in Standard mode*

Security

You can select the appropriate security configuration as shown in the following table:

Settings	Choices
Enable binary authorization	Adds an extra layer of security by requiring container images to be signed before deployment, preventing unauthorized or unverified code from running. **Example choices**: You can enable binary authorization to ensure that only signed container images are deployed in your GKE cluster. This feature helps in maintaining a secure and trusted container environment.
Shielded GKE nodes	Enhances the security of your GKE nodes by leveraging Shielded VM technology, providing protection against firmware and boot-level attacks. **Example choices**: Opting for shielded GKE nodes improves the overall security posture of your Kubernetes nodes. This is particularly useful for safeguarding against sophisticated attacks targeting the underlying infrastructure.
Workload identity	Facilitates the integration of Kubernetes workloads with Google Cloud IAM, allowing you to assign and manage permissions at the workload level. **Example choices**: Enabling Workload Identity lets your GKE workloads use Google Cloud IAM for secure access to other Google Cloud services. For instance, you have a user management service that needs to read data from a BigQuery dataset and store results in a Cloud Storage bucket. By leveraging workload identity, you can assign fine-grained permissions to the user management service directly, ensuring it only has the necessary access to read from BigQuery and write to cloud storage. This is done without granting overly broad permissions to the entire GKE cluster.
Vulnerability scanning	Automatically scans container images for known vulnerabilities before deployment, helping you identify and mitigate security risks. **Example choices**: Turning on vulnerability Scanning ensures that only images without critical vulnerabilities are deployed in your GKE cluster. Regularly scanning images is crucial for maintaining a secure container environment. **Additional costs**: Vulnerability scanning might incur additional costs based on the scanning frequency and the number of images scanned.
Legacy security option	May refer to deprecated or older security features. It is advisable to use newer, recommended security options for enhanced protection. **Example choices**: Choosing not to use legacy security options and opting for the latest and recommended security features available in GKE. Keeping security features up to date ensures protection against the latest threats and vulnerabilities.

***Table 3.10**: Security configuration*

The following figure shows the security settings:

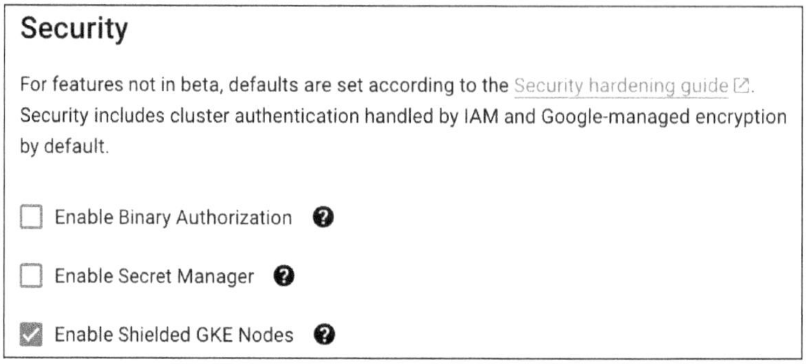

***Figure 3.20**: Cluster security in Standard mode*

Metadata

Please select the appropriate metadata configuration from the following table:

Settings	Choices
Description	This allows you to add a human-readable description for your GKE cluster. The description is typically used to provide more information about the purpose or characteristics of the cluster. **Example choices**: You can add a description like **`Production Cluster for Web Services`** to clearly convey the intended use of the cluster.
Labels	Labels are key-value pairs that you can attach to your GKE cluster. They are useful for organizing and categorizing clusters, making it easier to manage and query them. **Example choices**: You can add labels such as **`environment: production`** or **`team: devops`** to categorize and organize your GKE clusters based on specific criteria. Labels are valuable for implementing policies, automating tasks, and managing resources more efficiently within a Google Cloud environment.

***Table 3.11**: Metadata configuration*

The following are the metadata settings:

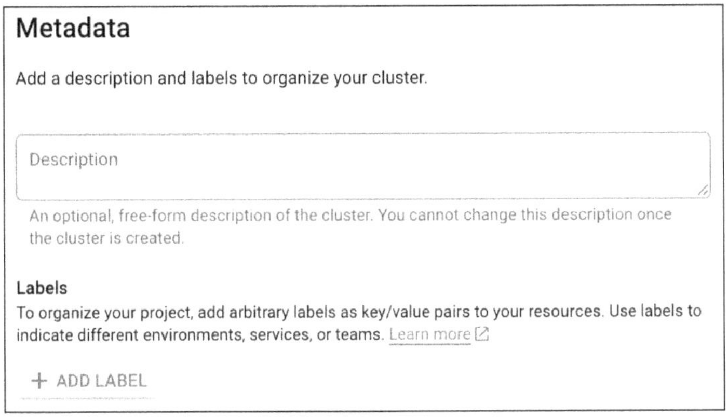

***Figure 3.21**: Cluster metadata in Standard mode*

Features

Please select the appropriate features from the following table:

Settings	Choices
Enable cloud monitoring	Enabling cloud monitoring integrates your GKE cluster with Google Cloud's monitoring service. This allows you to collect and analyze performance metrics, set up alerts, and gain insights into the health and performance of your cluster. **Example choices**: By enabling cloud monitoring, you can easily track metrics like CPU usage, memory usage, and network traffic for your GKE workloads. Setting up monitoring is crucial for proactive management and troubleshooting of your GKE cluster. Utilize dashboards and alerts to stay informed about your cluster's health. **Additional costs**: While enabling basic monitoring is usually free, there may be additional costs for advanced features or monitoring of specific resources.
Service mesh	Service mesh, often referring to Istio in the context of GKE, is a layer for managing communication between microservices. It provides features like traffic management, security, and observability, enhancing the capabilities of your GKE applications. **Example choices**: Integrating Istio as a service mesh to enable features such as traffic routing, load balancing, and monitoring between microservices in your GKE cluster. Service mesh helps in managing and securing communication between services, improving overall reliability and observability of your application.

Settings	Choices
Others (cloud TPU, cost allocation, backup for GKE, compute engine PD CSI Driver)	The additional options mentioned, including cloud TPU, cost allocation, backup for GKE, and CSI Drivers, offer specialized functionalities for optimizing and enhancing the capabilities of your GKE clusters. Cloud TPU support enables high-performance machine learning acceleration, cost allocation helps in tracking and attributing expenses, backup for GKE ensures data preservation and disaster recovery, and the Compute Engine PD CSI Driver allows seamless integration of PD for containerized workloads. Each option addresses specific needs, contributing to the efficiency, reliability, and cost-effectiveness of your GKE infrastructure.

Table 3.12: Feature configuration

The following figure shows the features settings:

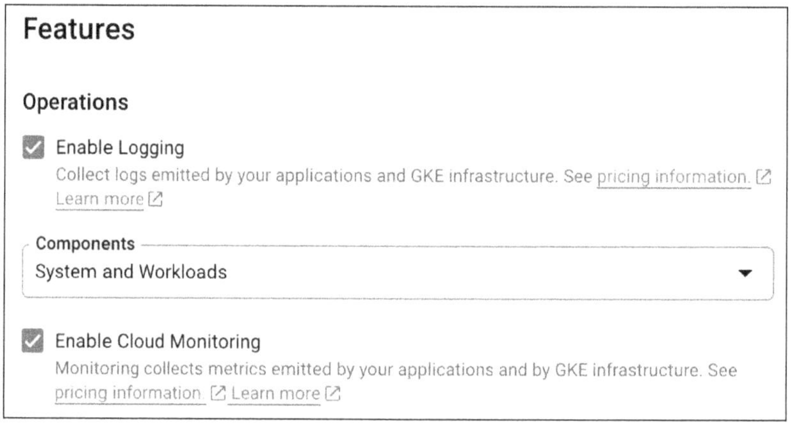

Figure 3.22: Cluster features in Standard mode

Conclusion

In conclusion, this chapter guided us through the creation of our first GKE cluster, offering various methods to achieve this.

We explored customizing cluster configurations and touched upon enabling and configuring GKE add-ons, providing additional functionalities to the cluster. We explored storage options within GKE, discussing PVs and the difference between stateful and stateless applications.

As we wrap up this chapter, you should feel confident in creating and customizing GKE clusters through different methods, optimizing performance, and integrating storage solutions tailored to their application requirements. This foundational knowledge serves as a valuable steppingstone for further exploration and mastery of GKE.

The next chapter focuses on the practical implementation of setting up a GKE environment. It bridges theory with real-world application, highlighting the value of hands-on experience in mastering GKE management.

Multiple choice questions

1. **In which scenario would you likely choose the GCP Console for creating a GKE cluster?**
    a. When you prefer automated cluster creation
    b. For a user-friendly walkthrough and visual representation
    c. When you want complete control through command line tools
    d. When you need to integrate GKE with AWS services
2. **When might you consider using Terraform for GKE cluster creation?**
    a. For manual and one-time cluster setups
    b. When you need a graphical interface
    c. When you want to automate cluster creation as code
    d. For managing GKE add-ons exclusively
3. **Which use case is most suitable for configuring different node pools in a GKE cluster?**
    a. Uniform application requirements across all nodes
    b. When applications have diverse resource needs
    c. For clusters with a fixed number of nodes
    d. Only when using the GCP Console for cluster creation
4. **In what situation would you enable and configure cluster auto-scaler in a GKE cluster?**
    a. For small clusters with consistent traffic
    b. In clusters with fixed and predictable workloads
    c. When you need automated scaling based on demand
    d. Exclusively for stateful applications

5. **Why is workload identity beneficial in a microservices architecture on GKE?**
    a. To replace traditional microservices with serverless functions.
    b. To organize microservices into fleets for better scalability.
    c. To securely manage access to Google Cloud services for individual microservices.
    d. To optimize network routing within GKE clusters.

Answer key

1.	b
2.	c
3.	b
4.	c
5.	c

Chapter 4
Setting Up Your GKE Environment

Introduction

This chapter discusses the practical aspects of setting up a GKE environment. It is designed to translate theoretical knowledge into real-world skills, emphasizing the importance of hands-on experience in understanding and managing GKE. This chapter begins with an overview of the necessary system preparations and requirements, ensuring the reader's environment is ready for GKE deployment. It starts with Google Cloud SDK (gcloud CLI), a set of tools that includes the gcloud command line tool for managing resources on GCP, essential for interacting with your GKE cluster. The focus shifts to essential Kubernetes tools like kubectl, which is crucial for interacting with the Kubernetes cluster. This chapter also covers K9s and OpenLens as well as advanced tools like kustomize, Helm, Argo CD, Prometheus, and Grafana to equip readers with the knowledge to manage Kubernetes resources effectively.

Structure

This chapter covers the following topics:

- Preparing your system
- Authenticating the local system with GKE cluster
- GKE management and automation tools

Objectives

By the end of this chapter, you will gain the practical knowledge and hands-on experience in setting up a GKE environment. You will understand the importance and process of preparing your system for GKE. You will have an understanding of essential tools like **gcloud CLI** and **kubectl**. You learn how to install **Visual Studio Code** (**VS Code**) for Kubernetes-related tasks and navigate advanced Kubernetes management tools like K9s and OpenLens. You get to learn the installation of advanced tools related to management and automation of GKE like kustomize, Helm, Argo CD, Prometheus, and Grafana.

Preparing your system

In this section, we will ensure your system is equipped with the essential tools and configurations needed for a seamless GKE setup and management.

Installing Visual Studio Code

VS Code is a popular open-source code editor developed by *Microsoft*. While it is not specifically required for GKE, many developers find it to be a convenient and powerful tool for working with Kubernetes clusters, including GKE. The installation steps are as follows:

- For Mac:
  1. Open Terminal.
  2. Install `Homebrew` (if not installed):
     ```
     /bin/bash -c "$(curl -fsSL https://raw.githubusercontent.com/Homebrew/install/HEAD/install.sh)"
     ```
  3. Install VS Code:
     ```
     brew install --cask visual-studio-code
     ```
- For Windows:
  1. Open PowerShell as administrator.
  2. Install Chocolatey (if not installed):
     ```
     Set-ExecutionPolicy Bypass -Scope Process -Force; [System.Net.ServicePointManager]::SecurityProtocol = [System.Net.ServicePointManager]::SecurityProtocol -bor 3072; iex ((New-Object System.Net.WebClient).DownloadString('https://chocolatey.org/install.ps1'))
     ```
  3. Install VS Code:
     ```
     choco install vscode
     ```

Note: Ensure you have administrative privileges on both MacBook and Windows for installation.

You can also download Visual Studio Code directly from the official website (https://code.visualstudio.com/) for both Mac and Windows, if you prefer not to use the package managers.

Installing gcloud SDK and kubectl

gcloud SDK is a set of tools that allows you to manage resources and applications hosted on GCP, including GKE. It is crucial for managing GKE clusters and for configuring Google Cloud settings.

kubectl is the primary command line tool for interacting with Kubernetes, including GKE. A system for automating the deployment, scaling, and management of containerized applications. It allows you to deploy applications, inspect and manage cluster resources, and view logs.

Installation steps: These installation steps ensure that you have the tools required to interact with Google Cloud and Kubernetes.

For Mac:

1. Open Terminal.
2. Run the command: **`curl https://sdk.cloud.google.com | bash`**
3. Restart your shell: **`exec -l $SHELL`**
4. Install **`kubectl`** using **`gcloud`**: **`gcloud components install kubectl`**

For Windows:

1. Open PowerShell as Administrator.
2. Run the cloud SDK installer script:
   ```
   (New-Object System.Net.WebClient).DownloadFile("https://dl.google.com/dl/cloudsdk/channels/rapid/GoogleCloudSDKInstaller.exe", "$env:Temp\GoogleCloudSDKInstaller.exe"); Start-Process -FilePath "$env:Temp\GoogleCloudSDKInstaller.exe"
   ```
3. Follow the installer's prompts to complete the installation.
4. After installation, use **`gcloud`** to install **`kubectl`**: **`gcloud components install kubectl`**

Note: Make sure to have administrative privileges for the installations and restart the shell or command prompt after installation for the changes to take effect.

Using Homebrew and Chocolatey for installation

You can also use Homebrew on a MacBook and Chocolatey on a Windows system, for the installation of the gcloud SDK and kubectl, use the following commands in VS Code's Terminal (open VS Code | Terminal | New Terminal) or any other command Terminal (Mac Terminal or Windows PowerShell):

For Mac:

1. Install **Homebrew**:

   ```
   /bin/bash -c "$(curl -fsSL https://raw.githubusercontent.com/
   Homebrew/install/HEAD/install.sh)"
   ```

2. Install **gcloud** SDK and **kubectl** using **Homebrew**:

   ```
   brew install --cask google-cloud-sdk && gcloud components install
   kubectl
   ```

For Windows:

1. Install Chocolatey:

   ```
   Set-ExecutionPolicy Bypass -Scope Process -Force; [System.
   Net.ServicePointManager]::SecurityProtocol = [System.Net.
   ServicePointManager]::SecurityProtocol -bor 3072; iex ((New-Object
   System.Net.WebClient).DownloadString('https://chocolatey.org/
   install.ps1'))
   ```

2. Install **gcloud** SDK and **kubectl** using Chocolatey: **choco install gcloudsdk && gcloud components install kubectl**

Verifying the installation of gcloud SDK and kubectl

Once the installations are complete, run **gcloud** and **kubectl** to check the outputs using the following commands:

The following figure displays the result of executing the **gcloud** command:

```
Command name argument expected.

Available command groups for gcloud:

  AI and Machine Learning
      ai                        Manage entities in Vertex AI.
      ai-platform               Manage AI Platform jobs and models.
      ml                        Use Google Cloud machine learning capabilities.
      ml-engine                 Manage AI Platform jobs and models.
      notebooks                 Notebooks Command Group.
      workbench                 Workbench Command Group.

  API Platform and Ecosystems
      api-gateway               Manage Cloud API Gateway resources.
      apigee                    Manage Apigee resources.
      endpoints                 Create, enable and manage API services.
      recommender               Manage Cloud recommendations and recommendation
                                rules.
      services                  List, enable and disable APIs and services.

  Anthos CLI
      anthos                    Anthos command Group.

  Batch
      batch                     Manage Batch resources.
```

Figure 4.1: Output of command gcloud

The following figure displays the result of executing the **`kubectl`** command:

```
User@DESKTOP-FP4OP26 MINGW64 ~
$ kubectl
kubectl controls the Kubernetes cluster manager.

 Find more information at: https://kubernetes.io/docs/reference/kubectl/

Basic Commands (Beginner):
  create          Create a resource from a file or from stdin
  expose          Take a replication controller, service, deployment or pod and expose it as a new Kubernetes servic
  run             Run a particular image on the cluster
  set             Set specific features on objects

Basic Commands (Intermediate):
  explain         Get documentation for a resource
  get             Display one or many resources
  edit            Edit a resource on the server
  delete          Delete resources by file names, stdin, resources and names, or by resources and label selector

Deploy Commands:
  rollout         Manage the rollout of a resource
  scale           Set a new size for a deployment, replica set, or replication controller
  autoscale       Auto-scale a deployment, replica set, stateful set, or replication controller

Cluster Management Commands:
  certificate     Modify certificate resources
  cluster-info    Display cluster information
  top             Display resource (CPU/memory) usage
  cordon          Mark node as unschedulable
  uncordon        Mark node as schedulable
  drain           Drain node in preparation for maintenance
  taint           Update the taints on one or more nodes
```

Figure 4.2: Output of command kubectl

Tip: To further ensure that both tools are correctly configured and functional:

- **For `gcloud`, use the command: `gcloud version`**
- **For `kubectl`, use the command: `kubectl version`**

Authenticating the local system with GKE Cluster

In your Terminal, run:

```
gcloud auth login
```

This command is used to authenticate your Google Cloud CLI to access your Google Cloud account. Now, run:

```
gcloud auth application-default login
```

This command sets up the default credentials for application development with GCP services. It is useful when running or testing applications locally that will eventually be deployed on GCP. Both commands open a web browser for you to log in and provide a verification code, which we need to click **Allow,** as shown in *Figure 4.3*:

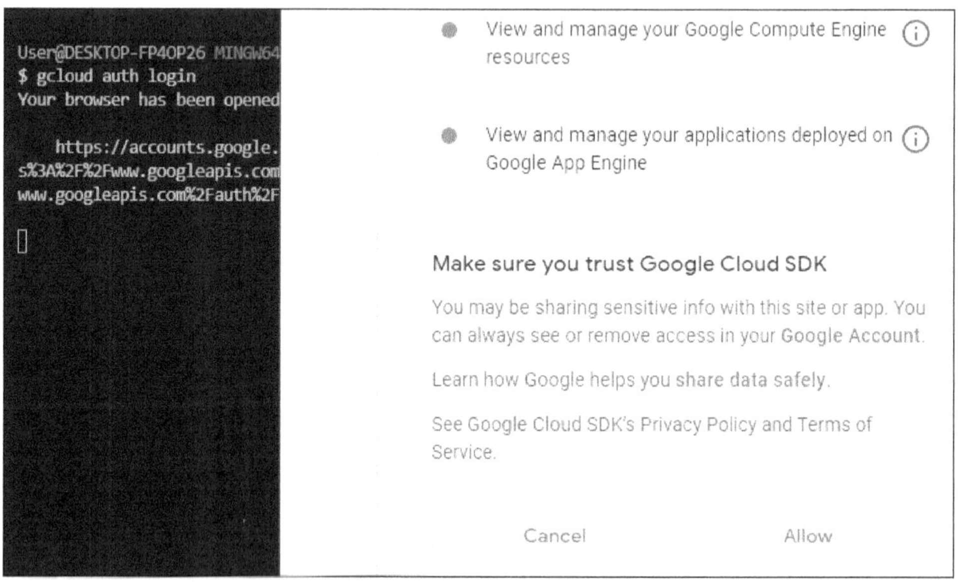

Figure 4.3: Authenticate Google Cloud SDK

Run: **`gcloud config set project [PROJECT_ID]`**

This command configures the Google Cloud CLI to use a specific Google Cloud project by its ID. Replace **`[PROJECT_ID]`** with your actual GCP project ID (which you can get from **Project info** or the top-left project panel).

Select the GCP project as shown in the following figure:

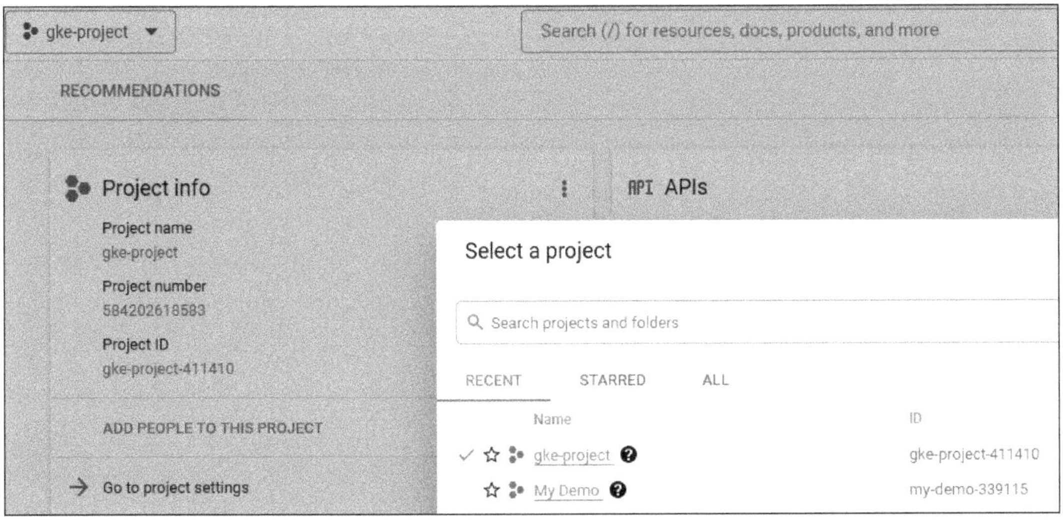

Figure 4.4: Select the GCP project

Now, run the following commands:

```
gcloud services enable compute.googleapis.com
gcloud services enable container.googleapis.com
```

These commands enable specific Google Cloud services for your project.

Here, **`compute.googleapis.com`** enables the Compute Engine service, and **`container.googleapis.com`** enables the Kubernetes Engine service.

You can create the cluster as explained in *Chapter 3, Creating and Configuring a GKE Cluster* with the following commands:

```
gcloud container clusters create [CLUSTER_NAME] --region [REGION]
gcloud container clusters create gke-cluster --region "us-west1"
```

The commands will create a new GKE cluster with the specified name in the specified region. Now, replace **`[CLUSTER_NAME]`** and **`[REGION]`** with your desired inputs, i.e., **`cluster name gke-cluster`** and **`region (us-west1)`**, respectively.

Once the GKE cluster is ready, click on the three dots icon on the right and click on **Connect** (circled for your reference in *Figure 4.5*):

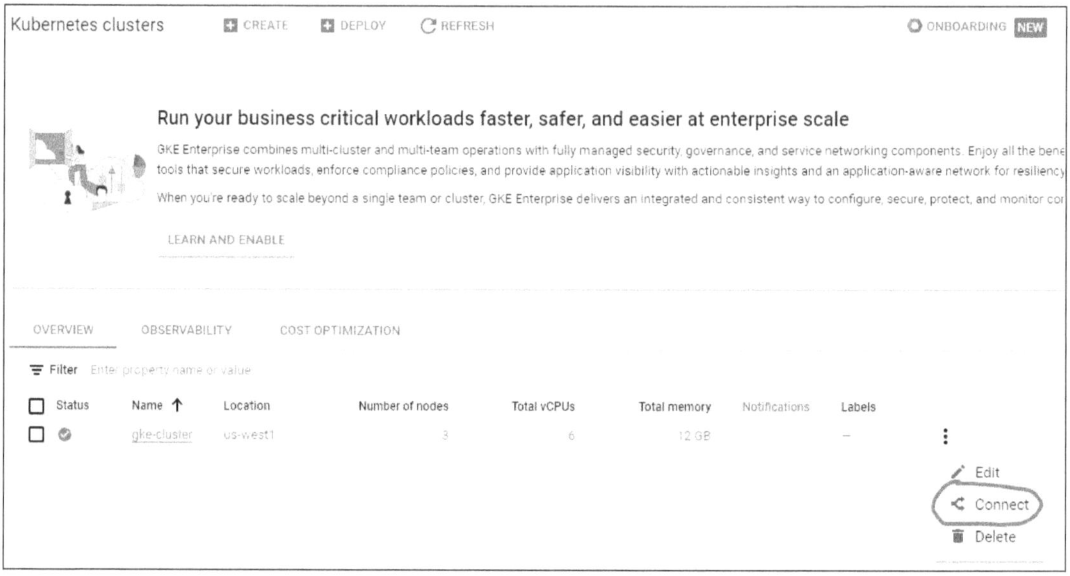

Figure 4.5: Connect to GKE cluster

```
gcloud container clusters get-credentials gke-cluster --region us-west1
--project [PROJECT_ID]
```

Copy the preceding command and paste it into our local command line Terminal, which will retrieve the credentials for the **gke-cluster** and configure **kubectl** to use them from the local system. It specifies the cluster in the **us-west1** region and associates it with the mentioned Google Cloud project.

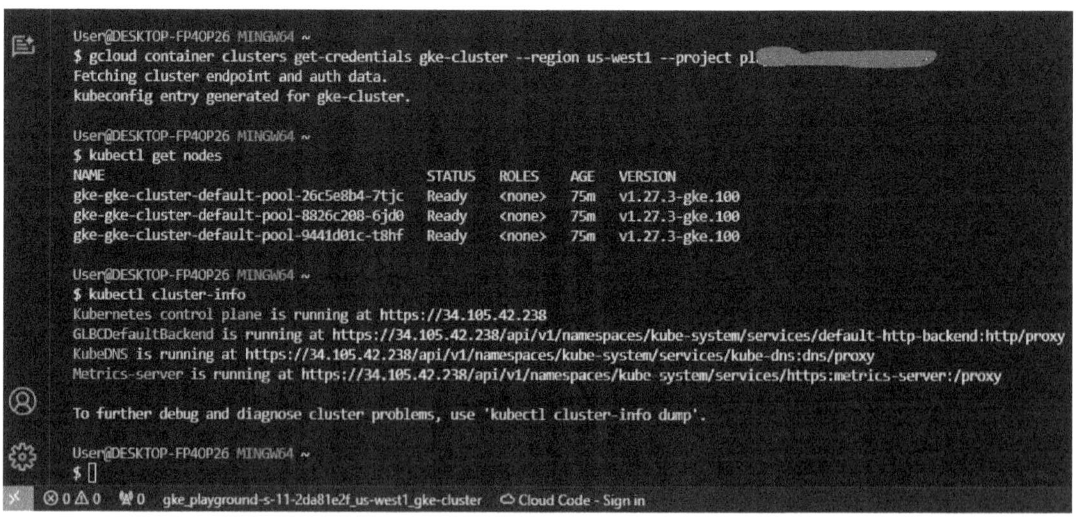

Figure 4.6: Running commands from the local system

Now, you can run all **`kubectl`** commands to perform and manage all the deployment and management inside the GKE cluster from your local system. Remember to **Connect to the cluster** from your local Terminal using the following command:

Figure 4.7: *Command to connect to GKE cluster*

GKE management and automation tools

Now, we will install the management and automation tools that would be required to manage the GKE Clusters from your local system (Windows and Mac/Linux).

The Google Cloud SDK and kubectl are the first prerequisite tools for managing GKE clusters. Kustomize, Argo CD, and Prometheus and Grafana stack are the rest of the essential tools for effectively managing GKE clusters from local Mac or Windows laptops. The gcloud SDK acts as a gateway, providing comprehensive command line access to Google Cloud resources, while kubectl is pivotal for direct interactions with the Kubernetes cluster. **Kustomize** enhances Kubernetes resource management through customizable deployments. **Argo CD** facilitates continuous delivery by automating the deployment process in alignment with GitOps principles. The **Prometheus-Grafana stack**, on the other hand, offers robust monitoring and visualization capabilities, crucial for maintaining cluster health and performance insights. Collectively, these tools form a powerful suite for seamless, efficient, and scalable management of GKE clusters.

Kustomize

Kustomize is a configuration management tool designed for Kubernetes. It allows users to customize raw, template-free **YAML Ain't Markup Language (YAML)** files for multiple purposes, maintaining the simplicity and declarative nature of Kubernetes resource configurations. The main advantages of using kustomize include:

- **Simplicity**: Kustomize operates directly on YAML files, eliminating the need for complex templating.
- **Flexibility**: It enables easy management of distinct configurations for different environments (development, staging, production) without duplication.
- **Ease of use**: Kustomize integrates seamlessly with kubectl, making it user-friendly and easily adoptable.
- **Safety**: By keeping configurations declarative, it reduces the risk of errors during deployment.

These qualities make kustomize an essential tool for Kubernetes users seeking an efficient and error-free way to manage their configurations.

Installation

The installation of kustomize is not required on the GKE cluster as it is a client-side tool. We will use kustomize on our local machine to deploy applications to GKE.

For Mac and Linux users:

You can install on your system with the following command:

```
curl -s "https://raw.githubusercontent.com/kubernetes-sigs/kustomize/master/hack/install_kustomize.sh" | bash
```

1. To find where kustomize is installed, run the following command from your home directory:

   ```
   find . -name kustomize
   ```

2. To move kustomize to a directory in your PATH, such as **/usr/local/bin/**, use the following command if kustomize is in your current directory:

   ```
   mv kustomize /usr/local/bin/
   ```

3. Ensure the binary is executable:

   ```
   chmod +x /usr/local/bin/kustomize
   ```

   Alternatively, you can also install it via Homebrew (in command Terminal or VS Code):

   ```
   brew install kustomize
   ```

4. Now, you can verify the installation by running:

   ```
   kustomize version
   ```

For Windows users:

Download kustomize for Windows from the official releases page (**https://kubectl.docs.kubernetes.io/installation/kustomize/**).

Now, extract the executable from the downloaded archive and add the path to the kustomize executable to your system's PATH environment variable.

Alternatively, you can also install it via Chocolatey (in PowerShell as Administrator or VS Code) using the following command:

```
choco install kustomize
```

Or via Scoop package manager:

```
scoop install kustomize
```

Now, you can verify the installation by running the following command:

```
kustomize version
```

For more detailed documentation, please refer the page: **https://kubectl.docs.kubernetes.io/installation/kustomize/**.

Helm

Helm is often described as the package manager for Kubernetes. It simplifies the process of managing and deploying applications on Kubernetes clusters. The main advantages of using Helm are:

- **Simplification**: Helm streamlines the installation and management of complex Kubernetes applications, turning potentially lengthy deployment scripts into a single command.
- **Manage dependencies**: Helm handles dependencies between different Kubernetes components, making it easier to maintain and update applications.
- **Reusable packages**: With Helm, you can create and share charts — packages of pre-configured Kubernetes resources, enabling reuse and standardization.
- **Version control**: Helm tracks the version history of your deployments, allowing you to rollback to previous versions easily.

Incorporating Helm into your Kubernetes workflow can significantly enhance efficiency and consistency, particularly for complex deployments.

Installation

The installation of Helm is not required on the GKE cluster as it is a client-side tool. We will use Helm on our local machine to deploy applications to GKE.

For Mac and Linux users:

Helm has an installer script that will automatically grab the latest version of Helm and install it locally through the following steps:

1. You can fetch that script and then execute it locally. It is well documented so you can read through it and understand what it is doing before you run it.

```
$ curl -fsSL -o get_helm.sh https://raw.githubusercontent.com/helm/helm/main/scripts/get-helm-3
$ chmod 700 get_helm.sh
$ ./get_helm.sh
```

Alternatively, you can also install it via Homebrew (in command Terminal or VS Code) using the following command:

```
brew install helm
or via Snap:
sudo snap install helm --classic
```

For Windows users:

1. You can install Helm via Chocolatey (in PowerShell as Administrator or VS Code):

```
choco install helm
```

Alternatively, you can also install it via Scoop:

```
scoop install helm
```

For more detailed documentation, please refer the page: **https://helm.sh/docs/intro/install/**.

Argo CD

Argo CD is a declarative, GitOps continuous delivery tool for Kubernetes. It automates the deployment process by syncing applications defined in a Git repository with the Kubernetes clusters. The main advantages of using Argo CD include:

- **Automated synchronization**: Automatically deploys applications as soon as the changes are pushed to the Git repository.
- **Declarative setup**: Uses Git to manage and store the desired state of applications, enhancing reproducibility and consistency.
- **Self-healing**: Automatically corrects any deviations from the desired state, ensuring the applications are always in the intended state.
- **Ease of use**: Simplifies complex deployment processes, making it easier to manage applications on Kubernetes.

Argo CD is popular for its ability to streamline deployment processes and maintain consistency across environments, making it a valuable tool for modern Kubernetes-based applications.

Installation

To install Argo CD in GKE Cluster, create an **argocd** namespace if not already done, using the following command:

```
kubectl create ns argocd
```

Once done, apply the Argo CD manifest:

```
kubectl apply -n argocd -f https://raw.githubusercontent.com/argoproj/argo-cd/stable/manifests/install.yaml
```

For Mac and Linux users:

1. We can install ArgoCD CLI via Homebrew (in command Terminal or VS Code) with the following command:

   ```
   brew install argocd
   ```

For Windows users:

1. You can install ArgoCD CLI via Chocolatey (in PowerShell as Administrator or VS Code):

   ```
   choco install argocd-cli
   ```

   Alternatively, you can also install via Scoop:

   ```
   scoop install argocd
   ```

For more detailed documentation, please refer the following pages:

- **https://argo-cd.readthedocs.io/en/stable/cli_installation/**
- **https://argo-cd.readthedocs.io/en/stable/operator-manual/installation/**

Prometheus and Grafana

The Prometheus-Grafana stack is a popular combination in cloud and container environments for monitoring and visualizing metrics. Prometheus collects and stores metrics as time series data, providing powerful querying capabilities. Grafana, on the other hand, is used for visualizing this data, offering customizable dashboards for a clear view of what is happening in your system. The main advantages of using this stack include:

- **Comprehensive monitoring**: Together, they provide detailed insights into the performance and health of applications and infrastructure.
- **Customization and flexibility**: Grafana offers extensive customization for dashboards, and Prometheus has a flexible query language.
- **Scalability**: Both of these tools are designed to handle large-scale data, making them suitable for growing systems.

This stack is ideal for those needing in-depth, real-time monitoring, and visualization capabilities in their technological environment.

Installation

In GKE cluster, there are multiple ways to install Prometheus-Grafana stack in Kubernetes. But in our GKE cluster, we will be installing Prometheus-Grafana stack using Helm, which is one of the easier options available.

We will add the Prometheus community repository to Helm with the help of the following command:

```
helm repo add prometheus-community https://prometheus-community.github.io/
helm-charts
```

We will now update Helm's local repository list to ensure it has the latest versions with the aid of the following command:

```
helm repo update
```

Now, let us type the following command to create a new namespace in Kubernetes named **Prometheus**:

```
kubectl create namespace Prometheus
```

To install the **Prometheus** stack in the **prometheus** namespace using Helm will use the following command:

```
helm install prometheus prometheus-community/kube-prometheus-stack -n
Prometheus
```

To retrieve all the newly created resources (like Pods, services, etc.) in the **prometheus** namespace:

```
kubectl get all -n Prometheus
```

The following command filters and checks for the specific Prometheus Pod which we need to access Prometheus UI:

```
kubectl get pods -n prometheus | grep prometheus-prometheus-kube-
prometheus-prometheus-0
```

The following command forwards port **9090** from the local machine to the **Prometheus** Pod for UI access:

```
kubectl port-forward prometheus-prometheus-kube-prometheus-prometheus-0
9090 -n Prometheus
```

Now, you can access Prometheus UI via 127.0.0.1:9090 or localhost:9090, as shown in the following figure:

Figure 4.8: Prometheus homepage

The following command lists all services in the **`Prometheus`** namespace to get the details of Grafana service:

```
kubectl get svc -n Prometheus
```

We will modify the Grafana service type from ClusterIP to LoadBalancer:

Service manifest: Here is an example of the service manifest before and after changing the type from **`ClusterIP`** to **`LoadBalancer`**. This allows external access to Grafana UI.

- **Before (ClusterIP)**: The following is the service manifest prior to making any changes:

  ```
  apiVersion: v1
  kind: Service
  metadata:
    name: prometheus-grafana
    namespace: prometheus
  spec:
    type: ClusterIP
    ports:
      - port: 3000
        targetPort: 3000
    selector:
      app: Grafana
  ```

  Then run the command **`kubectl edit service prometheus-grafana -n Prometheus`** and update the service manifest as given below. The changes will be applied automatically after you save the file within the editor.

```
apiVersion: v1
kind: Service
metadata:
  name: prometheus-grafana
  namespace: prometheus
spec:
  type: LoadBalancer
  ports:
    - port: 3000
      targetPort: 3000
  selector:
    app: Grafana
```

Note: Here, we could have accessed Grafana UI by port-forward method like Prometheus, but we will access Grafana using another service type called LoadBalancer.

We can use the following command for real-time watching the updated service type for Prometheus-Grafana service and get the LoadBalancer IP:

```
kubectl get service -n prometheus -watch
```

The following command retrieves the decoded Grafana admin password:

```
kubectl get secret prometheus-grafana -o jsonpath="{.data.admin-password}"
-n prometheus | base64 --decode ; echo
```

Now, you can access Grafana UI via [LoadBalancer:portnumber]:

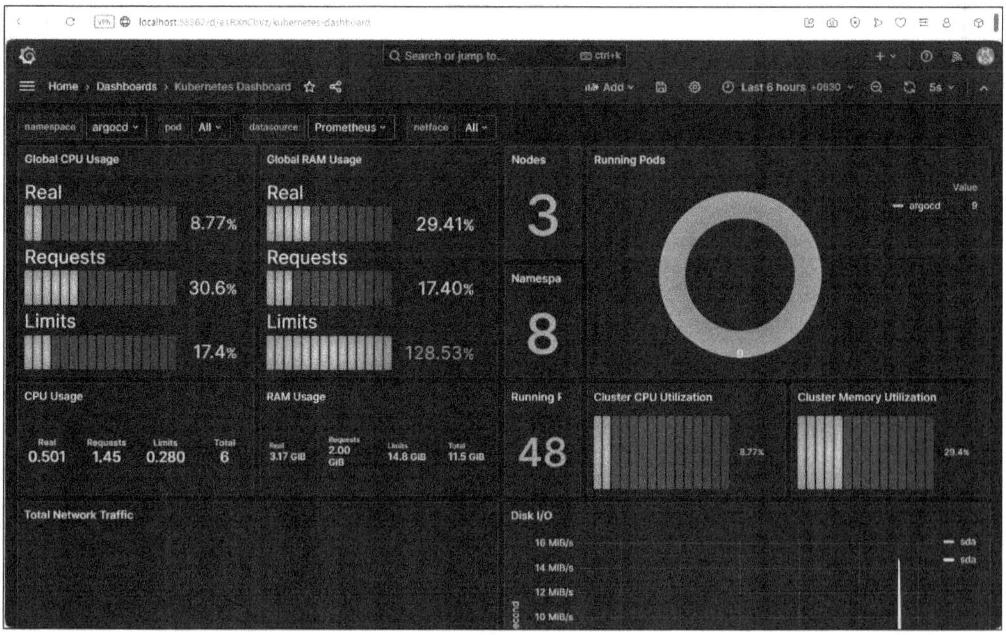

Figure 4.9: Grafana homepage

In enterprise environment, we do not install Prometheus-Grafana stack in our local (mac or windows) system. As shown in *Figure 4.9*, we install these directly as a service inside the GKE cluster.

OpenLens and K9s

OpenLens is a highly intuitive desktop application designed for Kubernetes cluster management. It offers a user-friendly interface, simplifying interactions with your Kubernetes clusters. OpenLens enhances visibility into cluster operations, making it easier to deploy, monitor, and troubleshoot applications within Kubernetes.

On the other hand, K9s is a Terminal-based tool that provides a text-based user interface to interact with your Kubernetes clusters. It focuses on simplifying cluster management through a command-line interface, offering efficient navigation and operation within Kubernetes environments. K9s is particularly favoured for its streamlined approach to cluster monitoring and management tasks.

Both tools do the same tasks, hence, you can use either to manage your GKE or any other Kubernetes clusters from your laptop.

Installation (OpenLens)

For Windows users:

We can install it using the command: `choco install openlens --version=6.1.12`

For Mac and Linux users:

This command will help us with the installation: `brew install --cask openlens`

Once your GKE cluster is ready and accessible from your local system, you can open OpenLens, which will give you the interface shown in *Figure 4.10*. You can take a full tour of the tool to see the comprehensive features and tasks that you can perform.

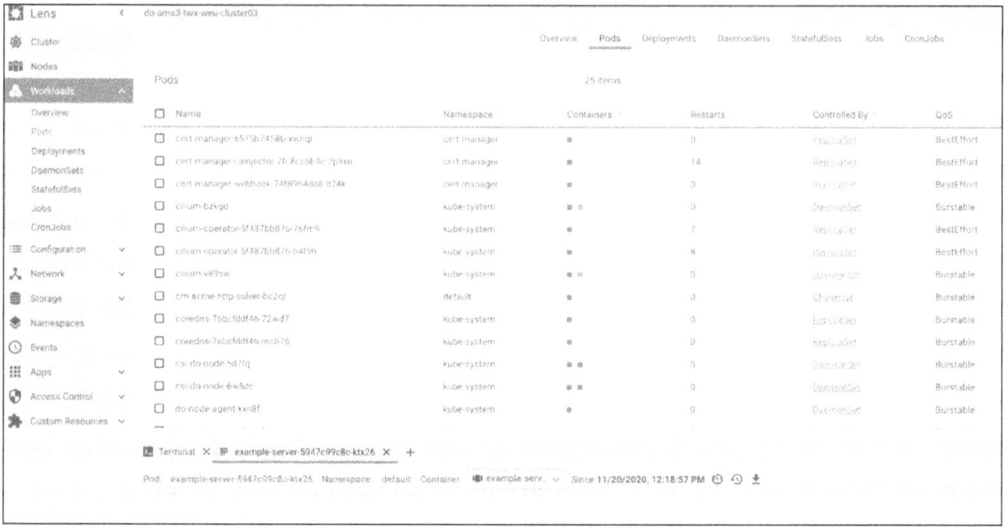

Figure 4.10: OpenLens homepage

For comprehensive documentation, visit the link: **https://docs.k8slens.dev/how-to/**.

Installation (K9s)

For Windows users:

This command will help us with installation: **`choco install k9s`**

For Mac and Linux users:

We can install it with this command: **`brew install k9s`**

Once your GKE cluster is ready and accessible from your local system, you can type the command **`k9s`** in your Terminal, which will give you the interface as shown in *Figure 4.11*. You can take a full tour of the tool to see the comprehensive features and tasks that you can perform.

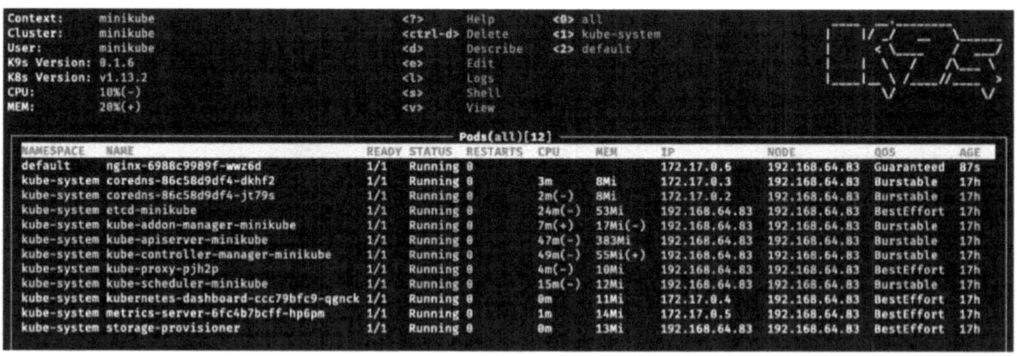

Figure 4.11: K9s Terminal

For comprehensive documentation, visit the link: **https://k9scli.io/topics/commands/**

Conclusion

This chapter focuses on setting up your development environment for effective work with GKE. It covers the installation and configuration of essential tools, automation utilities, and management solutions. This is a foundational chapter that equips developers with the essential tools and configurations needed to work efficiently with GKE. By installing VS Code, gcloud SDK, kubectl, and other automation and management tools, developers can streamline their development workflows, enhance cluster management, and improve the overall experience of developing, deploying, and monitoring applications on GKE.

Multiple choice questions

1. **What is the primary purpose of kustomize in the context of GKE development?**
    a. Monitoring Kubernetes clusters
    b. Customizing Kubernetes manifests without modifying original files
    c. Managing Helm charts
    d. Visualizing cluster metrics with Grafana
2. **Which tool is introduced as a package manager for Kubernetes in the chapter?**
    a. Argo CD
    b. Kustomize
    c. Helm
    d. OpenLens
3. **What does Argo CD specialize in within a GKE environment?**
    a. Monitoring applications on GKE clusters
    b. Continuous delivery and management of Kubernetes applications
    c. Customizing Kubernetes manifests
    d. Configuring authentication with GKE clusters
4. **Which tool is recommended for visualizing and monitoring cluster metrics within GKE?**
    a. K9s
    b. Prometheus
    c. OpenLens
    d. Helm

5. **What is the role of OpenLens in the context of GKE development?**
   a. Customizing Kubernetes manifests
   b. Monitoring Kubernetes clusters
   c. A Kubernetes-native IDE for cluster management
   d. Package management for Kubernetes applications

Answer key

1.	b
2.	c
3.	b
4.	b
5.	c

CHAPTER 5

Deploying Applications on GKE

Introduction

Deploying applications on GKE requires a structured approach to ensure your applications run efficiently and reliably. This chapter walks you through the important steps and knowledge about essential tools required for deployments.

Structure

This chapter covers the following topics:

- Basics of YAML
- GKE basics for deployment
- Deploying applications
- Managing deployments with Argo CD

Objectives

This is a foundational topic that would cover the essential concepts and steps needed to deploy applications on GKE. Key points would include understanding **YAML Ain't Markup Language** (**YAML**), and how to deploy applications in GKE using kubectl, Helm, Argo CD and kustomize. The aim is to provide readers with the knowledge to deploy applications such as web apps, APIs, or microservices, on GKE efficiently. You can manage deployments for multi-tier architectures, and handle environment-specific configurations using tools like kustomize. These skills empower developers to confidently build, deploy, and manage applications on GKE in real-world scenarios.

Basics of YAML

For deploying applications in GKE, we first need to understand YAML. It is a way to describe data in a structured format that is easy to read. If you wanted to describe a list of fruits in YAML, it would look like:

```
fruits:
  - apple
  - banana
  - grape
```

Dictionary is a collection of key-value pairs, for example:

```
fruit:
  name: apple
  color: red
  taste: sweet
```

Example of dictionary with list values:

```
fruits:
  apple: [red, sweet, crunchy]
  banana: [yellow, sweet, soft]
  grape: [green, sour, small]
```

A mixed example:

```
fruits:
  - name: apple
    attributes: [red, sweet, crunchy]
  - name: banana
    attributes: [yellow, sweet, soft]
  - name: grape
    attributes: [green, sour, small]
```

When writing YAML, some best practices for indentation include:

- **Consistency**: Always use the same number of spaces for each indentation level throughout the YAML file.
- **Spaces, not tabs**: Use spaces instead of tabs for indentation; tabs can be interpreted differently by various tools and can cause errors.

- **Two-space indentation**: Although YAML allows any number of spaces, the common convention is to use two spaces for each indentation level for readability.
- **Validation**: Use a linter or validator to check for syntax errors, which can easily occur due to incorrect indentation. An example of a linter for YAML in VS Code is the YAML Language Server extension.
- **Alignment**: Ensure that items that are at the same level of the hierarchy are aligned vertically with the same number of spaces.

By following these practices, you will create YAML files that are both readable and less prone to errors, which is particularly important in configuration files for systems like Kubernetes.

To install a YAML extension in VS Code, follow these steps:

1. Open VS Code.
2. Go to the Extensions view by clicking on the square icon on the sidebar or pressing *Ctrl+Shift+X*.
3. In the search bar at the top, type **`YAML`** to find YAML extensions.
4. Look for the YAML Language Support by *Red Hat* or another preferred YAML extension.
5. Click on the **Install** button next to the extension to install it, shown as follows:

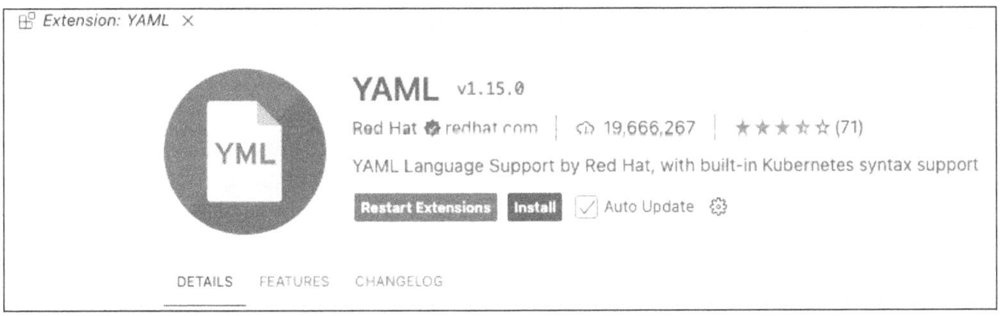

Figure 5.1*: VS Code YAML extension*

YAML files are used to define Kubernetes resources such as Pods, deployments, services, and more. Understanding YAML syntax is essential for configuring and deploying applications on GKE.

GKE basics for deployment

YAML is utilized to define the components of GKE. To review their definitions, please revisit the section titled *Common terms in the Kubernetes ecosystem* in *Chapter 1, Introduction to Kubernetes and Containerization*.

We will use manifest written in YAML format to create Kubernetes resources based on these definitions.

Manifest are configuration files written in YAML or JSON format that describe the desired state of Kubernetes resources. These files define the characteristics and specifications of various Kubernetes objects, such as Pods, deployments, services, Ingress controllers, and more. Manifest typically includes key sections such as apiVersion, kind, metadata, and spec:

- **apiVersion** specifies the Kubernetes API version being used.
- **kind** defines the type of resource being created (e.g., deployment, service).
- **metadata** provides additional information like the name and labels of the resource.
- **spec** outlines the desired configuration parameters and settings for the resource.

When applied to a Kubernetes cluster using the **kubectl apply** command, Kubernetes compares the current state of the cluster to the state described in the manifest files and takes actions to reconcile any differences, ensuring that the cluster matches the desired state specified in the manifests. This allows for easy management and automation of deployments, updates, and configurations within Kubernetes environments.

Skeletal structure of the manifest without any values looks like this:

```
apiVersion:
kind:
metadata:
spec:
```

Now, let us see how to create a Pod using this above template.

Manifest for Pod

Here is a basic example of a Kubernetes Pod manifest that defines a simple Pod running an **nginx** container:

```
apiVersion: v1
kind: Pod
metadata:
  name: example-pod-name
spec:
  containers:
  - name: example-container-name
    image: nginx
```

To summarize, if we want to create and deploy a Pod in a GKE cluster, we need to follow the steps shown in *Figure 5.2*:

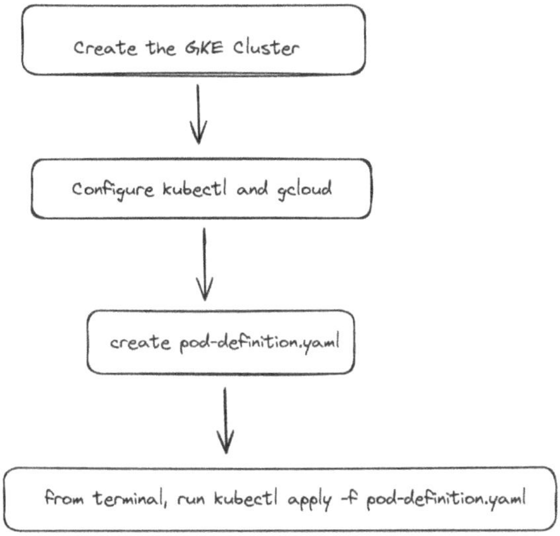

***Figure 5.2**: Steps to deploy Pod in GKE cluster*

To deploy a Pod in your GKE cluster, follow these steps to set up the environment and apply the Pod manifest:

1. **Set up GKE environment**: Ensure you have Google Cloud SDK installed and authenticated.
2. **Configure kubectl**: Use gcloud to set the default cluster for **`kubectl`** commands.
3. **Create the manifest in YAML**: Write a Pod definition in a YAML file using the provided template.
4. **Apply YAML file**: Use **`kubectl apply -f your-pod definition.yaml`** or **`kubectl create -f your-pod-definition.yaml`** to create the Pod in your GKE cluster.

Note: Please note that `kubectl create` is used to create new resources in a Kubernetes cluster.

If the resource already exists, **`kubectl create`** will return an error as given in the following figure:

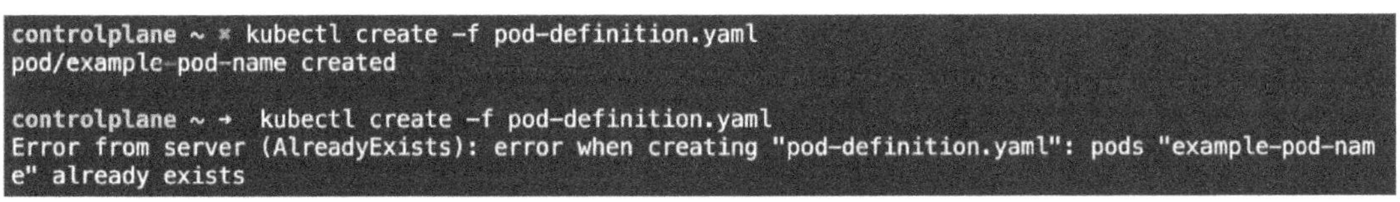

***Figure 5.3**: Error indicates that kubectl create cannot be used for existing resources*

It is commonly used for creating resources for the first time, but not for updating existing resources. For example: **`kubectl create -f my-resource.yaml`**.

To verify Pod creation: Check the Pod's status with the aid of this command:

```
kubectl get pods
```

This will list all the Pods running in the default namespace.

To verify Pod creation in a specific namespace, use the following command to check the Pod's status:

```
kubectl get pods -n <namespace>
```

Replace **<namespace>** with the appropriate namespace name to list the Pods within that namespace.

Manifest for ReplicaSet

To manage the deployment of multiple identical Pods in Kubernetes, a ReplicaSet is used. It ensures a specified number of Pod replicas are running at all times, providing scalability and resilience. Below is a basic example of a Kubernetes ReplicaSet manifest. This manifest defines a simple Pod running an NGINX container. Once the YAML file is created, you can use the command **kubectl apply -f replicaset-definition.yaml** to create the ReplicaSet.

Here is the example:

```
apiVersion: apps/v1
kind: ReplicaSet
metadata:
  name: example-replicaset
spec:
  replicas: 3
  selector:
    matchLabels:
      app: example
  template:
    metadata:
      labels:
        app: example
    spec:
      containers:
      - name: example-container
        image: nginx
```

Manifest for Deployment

A **Deployment** in Kubernetes is a higher-level abstraction for managing application updates, scaling, and ensuring a desired state for your Pods. It provides rolling updates, rollback capabilities, and more. Below is an example of a **Deployment** manifest. This YAML file defines a **Deployment** that ensures three replicas of a Pod running an NGINX container are maintained. Once the file is created, you can apply it using the command **kubectl apply -f deployment-definition.yaml**. Here is the example:

```
apiVersion: apps/v1
kind: Deployment
metadata:
  name: example-deployment
spec:
  replicas: 3
  selector:
    matchLabels:
      app: example
  template:
    metadata:
      labels:
        app: example
    spec:
      containers:
      - name: example-container
        image: nginx
```

Manifest for Service

A **Service** in Kubernetes is used to expose a set of Pods as a network service, enabling communication between components or external access to your application. Below is a simple **Service** manifest that routes traffic to Pods with the label app: **example**. You can create it using the command **kubectl apply -f service-definition.yaml**. Here is the example:

```
apiVersion: v1
kind: Service
metadata:
  name: example-service
spec:
  selector:
    app: example
  ports:
  - protocol: TCP
    port: 80
    targetPort: 80
  type: LoadBalancer
```

Manifest for ConfigMap

A **ConfigMap** in Kubernetes can store multiple key-value pairs, making it easy to manage application settings, **environment** variables, and other configurations separately from your application code. Below is an example **ConfigMap** manifest with multiple configuration values. Apply it using the command **kubectl apply -f configmap-definition.yaml**. Here is the example:

```
apiVersion: v1
kind: ConfigMap
metadata:
  name: example-configmap
data:
  app.name: MyApp
  app.environment: production
  app.version: "1.0.0"
  database.url: jdbc:mysql://example-db:3306/mydb
  database.username: admin
  database.password: secret
```

Manifest for Secret

A **Secret** in Kubernetes is used to securely store sensitive information, such as passwords or API keys, and can be accessed by Pods or other Kubernetes resources. The data is stored in base64-encoded format to ensure it is safely handled. Below is an example **Secret** manifest, which can be applied using **kubectl apply -f secret-definition.yaml**.

Here is the example:

```
apiVersion: v1
kind: Secret
metadata:
  name: example-secret
type: Opaque
data:
  secretKey: base64EncodedValue
```

Manifest for PersistentVolume

A **PersistentVolume** (**PV**) in Kubernetes provides storage resources for Pods, ensuring data persists even if the Pod is deleted or rescheduled. Below is an example **PersistentVolume** manifest that defines a storage volume with specific capacity, access modes, and reclaim policy. You can apply it using **kubectl apply -f persistentvolume-definition.yaml.**

Here is the example:

```
apiVersion: v1
kind: PersistentVolume
metadata:
  name: example-pv
spec:
  capacity:
    storage: 1Gi
  accessModes:
    - ReadWriteOnce
  persistentVolumeReclaimPolicy: Retain
  storageClassName: standard
  hostPath:
    path: /path/to/storage
```

This example shows a **PersistentVolume** that uses a local directory (**hostPath**) to store data, with a reclaim policy of **Retain** to keep the volume after it is released.

Manifest for PersistentVolumeClaim

A **PersistentVolumeClaim** (**PVC**) in Kubernetes is used by Pods to request storage resources. It allows Pods to access the storage provided by a PV. Below is an example **PersistentVolumeClaim** manifest that requests **1Gi** of storage with a specified access mode. You can apply it using **kubectl apply -f persistentvolumeclaim-definition.yaml.**

Here is the example:

```
apiVersion: v1
kind: PersistentVolumeClaim
metadata:
  name: example-pvc
spec:
  accessModes:
    - ReadWriteOnce
  resources:
    requests:
      storage: 1Gi
  storageClassName: standard
```

This example demonstrates how a PVC can request a PV that meets the specified storage and access requirements.

Manifest for Ingress

An **Ingress** in Kubernetes is used to manage external access to services within a cluster, typically HTTP and HTTPS traffic. It defines rules for routing traffic to different services based on hostnames and paths. Below is an example **Ingress** manifest that routes traffic for **example.com** to a service named **example-service**. You can apply it using **kubectl apply -f Ingress-definition.yaml**.

Here is the example:

```
apiVersion: networking.k8s.io/v1
kind: Ingress
metadata:
  name: example-Ingress
spec:
  rules:
  - host: example.com
    http:
      paths:
      - path: /
        pathType: Prefix
        backend:
          service:
            name: example-service
            port:
              number: 80
```

This example shows how to route incoming requests for **example.com** to the specified service on port **80**.

Manifest for StatefulSet

A **StatefulSet** in Kubernetes is used to manage stateful applications that require persistent identities, stable network names, and ordered deployments. Unlike Deployments, StatefulSets ensure that each Pod has a unique, persistent identity across reschedules. Below is an example StatefulSet manifest that runs three replicas of an NGINX container. You can apply it using **kubectl apply -f statefulset-definition.yaml.**

Here is the example:

```
apiVersion: apps/v1
kind: StatefulSet
metadata:
  name: example-statefulset
spec:
```

```
  serviceName: "example"
  replicas: 3
  selector:
    matchLabels:
      app: example
  template:
    metadata:
      labels:
        app: example
    spec:
      containers:
      - name: example
        image: nginx
```

This example shows how to define a **StatefulSet** with three replicas, each running an NGINX container, and ensures each Pod has a stable identity.

Manifest for DaemonSet

A **DaemonSet** in Kubernetes ensures that a copy of a specific Pod is running on all (or selected) nodes in the cluster. It is useful for deploying system-level applications, like logging agents or monitoring tools. Below is an example `DaemonSet` manifest that runs an NGINX container on every node. You can apply it using **kubectl apply -f daemonset-definition.yaml.**

Here is an example:

```
apiVersion: apps/v1
kind: DaemonSet
metadata:
  name: example-daemonset
spec:
  selector:
    matchLabels:
      name: example
  template:
    metadata:
      labels:
        name: example
    spec:
      containers:
      - name: example
        image: nginx
```

This example shows how a **DaemonSet** ensures that an NGINX container is deployed on every node in the cluster.

Manifest for NetworkPolicy

In GKE, a **NetworkPolicy** is a specification of how groups of Pods are allowed to communicate with each other and with other network endpoints. It is essentially a set of rules that define the **Ingress** (incoming) and **Egress** (outgoing) traffic for your Pods. By default, Pods are non-isolated; they accept traffic from any source. When a Pod selector is applied within a **NetworkPolicy**, the Pods become isolated and only accept traffic defined by the policy. This is crucial for enforcing a secure networking posture within your Kubernetes environment.

Here is the example:

```
apiVersion: networking.k8s.io/v1
kind: NetworkPolicy
metadata:
  name: example-networkpolicy
spec:
  podSelector:
    matchLabels:
      role: db
  policyTypes:
  - Ingress
  - Egress
  Ingress:
  - from:
    - podSelector:
        matchLabels:
          role: frontend
    ports:
    - protocol: TCP
      port: 6379
```

This example demonstrates how to control Ingress traffic to Pods labeled **role: db** from Pods labeled **role: frontend** on **TCP** port **6379**, enforcing network security within the Kubernetes environment.

Manifest for ResourceQuota

A **ResourceQuota** provides constraints that limit aggregate resource consumption per namespace. It can control the consumption of resources like CPU, memory, storage, and even the number of objects such as Pods, Services, or PVC. When a **ResourceQuota** is active for a namespace, it ensures that the namespace cannot use more of a given resource than the quota allows. This helps cluster administrators manage the resources their cluster provides more effectively by avoiding over-consumption by a single namespace.

Here is the example:

```
apiVersion: v1
kind: ResourceQuota
metadata:
  name: example-resourcequota
spec:
  hard:
    requests.cpu: "1"
    requests.memory: 1Gi
    limits.cpu: "2"
    limits.memory: 2Gi
```

Manifest for LimitRange

A **LimitRange** is a policy that allows administrators to specify constraints on resource use per **Pod** or **Container** in a namespace. It can set default and maximum limits on resources like CPU and memory, preventing individual Pods or Containers from consuming too much of a shared resource. This ensures a more efficient and fair use of resources among all the applications within a namespace, preventing any single application from monopolizing resources and potentially affecting other applications in the same namespace.

Here is the example:

```
apiVersion: v1
kind: LimitRange
metadata:
  name: example-limitrange
spec:
  limits:
  - type: Pod
    max:
      cpu: "2"
      memory: 2Gi
    min:
      cpu: "200m"
      memory: 6Mi
  - type: Container
    defaultRequest:
      cpu: "200m"
      memory: 10Mi
```

```
default:
  cpu: "300m"
  memory: 100Mi
max:
  cpu: "2"
  memory: 2Gi
min:
  cpu: "100m"
  memory: 3Mi
```

Deploying applications

Deploying applications on GKE involves creating Kubernetes resources such as deployments, services, Ingresses, and more by applying the manifest files as shown above.

To deploy a NGINX web application in GKE, follow these steps:

1. Create a Deployment YAML file for **nginx**.

   Use **kubectl apply -f nginx-deployment.yaml** to create the deployment in GKE.

2. Create a Service YAML file to expose **nginx**.

   Use **kubectl apply -f nginx-service.yaml** to expose the NGINX application.

3. Create an Ingress YAML file if advanced routing or TLS termination is needed(optional).

   Use **kubectl apply -f nginx-Ingress.yaml** for external access with HTTP/S.

This process deploys NGINX as a scalable web application in your GKE cluster, making it accessible as specified in your service and Ingress configurations.

These files collectively describe the desired state of your application in the cluster, enabling Kubernetes to manage and maintain your application automatically.

To rollback a deployment to a previous revision using **kubectl**, you can use the **kubectl rollout undo** command. Here is how you can do it:

- **Check deployment revisions**: First, list the revisions of your deployment to identify the revision you want to rollback to:

  ```
  kubectl rollout history deployment <deployment-name>
  ```

- **Rollback to a specific revision**: Once you have identified the revision you want to rollback to use the **kubectl rollout undo** command to rollback the deployment:

  ```
  kubectl rollout undo deployment <deployment-name> --to-
  revision=<revision-number>
  ```

Rolling back a deployment using **kubectl rollout undo** reverts the deployment to the specified revision, effectively undoing any changes made since that revision. This can be useful for quickly recovering from deployment issues or rolling back to a known stable state.

Deploy applications using kustomize, Helm and Argo CD

Kustomize, Helm, and Argo CD are popular tools used for managing Kubernetes configurations and deploying applications. Each tool offers unique features and benefits for streamlining the deployment process on GKE.

Using Kustomize with GKE

Kustomize is a built-in tool for Kubernetes that allows you to customize, patch, and manage Kubernetes resource configurations. It provides a simple yet powerful way to manage complex configurations and customize deployments for different environments.

1. **Install kustomize**: Refer to *Chapter 4, Setting Up Your GKE Environment* for installation steps

2. **Create your application manifests**: Organize your Kubernetes manifests (YAML files) into a directory structure. These manifests should include resources like deployments, services, ConfigMap, and any other necessary objects for your application.

   Let us say you have a simple web application consisting of a deployment, a service, and a ConfigMap. You can organize your Kubernetes manifests into a directory structure like this:

   ```
   my-web-app/
   ├── deployments/
   │   └── web-deployment.yaml
   ├── services/
   │   └── web-service.yaml
   ├── configmaps/
   │   └── web-configmap.yaml
   └── kustomization.yaml
   ```

3. **Create a kustomization file**: In the root directory of your application manifests, create a **kustomization.yaml** file. This file serves as the configuration for Kustomize and specifies which resources to include in the final deployment, as well as any customization options, shown as follows:

```
apiVersion: kustomize.config.k8s.io/v1beta1
kind: Kustomization
resources:
- deployment.yaml
- service.yaml
# Add more resources as needed
```

4. **Add customizations (optional)**: If you need to make customizations to your base manifests for different environments or specific configurations, you can use overlays. Create overlay directories (e.g., **dev**, **prod**) and add additional manifest files with the desired changes. Then, reference these overlays in your **kustomization.yaml**, shown as follows:

```
apiVersion: kustomize.config.k8s.io/v1beta1
kind: Kustomization
resources:
- deployment.yaml
- service.yaml
# Add base resources
bases:
- ../base
# Add overlays for customization
- ../overlays/dev
```

If you are using overlays in kustomize, your directory structure might look something like this:

```
my-web-app/
├── base/
│   ├── deployments/
│   │   └── web-deployment.yaml
│   ├── services/
│   │   └── web-service.yaml
│   ├── configmaps/
│   │   └── web-configmap.yaml
│   └── kustomization.yaml
└── overlays/
    ├── dev/
    │   ├── kustomization.yaml
    │   └── patches/
    │       ├── deployment-patch.yaml
    │       └── service-patch.yaml
    ├── prod/
    │   ├── kustomization.yaml
```

```
│   └── patches/
│       ├── deployment-patch.yaml
│       └── service-patch.yaml
└── staging/
    ├── kustomization.yaml
    └── patches/
        ├── deployment-patch.yaml
        └── service-patch.yaml
```

Here is a breakdown of the directory structure:

- **base/**: This directory contains the base Kubernetes manifests for your application. It includes the deployment, service, ConfigMap YAML files, and a **kustomization.yaml** file that specifies the resources to include in the base configuration.
- **overlays/**: This directory contains subdirectories for different environments or scenarios where you want to apply customizations. Each environment overlay directory contains its own **kustomization.yaml** file and a **patches/** directory for customization patches specific to that environment.
- **dev/**: It contains overlays specific to the development environment.
- **prod/**: This directory contains overlays specific to the production environment.
- **staging/**: It contains overlays specific to the staging environment.
- **patches/**: This directory within each overlay contains patch files (e.g., **deployment-patch.yaml**, **service-patch.yaml**) that specify modifications or additions to the base configuration for the corresponding environment. These patches are applied on top of the base configuration to customize it for the specific environment.

Each **kustomization.yaml** file within the base and overlay directories specifies the resources to include and any additional customization options. The overlays allow you to manage environment-specific configurations and keep your deployment configuration organized and modular.

Build your deployment

Use the **kustomize build** command to generate the final Kubernetes manifests based on your configuration. This command outputs the merged manifests to **stdout**, which you can apply to your GKE cluster:

```
kustomize build path/to/your/app
```

1. **Apply manifests to GKE**: Once you have the final manifests generated by **kustomize**, you can apply them to your GKE cluster using **kubectl apply** command:

   ```
   kustomize build path/to/your/app | kubectl apply -f -
   ```

2. **Verify deployment**: After applying the manifests, use **`kubectl`** commands to verify that your application has been deployed successfully and is running as expected on your GKE cluster.

   ```
   kubectl get pods
   kubectl get services
   ```

   Check other resources as needed (e.g., Deployments, Ingress).

3. **Update and rollback**: If you need to make changes to your application or rollback to a previous version, simply update your manifests, rebuild with kustomize, and reapply to the cluster using **`kubectl apply`**.

Using kustomize with GKE offers a flexible and efficient way to manage Kubernetes deployments and configurations, allowing you to customize deployments for different environments while maintaining consistency and repeatability in your deployment process.

Helm charts for GKE applications

It is a special tool that makes deploying and managing applications super easy. Instead of creating and applying each YAML file manually, Helm gives us pre-made bundles called **Helm charts**. These charts contain all the necessary configuration files for our application, neatly packaged and ready to use. With Helm, we can quickly install and manage these charts using simple commands. This saves us time, reduces errors, and ensures consistency across different environments. In a nutshell, Helm charts are like ready-made solutions that make deploying on Kubernetes a breeze.

1. **Install Helm**: You can follow the instructions provided in *Chapter 4, Setting Up Your GKE Environment* in the section *GKE management and automation tools.*

2. **Initialize Helm**: Once Helm is installed, initialize Helm on your Kubernetes cluster using this command: **`helm init`**

3. **Create a Helm chart**: Create a Helm chart for your application. You can use the Helm CLI to generate a new chart: **`helm create my-web-app`**

   This command creates a new directory named **`my-web-app`** containing the basic structure of a Helm chart.

   The structure starts with the root directory, **`my-web-app/`**, which contains several folders (e.g., **`charts/`**, **`templates/`**) and files (e.g., **`Chart.yaml`**, **`values.yaml`**).

   Each folder can contain additional subfolders and files, reflecting the modular structure of a Helm chart.

   This tree-like structure helps to organize the components of the Helm chart in a clear, hierarchical manner, rather than just a flat list of files.

Explore the directory structure:

```
my-web-app/
├── charts/
├── templates/
│   ├── NOTES.txt
│   ├── _helpers.tpl
│   ├── deployment.yaml
│   ├── Ingress.yaml
│   ├── service.yaml
│   └── tests/
│       └── test-connection.yaml
├── Chart.yaml
├── values.yaml
└── values.schema.json
```

Here is a brief overview of each file and directory:

- **charts/**: This directory is used to store dependencies if your chart depends on other charts.
- **templates/**: This directory contains the templates for Kubernetes resources (e.g., deployments, services) defined using YAML and Helm's template language. Each template file ends with the `.yaml` extension.
- **NOTES.txt**: This file contains post-installation notes that are displayed after the chart is installed.
- **_helpers.tpl**: This file contains helper templates that can be used within other templates.
- **deployment.yaml**: This file contains the template for a Kubernetes Deployment resource.
- **Ingress.yaml**: This file contains the template for a Kubernetes Ingress resource (optional).
- **service.yaml**: This file contains the template for a Kubernetes Service resource.
- **tests/**: This directory contains YAML files defining test cases to be executed after the chart is installed.
- **Chart.yaml**: This file contains metadata about the chart, such as its name, version, description, maintainers, etc.
- **values.yaml**: This file contains default values for the configuration parameters used in the templates.
- **values.schema.json**: This file defines the schema for the values file, allowing for validation and autocompletion in Helm environments that support it.

Customizing and deploying a Helm chart

After creating a Helm chart, you can customize it to fit your application's needs before packaging and deploying it.

1. **Customize the Helm chart**: Edit the files in the `templates/` directory to define the Kubernetes resources for your web application. For example:
    - **deployment.yaml**: Define a Deployment resource for your web application, specifying the container image, ports, environment variables, etc.
    - **service.yaml**: Define a Service resource to expose your web application within the Kubernetes cluster.
    - **Ingress.yaml**: Optionally, define an Ingress resource if you want to expose your web application externally.
    - **values.yaml**: Additionally, you can utilize the `values.yaml` file to define configurable parameters such as image versions, resource limits, or any other variables specific to your deployment needs.
2. **Package the Helm chart**: Once you have customized the Helm chart, you can package it into a `.tgz` file using the following command:
    ```
    helm package my-web-app
    ```
    This command creates a `my-web-app-<version>.tgz` file in the current directory, containing your Helm chart and all its dependencies.
3. **Deploy the Helm chart**: Deploy the Helm chart to your Kubernetes cluster:
    ```
    helm install my-web-app-release my-web-app-<version>.tgz
    ```

The `helm install` command deploys the chart using the name `my-web-app-release` (you can choose any name for your release).

In addition to managing Helm charts locally or within private repositories, Helm provides access to the Helm Hub, a centralized repository of Helm charts maintained by the Helm community. The Helm Hub hosts a wide range of pre-configured Helm charts for various applications and services, allowing users to easily discover and install them directly from the Helm CLI. This simplifies the process of deploying applications by providing a convenient way to access and install Helm charts without needing to manage chart repositories manually.

Let us say you want to deploy the NGINX Ingress Controller to your Kubernetes cluster. You can install it directly from the Helm Hub using the following command:

```
helm repo add Ingress-nginx https://kubernetes.github.io/Ingress-nginx
helm repo update
helm install my-Ingress Ingress-nginx/Ingress-nginx
```

4. **Verify deployment**: To verify that your application has been deployed successfully run the following command:

```
kubectl get pods -n <namespace>
kubectl get services -n <namespace>
# Check other resources as needed
```

   If issues arise, use the following command to troubleshoot:

```
kubectl describe <resource-type> <resource-name> -n <namespace>
(e.g., kubectl describe pod <pod-name> -n <namespace>
kubectl describe service <service-name> -n <namespace>)
```

   This command provides detailed information about the resource, including events and potential error messages.

5. **Update the Helm chart (optional)**

   If you need to make changes to your application or Helm chart, you can update the chart and upgrade the release with the aid of this command: **helm upgrade my-release my-web-app-<version>.tgz**

6. **Uninstall the Helm chart (optional)**

   If you want to remove the deployed application, you can uninstall the Helm release with this command: **helm delete my-release**

These are the basic steps for deploying applications using Helm charts. Helm simplifies the process of packaging, deploying, and managing applications on Kubernetes by providing a templating engine and package manager for Kubernetes manifests.

In summary, kustomize is better for lightweight, straightforward YAML customization, while Helm is more suited for managing and deploying pre-packaged, complex applications.

Here is the difference between kustomize and Helm:

Feature	Kustomize	Helm
Purpose	Customizes existing YAML files using overlays and patches.	Provides pre-packaged application configurations via charts.
Templating	Does not use templating; relies on plain YAML transformations.	Uses templates and values files to generate YAML dynamically.
Ease of use	Simple and straightforward; ideal for small to medium setups.	Offers flexibility but can be more complex due to templating logic.
Reusability	Focuses on customizing existing manifests rather than reusable packages.	Helm charts are reusable, versioned packages.
Use case	Best for managing variations across environments.	Ideal for deploying complex applications or using pre-made charts.

***Table 5.1**: Difference between kustomize and Helm*

Managing deployments with Argo CD

It is a special tool that helps you deploy your applications automatically. It keeps an eye on your code stored in Git repositories and makes sure that your applications are always in the right state on your Kubernetes cluster. Whenever you make changes to your code, **Argo CD** automatically updates your applications to match those changes. This makes deploying applications super easy and saves you time. Plus, it encourages teamwork and makes sure everyone is using the same version of your application's configuration.

Argo CD is primarily designed to work with Git repositories as a source of truth for application configurations. However, it is technically possible to use Argo CD without Git, but it is not recommended, and it would limit the capabilities and benefits of using Argo CD.

To deploy Argo CD in your Kubernetes cluster, follow these essential steps below.

Install Argo CD on your Kubernetes cluster

Refer to *Chapter 4, Setting Up Your GKE Environment* for the installation steps

1. Configure a Git repository with your application manifests: If you have not already, create a Git repository to store your application manifests. You can use popular Git hosting platforms like **GitHub**, **GitLab**, or **Bitbucket**.

   To create a Git repository on GitHub, follow these steps:

   a. **Sign in to GitHub**: Open your web browser and go to GitHub. Sign in to your GitHub account if you have not already.
   b. Create a New Repository.
   c. Click on the + icon in the top-right corner of the page.
   d. Select New repository from the dropdown menu.
   e. Fill out the Repository Information.

2. Enter a name for your repository in the Repository name field. Choose a descriptive name that reflects the purpose of your project.

Once your repository is created, you will be redirected to its homepage on GitHub. From there, you can clone the repository to your local machine, push existing code to the repository, or start adding files and making commits directly on GitHub's web interface. You can also manage repository settings, collaborate with others, track issues and pull requests from the repository's homepage.

Create Argo CD Application from Git

To create an Argo CD `Application` resource referencing your Git repository, you will need to create a YAML manifest file that defines the application configuration. Here is an example of how you can create an Argo CD **Application** resource for deploying your web app:

```
apiVersion: argoproj.io/v1alpha1
kind: Application
metadata:
  name: my-web-app
spec:
  destination:
    server: https://kubernetes.default.svc
    namespace: default
  project: default
  source:
    repoURL: https://github.com/your-username/your-repo
    targetRevision: HEAD
    path: my-web-app
  syncPolicy:
    automated:
      prune: true
      selfHeal: true
    syncOptions:
    - Validate=true
```

Argo CD will continuously monitor the Git repository specified in the application resource for changes. When changes are detected, Argo CD will automatically sync the application with the changes from the Git repository and deploy or update the application as necessary to match the desired state defined in the manifests.

Therefore, after creating the Argo CD **Application** resource manifest, there is no need to manually apply it using **kubectl**. Argo CD will handle the deployment process for you based on the configuration specified in the manifest.

Deploy Helm charts using Argo CD

To deploy Helm charts using Argo CD, you can define an Argo CD Application resource that references the Helm chart repository and the specific Helm chart you want to deploy. Here is how you can do it:

1. **Create a Helm chart**: First, ensure that you have a Helm chart for your application. If you do not have one already, create a Helm chart for your application following the Helm chart structure.

2. **Add Helm repository**: If your Helm chart is hosted in a Helm repository (such as Helm Hub or a private repository), ensure that Argo CD has access to this repository.

3. **Define Argo CD application**: Create an Argo CD Application resource that references your Helm chart.

   Here is an example of how you can define an Argo CD `Application` resource to deploy a Helm chart:

```
apiVersion: argoproj.io/v1alpha1
kind: Application
metadata:
  name: my-helm-app
spec:
  destination:
    server: https://kubernetes.default.svc
    namespace: default
  source:
    helm:
      chart: my-helm-chart
      version: 1.0.0
      sourceRef:
        kind: HelmRepository
        name: stable
        namespace: argocd
  project: default
  syncPolicy:
    automated:
      prune: true
      selfHeal: true
```

4. Replace the placeholders (`my-helm-chart`, `1.0.0`, `stable`, `argocd`) with the appropriate values for your Helm chart and Helm repository. Ensure that Argo CD has access to the Helm repository where your Helm chart is hosted.

Once you have defined the Argo CD Application resource, Argo CD will automatically deploy the Helm chart to your Kubernetes cluster based on the configuration specified in the resource.

Conclusion

In this chapter, we saw how to deploy applications on GKE require a solid understanding of Kubernetes concepts, YAML configuration and deployment tools such as kubectl, kustomize, Helm, and Argo CD. By mastering these fundamentals and leveraging the capabilities of GKE, you can streamline the deployment process and ensure the reliability and scalability of your applications running on Kubernetes.

Multiple choice questions

1. **Which tool is best suited for deploying applications that require customized configuration based on different environments (e.g., development, staging, production)?**
    a. Kustomize
    b. Helm
    c. Docker
    d. Argo CD
2. **You have a complex application composed of multiple microservices that need to be deployed and managed as a single unit. Which tool is most appropriate for this scenario?**
    a. Docker
    b. Kubernetes
    c. Argo CD
    d. Helm
3. **Your team wants to automate the deployment process for applications and ensure consistency across different environments using a GitOps approach. Which tool would you use?**
    a. Docker
    b. Argo CD
    c. Kustomize
    d. Kubernetes
4. **You are tasked with deploying a new application onto your Kubernetes cluster using kubectl. Which command would you use to apply the application's Kubernetes manifests stored in a directory named app-manifests?**
    a. kubectl deploy -f app-manifests
    b. kubectl apply -f app-manifests
    c. kubectl create -f app-manifests
    d. kubectl run -f app-manifests

5. **You want to apply environment-specific configurations to your Kubernetes manifests without modifying them directly. Which tool provides a way to overlay configurations onto base manifests for different environments?**
   a. Helm
   b. Kustomize
   c. Docker
   d. Argo CD

Answer key

1.	a.
2.	d.
3.	b.
4.	b.
5.	b.

Join our book's Discord space

Join the book's Discord Workspace for Latest updates, Offers, Tech happenings around the world, New Release and Sessions with the Authors:

https://discord.bpbonline.com

CHAPTER 6
Networking in GKE

Introduction

Networking within GKE is a critical aspect that directly impacts the performance, scalability, and security of applications running on the platform. This chapter delves into the intricacies of GKE networking, offering readers a comprehensive understanding of its features and functionalities.

Structure

In this chapter we will learn the following concepts:

- Services
- Different types of Services and their roles
- Commands to interact with Services
- Load balancing with GKE
- Types of load balancers in GKE
- Identity-Aware Proxy for GKE
- Network policies in GKE
- DNS and service discovery in GKE
- Ingress and Ingress controllers in GKE

Objectives

This chapter is focused on covering networking intricacies by allowing you to gain a comprehensive understanding of networking concepts in GKE. You will learn to configure and manage Services for efficient communication. As you proceed further in this chapter, you will understand load balancing mechanisms and their implementation in GKE. Towards the end of this chapter, you will be able to master the use of network policies for traffic control and security and explore DNS configuration and Service discovery best practices in GKE clusters.

Services

Kubernetes Services in GKE play a critical role in exposing, managing, and securing containerized applications. This chapter dives into the essentials of Kubernetes Services within GKE, outlining their types, functionalities, and how they facilitate Pod-to-external communication.

Overview of Kubernetes Services

In GKE Services abstract the way applications are exposed, both internally and externally, offering a unified method of accessing a set of running Pods. This abstraction is key in managing Pod lifecycles and ensuring application availability.

Key concepts

Here are the key concepts which will be covered:

- **Stable endpoint**: Services provide a stable IP address and DNS name by which Pods can be accessed, regardless of Pod changes.
- **Load distribution**: Automatically distributes traffic across all Pods associated with the Service, achieving load balancing.
- **Discovery and connectivity**: Facilitates Service discovery within the cluster and manages external connectivity to Services.

The following *Figure 6.1* illustrates the relationship between a Service, its selector, and the Pods it routes traffic to:

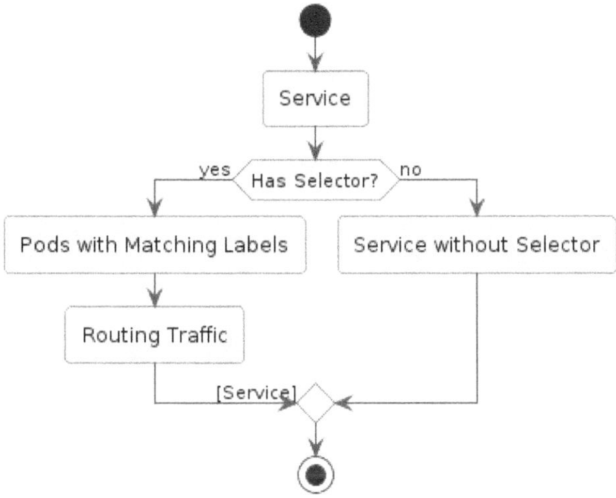

***Figure 6.1**: Kubernetes Service architecture*

The flowchart in the *Figure 6.1* outlines the following process:

1. **Service**: The starting point for defining how to access a set of Pods.
2. **Has selector?**: Determines whether the Service is defined with a selector to identify the Pods:
   a. If the output is **Yes**, then Service uses a selector to find Pods with matching labels:
      i. **Pods with matching labels**: Pods that match the labels specified by the Service's selector.
      ii. **Routing traffic**: The Service routes traffic to these matching Pods, creating a connection between the Service and the Pods based on the labels.
   b. If the output is **No**, then it results in a Service without a selector, indicating a special case where the Service might be manually directing traffic to specific endpoints or another advanced configuration.

This visualization demonstrates how Kubernetes Service acts as an abstract way to expose an application running on a set of Pods as a network Service, and how the selector mechanism is used to automatically find and route traffic to the appropriate Pods.

Different types of Services and their roles

Kubernetes offers several types of Services, each tailored for specific use cases. Let us study them:

- **ClusterIP**:
    - **Description**: This is the default Kubernetes Service that gives a Service a stable internal IP address which is accessible only within the cluster.
    - **Use case**: It is ideal for when you need to enable communication between different Services within a cluster, like a backend Service that needs to be reachable from a frontend Service, however not from outside the cluster.

  This code defines a ClusterIP Service in Kubernetes, which allows internal communication within the cluster. The Service exposes port **80** and routes traffic to port **9376** on the selected Pod, **my-app**. It ensures that the Service is only accessible from within the cluster.

```
apiVersion: v1
kind: Service
metadata:
  name: my-internal-Service
spec:
    selector:
      app: my-app
    ports:
        - protocol: TCP
          port: 80
          targetPort: 9376
  type: ClusterIP
```

- **NodePort**:
    - **Description**: This Service exposes the Service on each node's IP at a specific static port, making it accessible from outside the cluster using **<NodeIP>:<NodePort>**.
    - **Note**: The NodePort value must be within the range of 30000-32767, which is the default NodePort range in Kubernetes. This range can be adjusted by modifying the Kubernetes API server configuration if needed.
    - **Use case**: It is useful for temporary external access to a Service for development or testing purposes before setting up a more secure LoadBalancer or Ingress.

  This code defines a NodePort Service in Kubernetes, which exposes the Service on a specific port (**30007**) across all nodes in the cluster. The Service routes traffic from port **80** to the selected Pod **my-app**, making it accessible externally through the node's IP address on the specified node port.

```
apiVersion: v1
kind: Service
metadata:
  name: my-nodeport-Service
```

```
spec:
    selector:
        app: my-app
  ports:
       - protocol: TCP
         port: 80
         nodePort: 30007
  type: NodePort
```

- **LoadBalancer**:
  - **Description**: This Service provisions an external IP from GCP to route external traffic directly to the Kubernetes Service, bypassing the need for a NodePort.
  - **Use case**: It is perfect for applications that require exposure to the internet, providing an easy way to get an external IP linked to your Service.

  This code defines a LoadBalancer Service in Kubernetes, which exposes the Service to external traffic. It routes traffic on port **`80`** to the selected Pod **`my-app`**. The Service is assigned an external IP by a cloud provider's load balancer, making it accessible from outside the cluster.

```
apiVersion: v1
kind: Service
metadata:
  name: my-loadbalancer-Service
spec:
  selector:
      app: my-app
  ports:
      - protocol: TCP
      port: 80
  type: LoadBalancer
```

These Service types and their use cases have been summarized in the following *Table 6.1*:

Service type	Description	Use case
ClusterIP	Stable internal IP only accessible within the cluster	Internal Service communication
NodePort	Exposes the Service on each node's IP at a specified port	External access for development/ testing
LoadBalancer	External IP to route external traffic to the Service	Internet-facing applications

***Table 6.1**: Types of Kubernetes Services*

Enabling communication between Pods and external clients

To ensure smooth interaction between your Kubernetes Pods and external clients, it is essential to establish proper communication mechanisms. These methods allow both internal communication among Pods within the cluster and external access for clients outside the cluster. Let us explore the two types of communication in Kubernetes: internal and external:

- **Internal communication**: The communication which happens between Pods within a cluster among each other through Services using the internal ClusterIP of the Service is termed as internal communication.
- **External communication**: For external access, NodePort and LoadBalancer Services provide mechanisms to expose Services to traffic outside the cluster. This is known as external communication.

Commands to interact with Services

When working with Services in Kubernetes, it is essential to understand the various commands that allow you to create, manage, and troubleshoot Services. The following are some common commands for interacting with Services:

Create a Service:

The following code defines a Kubernetes Service that exposes an application running within a cluster to external traffic. Specifically, it creates a LoadBalancer Service that directs incoming TCP traffic on port `80` to the target port `8080` of the application Pods labeled with app: `my-app`. This configuration allows external clients to access the application. Here is the code snippet:

```
apiVersion: v1
kind: Service
metadata:
  name: my-app-Service
spec:
  type: LoadBalancer
  selector:
      app: my-app
  ports:
      - protocol: TCP
      port: 80
      targetPort: 8080
```

To create a Service that exposes an application running within a cluster to external traffic, use the following command:

```
kubectl apply -f Service-definition.yaml
```

To view all Services in your cluster, you can use the following command:

```
kubectl get Services
```

This will list all the Services, along with their details like IP addresses and port mappings.

For more detailed information about a specific Service, use:

```
kubectl describe Service my-Service
```

This command provides a comprehensive breakdown of the Service, including its endpoints, selectors, and other associated configurations.

Scenarios and solutions

Let us look at couple of scenarios and how they can be solved, and which Service needs to be used:

- **Scenario**: You need to expose a web application to the internet securely.

  Solution: Use a LoadBalancer Service to get an external IP address that routes traffic to your web application Pods securely.

- **Scenario**: An internal database Service needs to be accessible by other Services within the same GKE cluster.

  Solution: Deploy a ClusterIP Service for the database. This setup restricts access to the database within the cluster, enhancing security.

- **Scenario**: A temporary external endpoint is required for a testing environment within the GKE cluster.

  Solution: Implement a NodePort Service, which allows external access to a specific Service for testing before setting up a LoadBalancer for production.

- **Scenario**: A microservice architecture where different microservices within the cluster need to communicate with each other without exposing their endpoints to the outside world.

  Solution: Utilize ClusterIP Services for each microservice. This setup ensures that microservices can reach each other via stable internal endpoints, while keeping the communication internal and secure from external access.

Monitoring and logging

To ensure the reliability and security of Services and their communication pathways, it is important to implement monitoring and logging:

- **Monitoring**: Utilize tools like Prometheus and Grafana for real-time monitoring of Services. Metrics to monitor include request rate, error rate, and response times.
- **Logging**: Implement centralized logging with solutions like **Elasticsearch, Fluentd, and Kibana** (**EFK**) or Loki. Logging all requests to and from Services can help in troubleshooting and understanding traffic patterns.

Figure 6.2 shows how Services are monitored and how logs are collected, highlighting the integration with monitoring and logging tools:

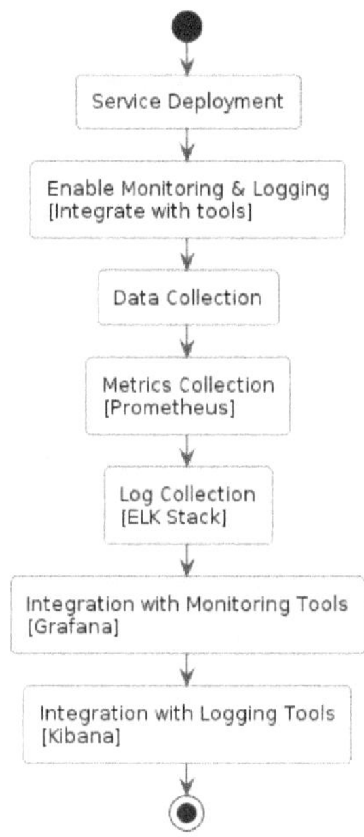

***Figure 6.2**: Service monitoring and logging flow*

The flowchart in *Figure 6.2* outlines these key stages:

1. **Service deployment**: Services that require monitoring and logging are deployed.
2. **Enable monitoring and logging**: Configuration steps are undertaken to integrate with monitoring and logging tools.
3. **Data collection**: This central step involves gathering both performance metrics and Service logs.
    a. **Metrics collection**: Utilizing Prometheus to collect performance metrics.
    b. **Log collection**: Using the ELK stack for log collection.
4. **Integration with monitoring tools**: Metrics collected by Prometheus are visualized through Grafana, providing insights into Service performance.
5. **Integration with logging tools**: Logs collected by the ELK stack are analyzed and visualized using Kibana, facilitating issue identification and troubleshooting.

This visualization emphasizes a streamlined approach to collecting and integrating data for Service monitoring and logging, employing specific tools to achieve comprehensive insight and analysis.

Best practices for Service management in GKE

Here are a few best practices for Service management in GKE:

- **Labeling and selector use**: Apply descriptive labels to your Pods and Services for clear identification and organization. Use selectors efficiently to target specific Pods with Services, facilitating precise control over traffic routing within your GKE cluster.
- **Optimize traffic distribution**: For Services that require more complex traffic routing than what is available through standard types, consider using GKE Ingress or a Service mesh like **Istio**. These tools offer advanced traffic management features such as path-based routing, traffic splitting, and canary deployments.
- **Define readiness and liveness probes**: Ensure that Pods are ready to handle requests before they are added to the Service load balancer and are removed if they become unresponsive.
- **Secure your Services**: Apply network policies to restrict the flow of traffic to and from your Services in accordance with the principle of least privilege. For Services exposed to the internet, ensure that you implement strong TLS encryption and consider using Google-managed certificates for ease of management.

Advanced integration scenarios

Now let us look at a few scenarios where advanced integration is needed:

- **Integrating with Cloud DNS for service discovery**: Utilize ExternalName Services and Google Cloud DNS to facilitate service discovery across GKE clusters and external resources, enabling a unified approach to managing internal and external Services.
- **Automating service deployments with continuous integration and continuous deployment (CI/CD):** Integrate your GKE Services with a CI/CD pipeline to automate the deployment and management of Services. Use GitOps practices to maintain versioned configurations of your Services in source control, ensuring reliable and reproducible deployments.
- **Leveraging ConfigMaps and Secrets for configuration:** Store Service configuration in ConfigMaps and sensitive information in Secrets. Reference these from your Service deployments to externalize configuration and credentials, improving security and flexibility.

Load balancing with GKE

Load balancing plays a pivotal role in distributing incoming network traffic across multiple backend Pods in GKE, enhancing the availability and reliability of applications. This section will explore the utilization of built-in load balancers in GKE, offering insights into configuring and optimizing load balancing for achieving high availability.

Utilizing built-in load balancers in GKE

GKE integrates seamlessly with Google Cloud's load balancing solutions, providing a robust and scalable way to distribute traffic among Pods.

Overview

Kubernetes offers different strategies for managing traffic across your Services, depending on whether the traffic is HTTP(S) or TCP/UDP. These strategies ensure high availability and efficient traffic distribution. The following are two common types of load balancing mechanisms:

- **Global load balancing**: Utilizes Google Cloud's global load balancing technology to distribute external HTTP(S) load balanced traffic intelligently across multiple regions.
- **Regional load balancing**: For TCP/UDP traffic, regional load balancing distributes traffic among Pods within a specific region, suitable for non-HTTP(S) workloads.

The following *Figure 6.3* shows how external traffic is distributed to Pods across different nodes and potentially across different regions:

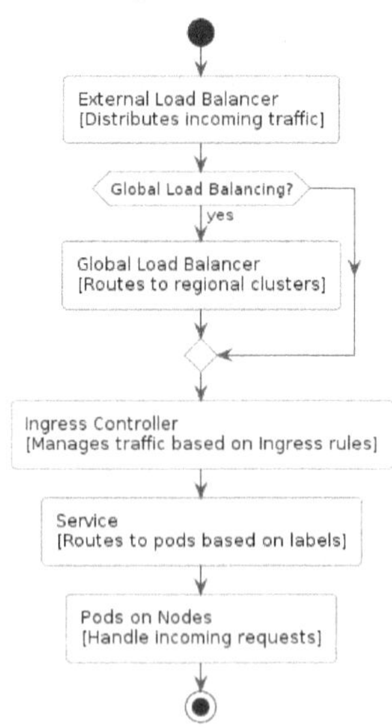

***Figure 6.3**: GKE load balancing architecture*

The flowchart in *Figure 6.3* outlines the following process:

- **External load balancer**: It acts as the entry point, distributing incoming traffic to the GKE cluster.
- **Global load balancer (optional)**: For multi-regional deployments, it routes traffic to regional clusters based on criteria like geography or workload distribution.
- **Ingress controller (optional for HTTP/S)**: It manages traffic within the cluster based on Ingress rules, directing it to the appropriate Services.
- **Service**: It defines how traffic is routed to Pods within the cluster based on labels or selectors.
- **Pods on nodes**: The endpoints where incoming requests are finally processed, deployed across various nodes within the cluster.

This visualization clearly illustrates the flow of traffic from external sources through to the Pods handling the requests in GKE, highlighting the roles of different load balancing and traffic routing components.

Types of load balancers in GKE

Primarily we can categorize the load balancers in GKE in the following categories:

- **External HTTP(S) load balancer**
  - For HTTP(S) traffic, offering path-based routing and SSL termination.
  - Automatically scalable and highly available.
- **TCP/UDP load balancer**
  - For non-HTTP(S) traffic, providing a simple, regional distribution mechanism.
  - Ensures traffic is evenly distributed to all backend Pods.
- **Internal load balancer**
  - For distributing internal traffic within the same Google Cloud project.
  - Ideal for microservices communication where Services are split into multiple Pods.

These types of load balancer and their features and scope have been summarized in the *Table 6.2*:

Load balancer type	Traffic type	Scope	Features
External HTTP(S)	HTTP(S)	Global/ Regional	SSL termination, path-based routing
TCP/UDP	TCP/UDP	Regional	Simple load distribution
Internal	Any	Regional	Internal traffic management

Table 6.2: *GKE load balancer types and features*

Optimizing load balancing for high availability

Let us look at how we can configure the load balancers for high availability by optimizing them:

The configuration steps are as follows:

1. **Define a Service**:
   a. Create a Kubernetes Service of type LoadBalancer to expose your application.
   b. Specify the necessary ports and selector labels to target the right Pods.
2. **Optimize health checks**:
   a. Configure health checks to ensure only healthy Pods receive traffic.
   b. Utilize readiness and liveness probes within your Pod specifications.

   Example: Configuring an external HTTP(S) load balancer by running the following code:

```
apiVersion: v1
kind: Service
metadata:
  name: my-external-Service
spec:
  type: LoadBalancer
  selector:
 app: my-app
  ports:
 - protocol: TCP
       port: 80
       targetPort: 8080
```

Optimization techniques

Here are some optimization techniques:

- **Multi-zonal and cross-regional deployments**: Deploy your application across multiple zones or multiple regions to protect against zone or region failures.
- **Content-based routing**: Use HTTP(S) load balancers to route requests based on the URL path, distributing load based on content type or Service.
- **Autoscaling**: Implement Pod autoscaling based on CPU utilization or custom metrics to dynamically adjust the number of Pods based on traffic.

Commands

The following are the commands:

- **Creating a multi-zonal cluster**:

  ```
  gcloud container clusters create my-cluster --region us-central1
  --num-nodes 1 --node-locations us-central1-a, us-central1-b,us-
  central1-c
  ```

- **Enabling autoscaling**:

  ```
  kubectl autoscale deployment my-web-app --cpu-percent=80 --min=2
  --max=10
  ```

Scenarios and solutions

Let us look at a couple of scenarios and how they can be solved, and which load balancer needs to be used:

- **Scenario**: An e-commerce platform experiences variable traffic, with spikes during sales events.

  Solution: Use an external HTTP(S) load balancer with autoscaling configured for the backend Pods. This ensures the platform remains responsive and available during traffic spikes.

- **Scenario**: A global application needs to minimize latency for users in *Europe, Asia,* and *America*.

  Solution: Deploy the application in regions close to these user bases and configure a global HTTP(S) load balancer. Google Cloud's global load balancing automatically routes users to the nearest backend.

- **Scenario**: A web application needs to handle sudden spikes in traffic from users around the globe.

  Solution: Implement a global load balancer with autoscaling enabled for the GKE deployment. Optimize content delivery with Cloud CDN.

- **Scenario**: A multiplayer game server hosted on GKE requires low latency and high throughput for players.

  Solution: Use a network load balancer to evenly distribute UDP traffic among game server instances deployed across multiple zones for redundancy and lower latency.

Monitoring and tuning load balancers

Regular monitoring and tuning of load balancers are crucial to maintaining high availability and optimal performance:

- **Monitoring**: Utilize Google Cloud Monitoring to track the performance and health of your load balancer and underlying resources.
- **Tuning**: Adjust load balancer settings based on monitoring data, such as tweaking health check parameters or adding/removing resource capacity.

Figure 6.4 illustrates the cycle of monitoring load balancer performance, analyzing metrics, and adjusting settings or resources:

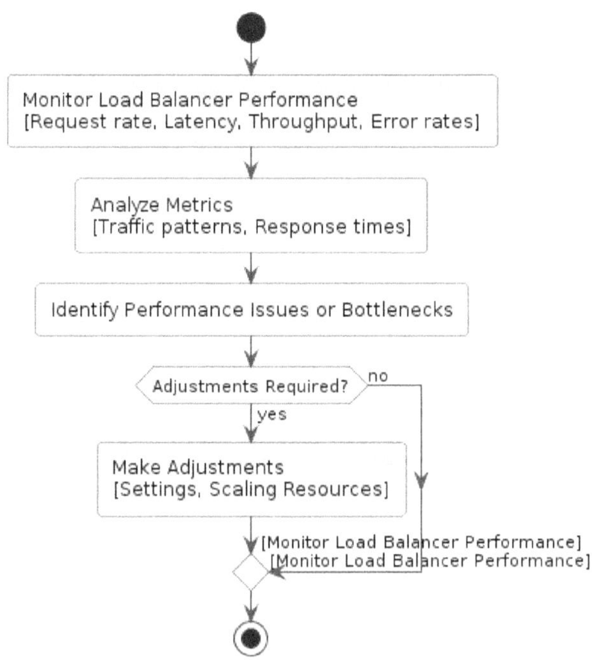

Figure 6.4: *Load balancing monitoring and tuning process*

The flowchart in the *Figure 6.4*, outlines these steps for an ongoing process:

- **Monitor load balancer performance**: Continuous monitoring of key metrics such as request rate, latency, throughput, and error rates.

- **Analyze metrics**: Detailed analysis of traffic patterns, average and peak response times, and resource utilization.
- **Identify performance issues or bottlenecks**: Identifying signs of performance degradation or capacity overload.
- **Adjustments required?**: Decision point based on analysis to determine the need for adjustments.
- **Make adjustments**: Implementing changes to load balancer settings or scaling resources behind the load balancer to address identified issues.
- **Monitor performance again**: Resuming performance monitoring to observe the effects of adjustments, continuing the routine monitoring cycle.

This visualization enhances understanding of the cycle of monitoring, analyzing, and tuning load balancer performance to ensure optimal operation.

Best practices for load balancing in GKE

Here are a few best practices for load balancing in GKE:

- **Use anycast IPs**: Leverage Google Cloud's global load balancing with Anycast IPs to reduce latency and improve the resilience of your applications.
- **SSL offloading**: Utilize the load balancer's capability to terminate SSL traffic, reducing the computational load on your backend Pods.
- **Session affinity**: Configure session affinity for applications that require persistent sessions, ensuring users are consistently routed to the same backend Pod.

Identity-Aware Proxy for GKE

Identity-Aware Proxy (**IAP**) revolutionizes the way access to applications is secured by leveraging Google Cloud's robust authentication and authorization mechanisms. This section focuses on introducing IAP within the context of GKE and details the process of configuring IAP for enhanced security of GKE applications.

Introduction to IAP for secure access

IAP stands as a pivotal component in the realm of cloud security, acting as a guard at the gate, ensuring that only authenticated and authorized users gain access to your applications.

The following are the reasons for using IAP:

- **Context-aware access**: IAP makes decisions based on identity and context of the access request, such as the user's location and device security status.

- **Zero trust security model**: IAP embraces the principle of *never trust, always verify*, significantly reducing the risk surface compared to traditional network perimeter security models.
- **Integration with Google's security**: IAP seamlessly integrates with Google's robust security infrastructure, including support for 2-step verification and security keys.

Figure 6.5 illustrates how IAP intercepts access requests to validate user identity and permissions before granting access to a GKE application:

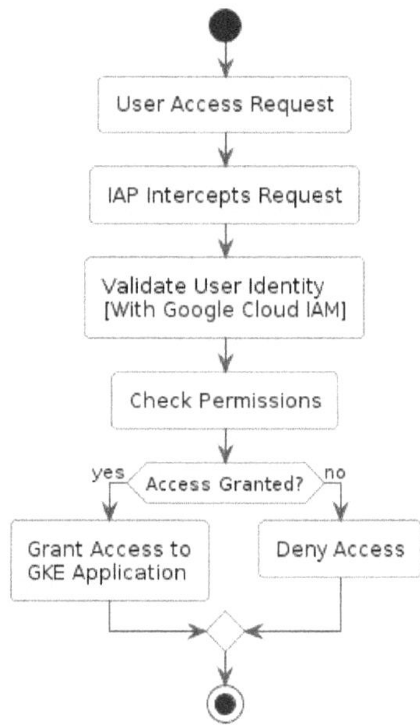

***Figure 6.5**: Access control with IAP*

The flowchart in the *Figure 6.5*, outlines these key steps:

1. **User access request**: The process begins with a user attempting to access a GKE application.
2. **IAP intercepts request**: IAP intercepts the access request to perform authentication and authorization checks.
3. **Validate user identity**: IAP utilizes Google Cloud IAM to validate the identity of the user making the request.
4. **Check permissions**: After identity validation, IAP checks the user's permissions to determine if they have the appropriate access rights.
5. **Access granted? Now, based on the permissions check**:

   If the output is **`Yes`**, IAP grants the user access to the GKE application.

   If the output is **`No`**, access to the application is denied.

This flowchart in *Figure 6.5* efficiently illustrates the role of IAP in securing GKE applications by ensuring that only authenticated and authorized users can access them.

Configuring IAP for GKE applications

Implementing IAP for your GKE applications involves several steps, from setting up OAuth credentials to configuring access policies.

Prerequisites:

- A GCP project.
- A GKE cluster with an application exposed through an Ingress or Service.

Steps to enable IAP:

1. Set up OAuth 2.0 credentials.
2. Navigate to the API and Services | Credentials page in the Google Cloud Console.
3. Click on Create credentials and select OAuth client ID.
4. Choose Web application as the application type and define a name.
5. Under Authorized redirect URIs, add the URI that will handle the authentication response.
6. **Enable IAP by**:
    a. Go to **Security** | **Identity-Aware Proxy** in the Cloud Console.
    b. Select the GCP project and enable IAP on the resource, such as a GKE Ingress or a particular Service as given in the following figure:

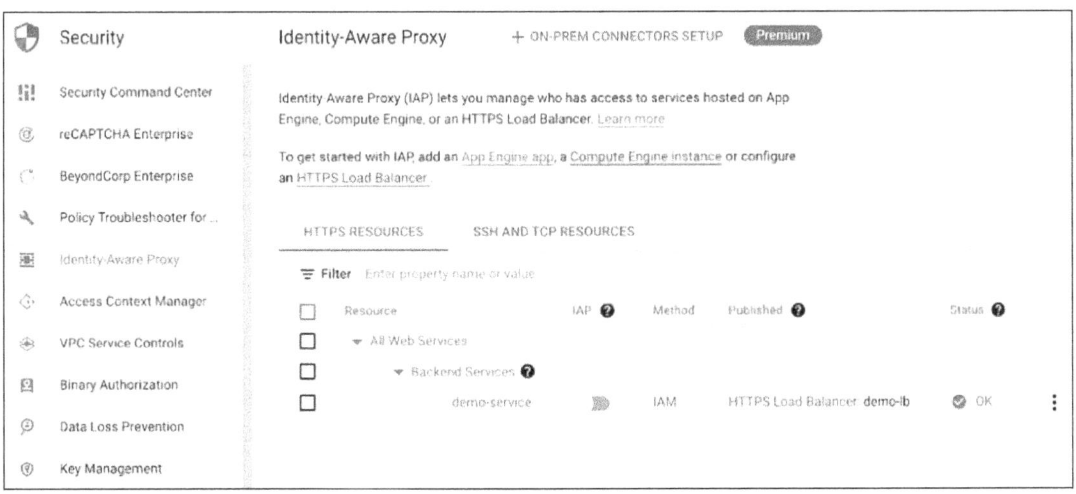

Figure 6.6: Identity-Aware Proxy page

Then check the configuration requirements and click **TURNING ON IAP**:

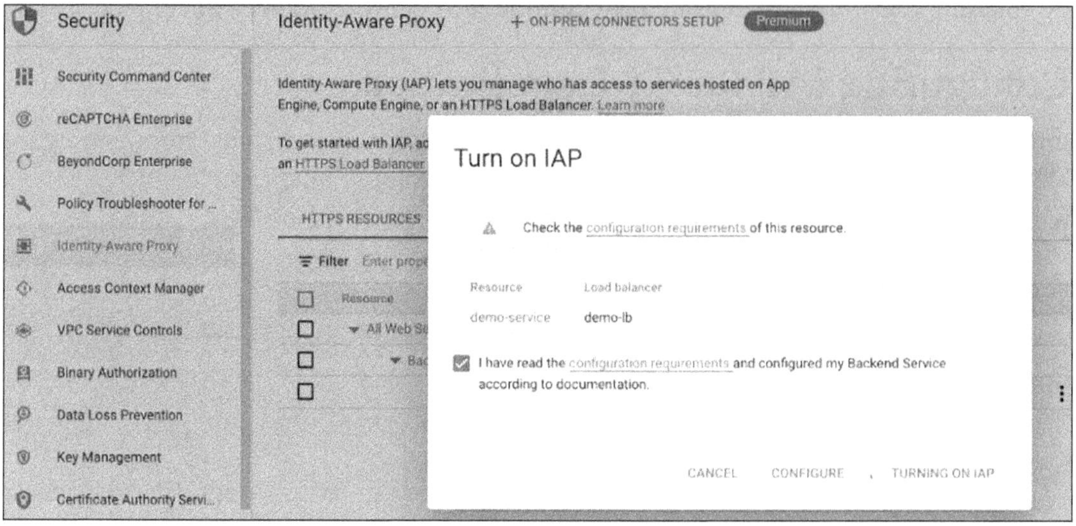

Figure 6.7: Enable Identity-Aware Proxy

7. **Configure IAP access policy**:
    a. In the IAP panel, configure access policies by specifying the Google Accounts or Google Groups allowed to access the application. Click on **Select a role** and choose **Cloud IAP | IAP-secured Web App User** as permission and then click save to apply the changes as given below:

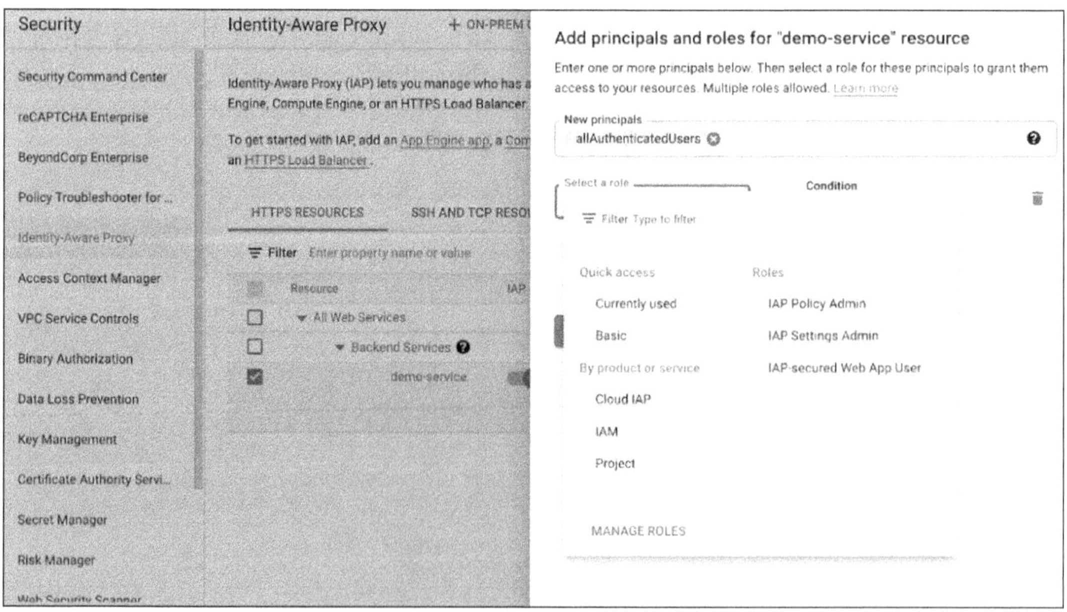

Figure 6.8: Manage roles in Identity-Aware Proxy

b. Ensure your GKE application is properly configured to work with IAP, including handling the X-Goog-Authenticated-User-Email header for user identity if needed.

Configuring access policies

Access policies are central to governing who can access your GKE application. IAP allows for fine-grained control over these policies. To configure access policies:

1. Navigate to the IAP page, select your resource, and click on Add Member to specify who can access the application.
2. Assign roles such as **IAP-secured Web App User** to the members to grant access.

Commands

List IAP-secured resources: `gcloud iap web list --project=YOUR_PROJECT_ID`

Set IAP Policy: `gcloud iap web set-iam-policy RESOURCE_NAME policy.yaml`

Example policy.yaml:

```
bindings:
- members:
  - user:user@example.com
  role: roles/iap.httpsResourceAccessor
```

Scenarios and solutions

Let us look at some scenarios and how they can be solved with IAP:

- **Scenario**: A company needs to securely expose an internal dashboard hosted on GKE to remote employees without VPN.

  Solution: Use IAP to secure the dashboard, enabling remote employees to securely access the dashboard using their corporate credentials without the need for a traditional VPN.

- **Scenario**: A healthcare application on GKE needs to ensure that only practitioners from certain locations can access patient data.

  Solution: Implement IAP with context-aware access controls to restrict access based on the user's location and secure their login process.

- **Scenario**: A company requires secure access to a GKE application for external consultants without exposing the application to the public internet.

  Solution: Use IAP with Cloud Identity to create accounts for external consultants, granting them access to the application while keeping it shielded from public access.

- **Scenario**: An organization needs to restrict access to its internal GKE-hosted application to only its employees, regardless of their location.

  Solution: Implement IAP for the GKE application, using Google Workspace accounts for authentication. Configure context-aware access policies to verify employee identities securely.

Best practices for IAP configuration

Here are a few best practices for IAP configuration in GKE:

- **Use strong authentication**: Enable 2-step verification for all users accessing applications protected by IAP.
- **Limit access with context-aware policies**: Apply context-aware access policies in IAP based on user location, device security status, and time of access.
- **Regularly update access policies**: Periodically review and update IAP access policies to reflect changes in user roles and responsibilities.
- **Monitor and audit access**: Utilize IAP's audit logs to monitor access patterns and investigate any suspicious activities.
- **Integrate with security command center**: Connect IAP logs with Google Cloud Security Command Center for centralized security management and insights.

Monitoring and logging

Effective monitoring and logging are crucial for maintaining security and gaining insights into application usage and access. With the right logging tools, you can track access requests and monitor interactions with your Services. Here are two key logging features for monitoring:

- **Audit logs**: Enable audit logs for IAP to keep track of access requests, granting insights into who is accessing your application and when.
- **Access transparency**: Use access transparency logs for an additional layer of insight into how Google personnel interact with your IAP configurations and data.

Network policies in GKE

Figure 6.9 illustrates how policies control traffic between Pods within a cluster:

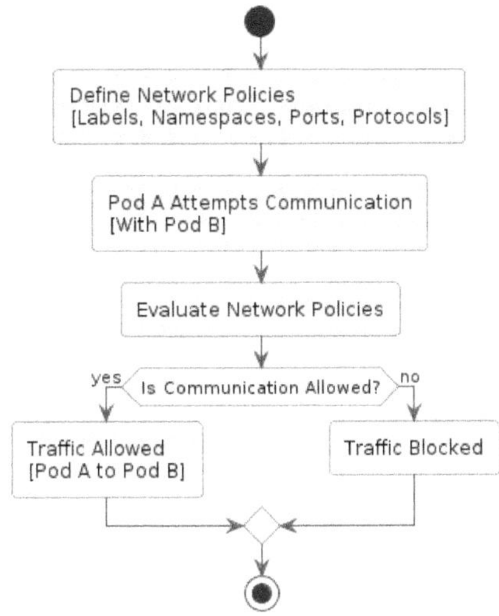

Figure 6.9*: Network policy enforcement in GKE*

The flowchart in *Figure 6.9* outlines the process as follows:

1. **Define network policies**: This is the initial step where network policies are created within the GKE cluster, specifying allowed communication patterns based on labels, namespaces, ports, and protocols
2. **Pod A attempts communication**: Demonstrating a scenario where Pod A attempts to communicate with another Pod (Pod B).
3. **Evaluate network policies**: The system evaluates the attempted communication against the defined network policies.
4. **Is communication allowed?**: Decision point based on the policy evaluation:
   a. If the output is **yes**, then the traffic is allowed to flow from Pod A to Pod B, indicating that the communication complies with the network policies.
   b. If the out is **no**, then the traffic is blocked, demonstrating the network policy's role in restricting communication within the cluster.

This visualization in *Figure 6.9* efficiently illustrates the critical steps involved in managing and enforcing network policies in GKE, ensuring secure and controlled communication between Pods.

Steps to define and apply network policies

You can follow these steps to define and apply network policies:

1. **Enable network policy logging**: Before defining network policies, ensure that your GKE cluster is configured to support them, and that network policy logging is enabled for audit purposes.

2. **Create a network policy**: Define a YAML file that specifies the policy rules. For example, to allow incoming traffic from Pods with the label `app: frontend` to Pods with the label `role: backend` on TCP `port: 80`:

```
apiVersion: networking.k8s.io/v1
kind: NetworkPolicy
metadata:
  name: backend-access-policy
spec:
  PodSelector:
      matchLabels:
      role: backend
  Ingress:
  - from:
      - PodSelector:
      matchLabels:
      app: frontend
      ports:
      - protocol: TCP
      port: 80
```

3. **Apply the network policy**: Use `kubectl` to apply the policy to your cluster: `kubectl apply -f backend-access-policy.yaml`

Use cases and best practices

Let us look at uses cases and best practices while applying network policies:

- **Use cases**:
    - **Isolating sensitive workloads**: To prevent unauthorized access to sensitive workloads by defining strict Ingress and egress rules.
    - **Microservice architecture security**: To enhance security in a microservice architecture by allowing only necessary communication between Services.
- **Best practices**:
    - **Default deny all traffic**: Start with a default deny all Ingress and egress policy and selectively allow traffic as needed.
    - **Explicitly define trust**: Only allow traffic between Pods that require communication for application functionality.
    - **Regular policy reviews**: Periodically review and update network policies to adapt to changes in the application architecture and security requirements.

Scenarios and solutions

Here are a few scenarios and how they can be solved using the network policies:

- **Scenario**: You want to restrict access to a database Service.

  Solution: Apply a network policy that only allows Ingress traffic from specific application Pods.

- **Scenario**: You want to prevent external access except for a gateway.

  Solution: Implement an egress policy that blocks all traffic except traffic to known external endpoints.

Monitoring and troubleshooting network policies

Effective monitoring and troubleshooting of network policies are essential to ensure the security and proper operation of your Services. By leveraging tools and logs, you can track policy enforcement and identify potential issues. Here are two key approaches:

- **Audit logs**: Monitor network policy audit logs to ensure policies are being applied as expected and to identify unauthorized access attempts.
- **Policy simulation**: Use tools like Calico's **`calicoctl`** to simulate policy effects without applying them, aiding in troubleshooting.

Figure 6.10 shows how logging and monitoring tools can be used to visualize and audit network policy enforcement:

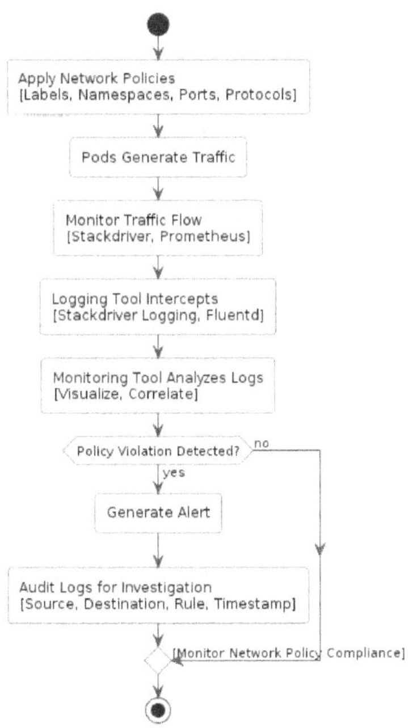

***Figure 6.10**: Monitoring network policy flow*

This visualization outlines the steps involved in monitoring network policy enforcement within a GKE cluster, including:

1. **Apply network policies**: Initial definition of network policies controlling Pod-to-Pod communication based on labels, namespaces, ports, and protocols.
2. **Pods generate traffic**: Pods within the cluster initiating communication, generating network traffic.
3. **Monitor traffic flow**: Utilizing monitoring tools like Stackdriver Monitoring and Prometheus to track and collect data on traffic flow.
4. **Logging tool intercepts**: Logging tools such as Stackdriver Logging and Fluentd capture detailed information on the traffic flow for analysis.
5. **Monitoring tool analyzes logs**: The analysis of logged data to visualize traffic patterns and identify potential policy violations.
6. **Policy violation detected?**: Decision point determining whether a policy violation has occurred, leading to alert generation and creation of detailed audit logs for investigation.

This cycle emphasizes the continuous nature of monitoring network policy compliance, ensuring the security and proper functioning of communications within the cluster.

Advanced integration scenarios

Now let us look at a few scenarios where advanced integration is needed:

- **Integrating with Cloud Armor**: Enhance security by integrating network policies with Google Cloud Armor for additional protection against DDoS attacks and other threats.
- **Automating policy management with CI/CD**: Integrate network policy definitions into your CI/CD pipeline for automated deployment and management, ensuring consistent policy enforcement across all environments.

DNS and service discovery in GKE

DNS and service discovery in GKE are fundamental components that facilitate communication between Services within and outside the Kubernetes cluster. This section explores the configuration of DNS resolution in GKE clusters and highlights best practices for DNS setup to ensure reliable Service discovery.

Configuring DNS resolution in GKE clusters

Kubernetes offers a built-in DNS Service for service discovery within the cluster, automatically creating DNS records for each Service and Pod. GKE enhances this capability with Cloud DNS, providing scalable and reliable DNS resolution.

Key concepts

Here are the key concepts which will be covered:

- **Cluster DNS**: Automatically assigns DNS names to Services and Pods, enabling internal Service discovery
- **Cloud DNS**: Integrates with GKE to manage DNS records for external Service discovery and resolution.

Figure 6.11 illustrates the process from DNS query initiation by a Pod to resolution by cluster DNS or Cloud DNS:

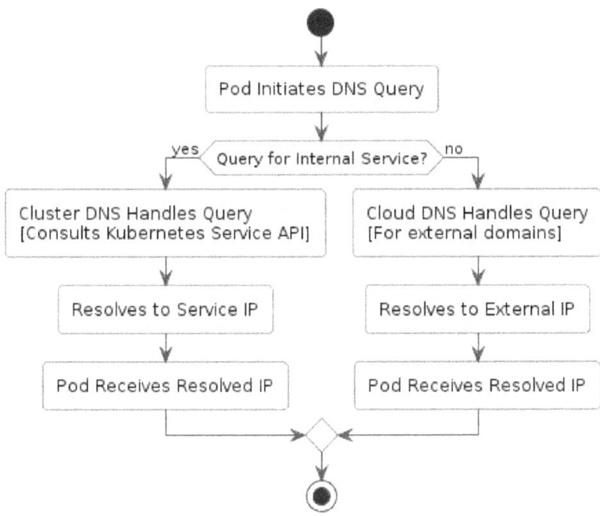

***Figure 6.11**: DNS resolution flow in GKE*

The flowchart in the *Figure 6.11*, details the process as follows:

1. **Pod initiates DNS query**: The process starts with a Pod in the GKE cluster initiating a DNS query.
2. **Query for internal service?**: The system checks if the query targets an internal service within the cluster.
   a. If the output is **yes**, then:
      i. **Cluster DNS handles query**: Cluster DNS resolves the query, consulting the Kubernetes Service API for details.
      ii. **Resolves to Service IP**: The Service's internal IP address is determined.
      iii. **Pod receives resolved IP**: The Pod gets the Service's internal IP for connection.

   b. If the output is **no**, then:

      i. **Cloud DNS handles query**: Cloud DNS takes over, resolving the query for external domains.

      ii. **Resolves to external IP**: An external IP address is obtained.

      iii. **Pod receives resolved IP**: The Pod receives the external IP to connect to the Service outside the cluster.

This visualization clearly illustrates the DNS resolution process in GKE, differentiating between internal services resolved by cluster DNS and external services handled by Cloud DNS.

The following are the steps to configure DNS in GKE:

1. **Verify cluster DNS configuration**: Ensure that `kube-dns` is running in your cluster. GKE clusters come with `kube-dns` pre-configured for internal DNS resolution: `kubectl get Pods -n kube-system -l k8s-app=kube-dns`
2. **Integrate cloud DNS for external DNS resolution**:
   a. Create a DNS zone in Cloud DNS for your domain.
   b. Update your domain's name servers to point to the Cloud DNS name servers.
   c. Configure DNS records in Cloud DNS to point to external IPs of Services exposed via Ingress or LoadBalancer.
3. **Utilize DNS policies for custom DNS configuration**: Apply DNS policies to control DNS resolution behavior within the cluster.
4. Create a DNSConfig option within the Pod spec to specify custom DNS settings, such as **nameservers** or search domains.

Best practices for DNS setup

Here are a few best practices for DNS setup:

- **Use short, descriptive service names**: This facilitates easier service discovery and minimizes potential DNS resolution issues.
- **Leverage subdomains for namespace isolation**: Use subdomains to logically separate Services within different namespaces, enhancing organization and security.
- **Monitor DNS queries and performance**: Utilize monitoring tools to track DNS query performance and identify potential bottlenecks or configuration issues.

The following table shows the DNS configuration options:

Configuration	Description	Use case
Cluster DNS	Resolves services and Pods within the cluster.	Internal service discovery
Cloud DNS Integration	Manages external DNS records for cluster services.	External access to cluster services
DNSConfig in Pods	Specifies custom DNS settings for individual Pods.	Custom DNS resolution requirements for Pods

Table 6.3: DNS configuration options in GKE

Scenarios and solutions

Kubernetes clusters often encounter unique networking and communication challenges based on application requirements. Below are common scenarios and their respective solutions:

- **Scenario**: A web application in GKE needs to communicate with an external API Service managed outside the cluster.

  Solution: Integrate Cloud DNS to resolve the external API service domain, ensuring reliable external service discovery.

- **Scenario**: Microservices within a GKE cluster need to communicate with each other using internal DNS names.

  Solution: Utilize cluster DNS for automatic service discovery, assigning DNS names to each service based on the service name and namespace for easy inter-service communication.

Monitoring and logging

Monitoring and logging are essential for ensuring the reliability and performance of your DNS configurations. By enabling logging and utilizing monitoring tools, you can proactively address issues and maintain optimal service. The following are two key practices:

- **Logging DNS queries**: Enable logging for DNS queries in Cloud DNS to audit and troubleshoot DNS resolution issues.
- **Monitoring DNS performance**: Use Google Cloud Monitoring to track the performance of DNS resolutions and identify latency or availability issues.

Figure 6.12 showcases how services are discovered via DNS and how queries are logged for auditing and troubleshooting purposes:

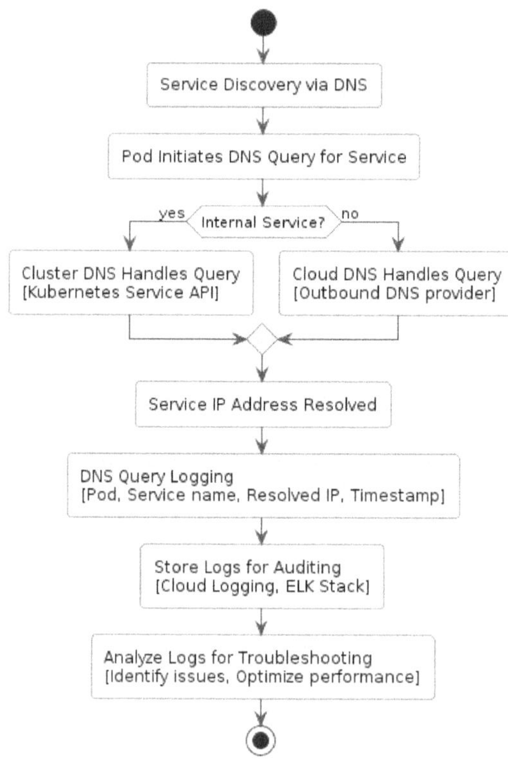

***Figure 6.12**: Service discovery and DNS logging*

The visualization in the preceding flowchart captures the following process:

1. **Service discovery via DNS**: A Pod needs to locate either an internal or external service.
2. **Pod initiates DNS query for service**: The Pod sends out a DNS query.
3. **Internal Service?**: Determines if the query is for an internal service.

   If the output is **yes**, then cluster DNS handles the query by consulting the Kubernetes Service API.

   If the output is **no**, then Cloud DNS processes the query as the outbound DNS provider.
4. **Service IP address resolved**: The DNS query is resolved to the IP address of the targeted Service.
5. **DNS query logging**: The details of the DNS query and its resolution are logged, including the Pod initiating the query, the queried Service name, the resolved IP address, and the timestamp.

6. **Store logs for auditing**: Logs are stored in a system like Cloud Logging or the ELK stack.
7. **Analyze logs for troubleshooting**: Logs are analyzed to identify issues with service discovery or DNS resolution and to optimize DNS performance.

This *Figure 6.12* effectively outlines the critical role of DNS in service discovery within GKE and the importance of DNS query logging for maintaining a robust and efficient networking environment.

Advanced integration scenarios

Now let us look at few scenarios where advanced integration is needed:

- **Hybrid Cloud DNS**: For hybrid cloud architecture, configure Cloud DNS to resolve Services across on-premises and cloud environments, ensuring seamless Service discovery.
- **DNS security**: Implement **DNS Security Extensions** (**DNSSEC**) in Cloud DNS to protect against DNS spoofing and ensure the integrity of DNS data.

Ingress and Ingress controllers in GKE

Ingress in GKE provides a powerful way to expose HTTP and HTTPS routes from outside the cluster to Services within the cluster. This section covers the fundamentals of deploying and configuring Ingress controllers in GKE for advanced traffic routing, enhancing control over how external traffic is managed and directed to the services.

Exposing HTTP and HTTPS routes using Ingress

Ingress allows you to easily expose your services to the internet, providing load balancing, SSL termination, and name-based virtual hosting without the need to configure each Service as a LoadBalancer.

Key concepts

Here are the key concepts which will be covered:

- **Ingress resources**: Define rules for routing external HTTP(S) traffic to internal services.
- **Ingress controllers**: Responsible for implementing Ingress, usually with a load balancer.

Figure 6.13 illustrates the path of external HTTP(S) traffic through an Ingress controller to the backend Services in the cluster:

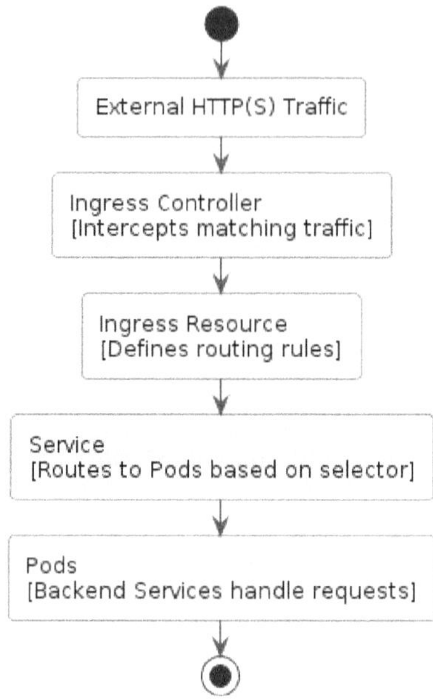

Figure 6.13: *Ingress traffic flow*

The flowchart in the *Figure 6.13*, illustrates these key steps:

- **External HTTP(S) traffic**: Initiates the process, representing requests from external clients aiming to access Services within the cluster.
- **Ingress controller**: It acts as the traffic gatekeeper, deployed within the cluster. It intercepts traffic that matches the routing rules defined in the Ingress resource.
- **Ingress resource**: A configuration object that specifies how incoming traffic should be routed. It includes routing rules based on hostnames, paths, and optionally SSL/TLS termination settings.
- **Service**: Receives traffic forwarded by the Ingress controller based on the matching rules. It acts as a load balancer, routing the traffic to the appropriate set of Pods based on label selectors.
- **Pods**: The backend services deployed as Pods within the cluster. These Pods process the incoming requests as per the service configuration.

Figure 6.13 effectively captures the critical role of the Ingress controller in managing external access to Services within a Kubernetes cluster, showcasing the routing of traffic based on predefined rules in the Ingress resource.

The following are the steps to deploy Ingress in GKE:

- **Enable HTTP(S) load balancing**: Ensure that the HTTP(S) load balancing component is enabled in your GKE cluster.

- **Deploy an Ingress resource**: Define an Ingress resource that specifies how traffic should be routed to your services.

```
apiVersion: networking.k8s.io/v1
kind: Ingress
metadata:
  name: example-Ingress
spec:
  rules:
  - host: example.com
      http:
      paths:
      - path: /
      pathType: Prefix
      backend:
      Service:
            name: example-Service
            port:
            number: 80
```

- **Configure TLS for HTTPS**: Secure your Ingress by specifying TLS secrets for your domains.

```
spec:
  tls:
  - hosts:
      - example.com
      secretName: example-tls
```

Deploying and configuring Ingress controllers

While GKE provides a default Ingress controller that utilizes Google Cloud Load Balancers, you can deploy custom Ingress controllers for advanced routing capabilities.

Selecting an Ingress controller

You can select any of the following Ingress controllers:

- **NGINX Ingress controller**: Offers rich features for HTTP routing, load balancing, and SSL termination.
- **Istio Ingress gateway**: Part of the Istio Service mesh, providing advanced traffic management features.

Configuration steps

Here are the configuration steps:

1. **Install the Ingress controller**: Deploy your chosen Ingress controller in the cluster. For NGINX, this might involve applying a deployment from the NGINX Ingress controller's official YAML.
2. **Configure Ingress resources**: Define Ingress resources tailored to the specific controller, utilizing annotations and controller-specific features for advanced routing.

Table 6.4 summarizes the key features of various Ingress controllers:

Ingress controller	Key features
GKE Ingress	Integrated with Google Cloud Load Balancers, automatic HTTPS, and global load balancing
NGINX Ingress controller	Customizable, support for WebSockets, sticky sessions, and rewriting
Istio Ingress gateway	Advanced traffic management, security policies, and observability

Table 6.4: *Ingress traffic flow*

Scenarios and solutions

The following are examples of scenarios and corresponding solutions to optimize routing and Service exposure:

- **Scenario**: A web application requires complex routing rules, including path-based routing and redirection.

  Solution: Deploy the NGINX Ingress controller to leverage its advanced routing capabilities, defining specific routing rules and redirections in the Ingress resource.
- **Scenario**: A Service needs to be exposed with both external internet access and internal cluster access.

  Solution: Configure an Ingress for external access and a ClusterIP service for internal access, ensuring secure and efficient traffic flow.

Monitoring and logging

To ensure the smooth operation of your Kubernetes cluster and its Services, monitoring and logging are essential. These practices help identify, troubleshoot, and resolve issues effectively. The following are a key aspect of logging to focus on:

- **Ingress controller logs**: Monitor logs from the Ingress controller to troubleshoot routing issues.
- **Metrics and observability**: Utilize Prometheus and Grafana to capture and visualize metrics from your Ingress controller for performance monitoring.

Figure 6.14 shows the integration of Ingress controllers with monitoring tools for insight into traffic patterns and performance:

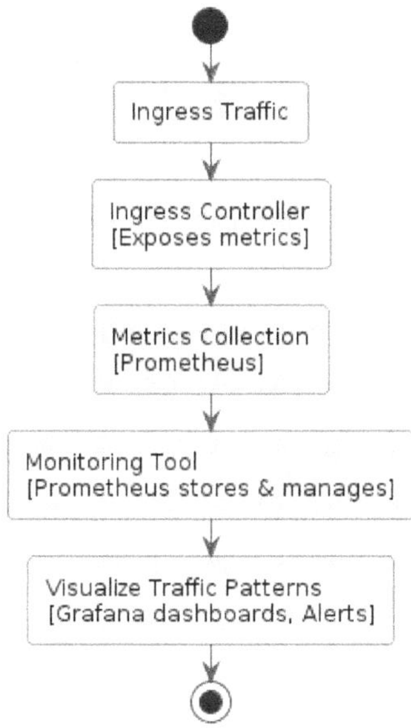

***Figure 6.14**: Monitoring Ingress traffic*

This visualization captures the essential steps for monitoring Ingress traffic within a Kubernetes cluster:

1. **Ingress traffic**: External HTTP(S) traffic is directed towards Services within the cluster.
2. **Ingress controller**: Central to processing incoming traffic, it also exposes critical metrics related to the traffic it handles, such as request rates, error rates, response times, and latency.
3. **Metrics collection**: Tools like Prometheus are employed to scrape these exposed metrics at regular intervals, gathering data to understand traffic patterns and performance.
4. **Monitoring tool (Prometheus)**: Acts as the central repository for the collected metrics, storing and managing the data for historical analysis and query.
5. **Visualize traffic patterns**: Visualization tools, notably Grafana, utilize the metrics data from Prometheus to construct insightful dashboards. These dashboards

enable administrators to observe traffic patterns over time, set up alerts based on predefined thresholds, and identify potential issues or bottlenecks in the traffic flow or Service performance.

Figure 6.14 effectively showcases the integration of Ingress controllers with monitoring tools, highlighting how metrics exposure, collection, and analysis provide deep insights into the health and performance of Ingress traffic, aiding in the optimization and management of cluster resources.

Best practices for Ingress configuration

Here are a few best practices for Ingress configuration:

- **Use annotations wisely**: Customize Ingress behavior with controller-specific annotations for tasks like authentication, SSL redirects, and more.
- **Regularly update your Ingress controllers**: Keep your Ingress controllers up to date to benefit from the latest features and security patches.
- **Secure your Services**: Always use TLS for Services exposed through Ingress and consider implementing network policies for additional security.

Conclusion

In conclusion, this chapter on networking in GKE has meticulously navigated through the critical components that constitute the networking landscape within GKE. From the foundational overview of Kubernetes Services to the advanced configurations of Ingress controllers and the strategic implementation of IAP for secure access, we have covered the gamut of functionalities essential for optimizing the performance, scalability, and security of applications. The insights provided not only illuminate the path for effective network management in GKE but also underscore the importance of a robust networking strategy in leveraging the full potential of cloud-native technologies.

The journey through the diverse networking features such as spanning services, load balancing, network policies, DNS and service discovery, to Ingress and Ingress controllers, equips practitioners with the necessary tools and knowledge to architect resilient and efficient systems. By embracing the best practices outlined, you are well-positioned to craft solutions that not only meet the immediate needs of their applications but also anticipate the dynamic challenges of the future. As networking continues to evolve within GKE, staying informed and adaptable will be key to unlocking new horizons of innovation and security in the cloud-native ecosystem.

Multiple choice questions

1. **What type of GKE Service is best suited for exposing a web application to the internet?**
    a. ClusterIP
    b. NodePort
    c. LoadBalancer
    d. ExternalName
2. **Which GKE feature allows you to control the flow of traffic to and from Pods within a Kubernetes cluster?**
    a. Ingress controllers
    b. Network policies
    c. DNS and service discovery
    d. Identity-Aware Proxy (IAP)
3. **When configuring DNS for Service discovery in GKE, which Kubernetes object automatically assigns DNS names to Services and Pods?**
    a. Cloud DNS
    b. kube-dns
    c. Ingress
    d. CoreDNS
4. **Which Ingress controller offers advanced traffic management features such as path-based routing and traffic splitting in GKE?**
    a. NGINX Ingress controller
    b. GKE Ingress
    c. Istio Ingress gateway
    d. Traefik
5. **Identity-Aware Proxy (IAP) in GKE is used to:**
    a. Automatically scale applications based on traffic
    b. Monitor and log network traffic
    c. Securely expose applications to the internet based on user identity
    d. Configure network policies between Pods

Answer key

1.	b.
2.	b.
3.	b.
4.	c.
5.	c.

Join our book's Discord space

Join the book's Discord Workspace for Latest updates, Offers, Tech happenings around the world, New Release and Sessions with the Authors:

https://discord.bpbonline.com

CHAPTER 7
Monitoring and Logging

Introduction

Monitoring and logging are crucial for keeping any workload running smoothly in production, especially in GKE. These tools help in two important ways:

- **Keeping an eye on system health**: By tracking things like uptime, error rates, and resource usage, you can quickly spot problems and make sure your applications are performing well. This helps you catch issues before they affect your users.
- **Understanding and improving performance**: Gathering detailed data about how your system is working, such as CPU usage, memory, and how often containers restart; to give you the information you need to fine-tune performance, use resources more efficiently, and fix problems faster.

Using Google Cloud operations suite, along with tools like Prometheus and Grafana, GKE offers everything you need to monitor and log your workloads, helping you keep your systems reliable and running at their best.

Structure

This chapter covers the following topics:

- Google Cloud operations suite

- Accessing Cloud Monitoring
- Monitoring GKE clusters using Prometheus and Grafana
- Visualizing metrics with Grafana
- Best practices for visualizing metrics with Grafana
- Log analysis and troubleshooting techniques

Objectives

This chapter covers critical aspects of monitoring and logging. You will understand the importance of monitoring and logging in GKE environments and learn how to set up comprehensive monitoring tools for tracking system health and performance. Then, as you will proceed in this chapter, you will explore best practices for managing and analyzing logs for efficient troubleshooting. You will also learn the use of Prometheus for custom alerting and Grafana for visualizing metrics and gain insights into optimizing resource usage and improving application performance through detailed metrics.

Google Cloud operations suite

Google Cloud operations suite, formerly known as **Stackdriver**, is a set of integrated tools that help users manage, monitor, and optimize their Google Cloud environments. It provides capabilities for monitoring, logging, error reporting, and trace for cloud-native applications.

Overview

Google Cloud operations suite provides a comprehensive set of observability tools designed to help users monitor, log, trace, and debug cloud-native applications, including those running on GKE. The suite includes:

- **Cloud Monitoring**: This helps you monitor and visualize the performance of your cloud applications and infrastructure.
- **Cloud Logging**: It aggregates logs from all Google Cloud services and third-party applications.
- **Cloud Trace**: It offers distributed tracing of requests across services.
- **Cloud Error Reporting**: It identifies and reports application errors in real-time.
- **Cloud Profiler**: It provides continuous profiling of your application performance.

Key features

Some of the key features of Google Cloud operations suite include:

- **Out-of-the-box monitoring for GKE**: Google Cloud operations suite automatically captures metrics from GKE including Pod status, container restarts, CPU, memory usage, and more.
- **Centralized log management**: It aggregates logs from all nodes and containers for easier troubleshooting.
- **Custom dashboards**: It also creates dashboards to visualize performance metrics and track health trends.
- **Proactive alerts**: One of the key features includes creating alerting policies to get notifications about performance or operational issues.

Since Cloud Monitoring and Cloud Logging are enabled by default while creating the GKE cluster, you can immediately start leveraging these tools to gain insights into your cluster's performance and application behavior. By accessing the monitoring dashboard and Logs explorer, setting up alerting policies, and creating custom dashboards, you ensure that your applications run smoothly and that you are promptly notified of any issues.

Accessing Cloud Monitoring

With Cloud Monitoring enabled, you can access a wealth of metrics and dashboards to keep an eye on your cluster's health and performance. The monitoring dashboard provides an overview of **key performance indicators** (**KPIs**) for your GKE cluster, such as CPU and memory utilization, network traffic, and Pod health. These metrics are visualized in real-time, allowing you to quickly identify any potential issues and take proactive steps. You can also drill down into specific components, such as nodes and individual Pods, to gain deeper insights into their behavior and performance.

In addition, Cloud Monitoring allows you to set up custom dashboards tailored to your specific use case, making it easier to track critical metrics and ensure your applications are running smoothly. By using this comprehensive suite of monitoring tools, you can maintain a high level of operational efficiency and address issues before they impact on your users.

Steps to access monitoring dashboard

Here are the steps to access monitoring dashboard:

1. **Navigate to Monitoring**:
    a. In the Google Cloud Console, on the search bar type **`monitoring`**, as shown in the following *Figure 7.1*:

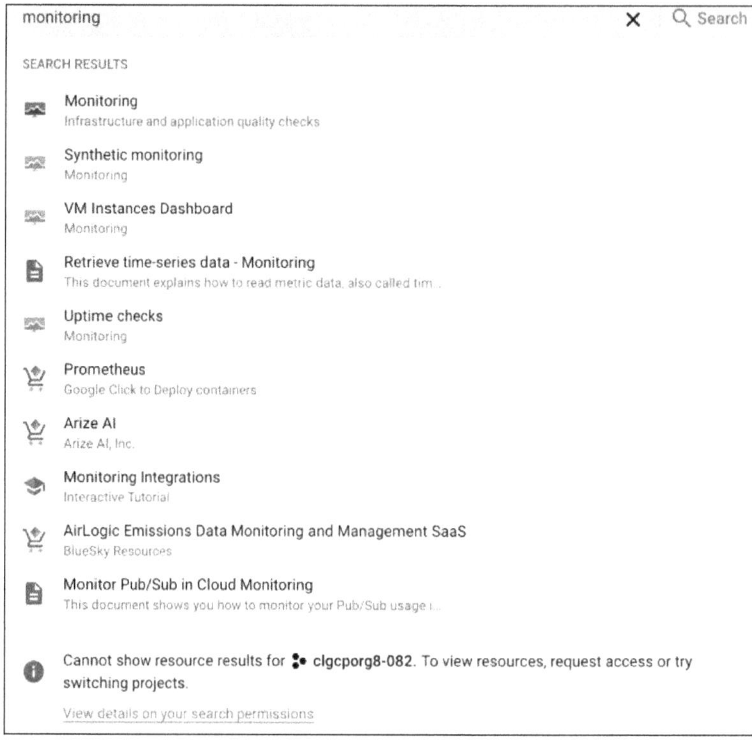

Figure 7.1: Search for Monitoring in GCP Console

b. Now, select **Monitoring | Dashboards** in the left side panel as shown in the following *Figure 7.2*:

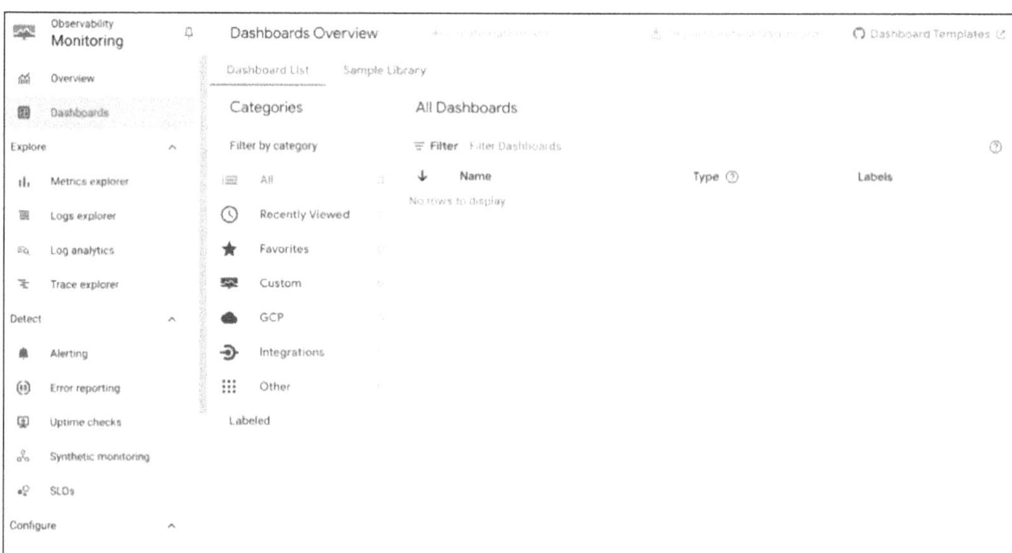

Figure 7.2: Search for Monitoring in GCP Console

2. **Explore pre-built dashboards**: Google Cloud provides pre-configured dashboards for GKE clusters. You need to look for dashboards named **GKE Cluster Monitoring** or similar.

   Now, let us understand the preceding dashboard shown in *Figure 7.3*:

   a. **CPU utilization**: It displays the average CPU usage across your clusters, nodes, namespaces, services, and Pods.

   b. **Memory usage**: It shows memory consumption trends.

   c. **Pod status**: It monitors the health and status of your Pods, including restarts.

   d. **Network traffic**: It visualizes Ingress and egress traffic for your services.

   e. **Adjusting timeframes**: You can use the time selector (usually at the top-right) to change the timeframe of the metrics displayed (for example, last hour, last 24 hours, and so on).

3. **Creating custom dashboards (optional)**: Click on **Create Dashboard** as given in the following figure to build a dashboard tailored to your specific monitoring needs:

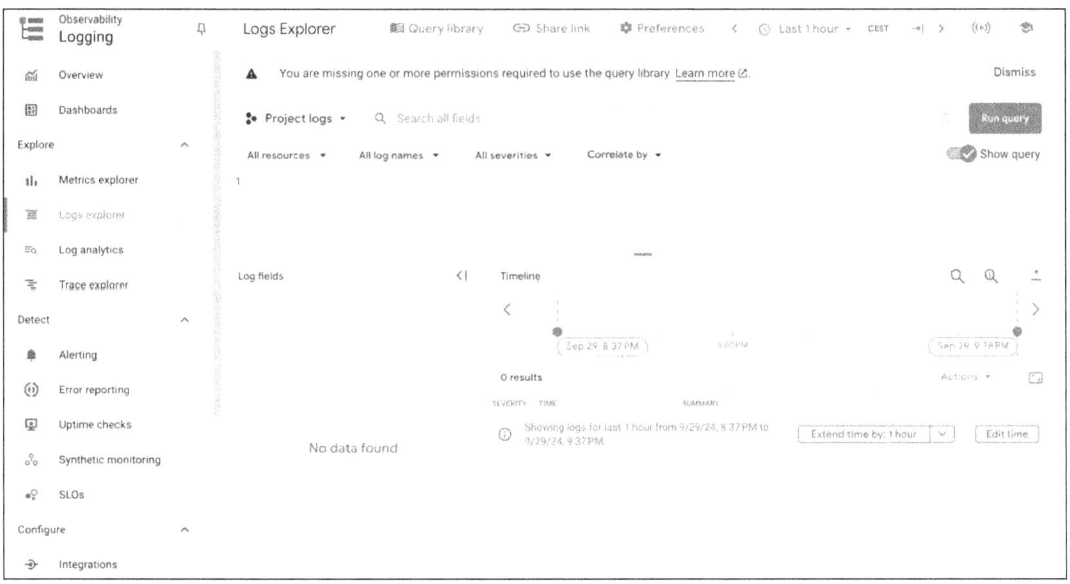

Figure 7.3: Create Custom Monitoring dashboard

You can add widgets for different metrics, charts, and logs as required.

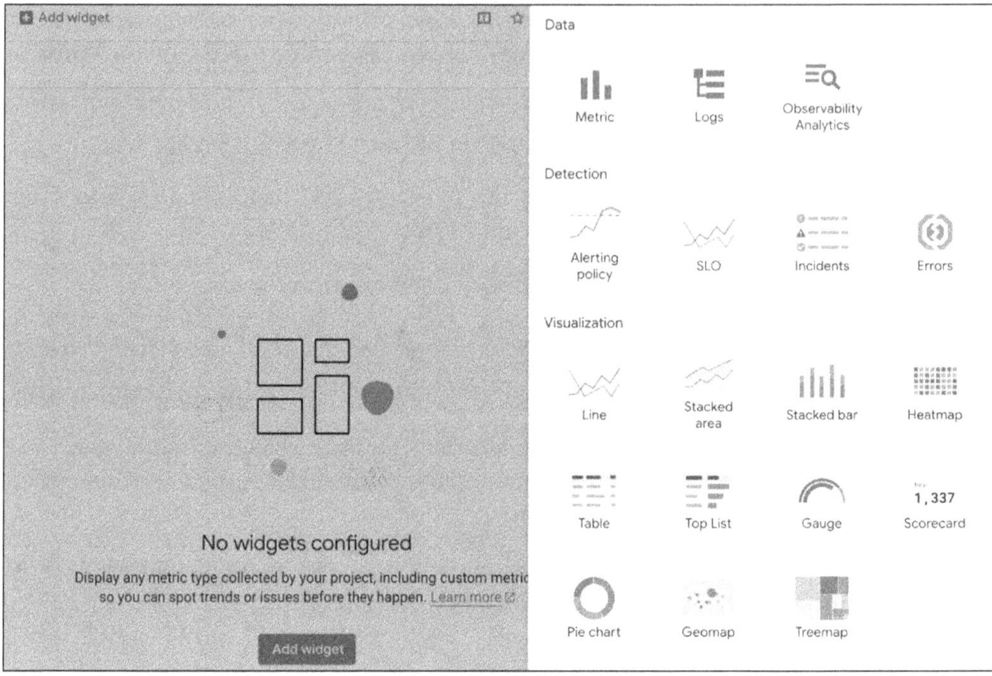

Figure 7.4: Add widgets to custom dashboard

Accessing Cloud Logging

Cloud Logging aggregates logs from your Kubernetes clusters, enabling you to troubleshoot and analyze application behavior effectively.

Steps to access logs explorer

Here are the steps to access logs explorer:

1. **Navigate to Logs explorer**:

   a. In the Google Cloud Console, search for **`logging`** as shown in the following figure:

Figure 7.5: Search for Logs explorer in the console

b. Now select **Logs explorer** as shown in the following *Figure 7.6*:

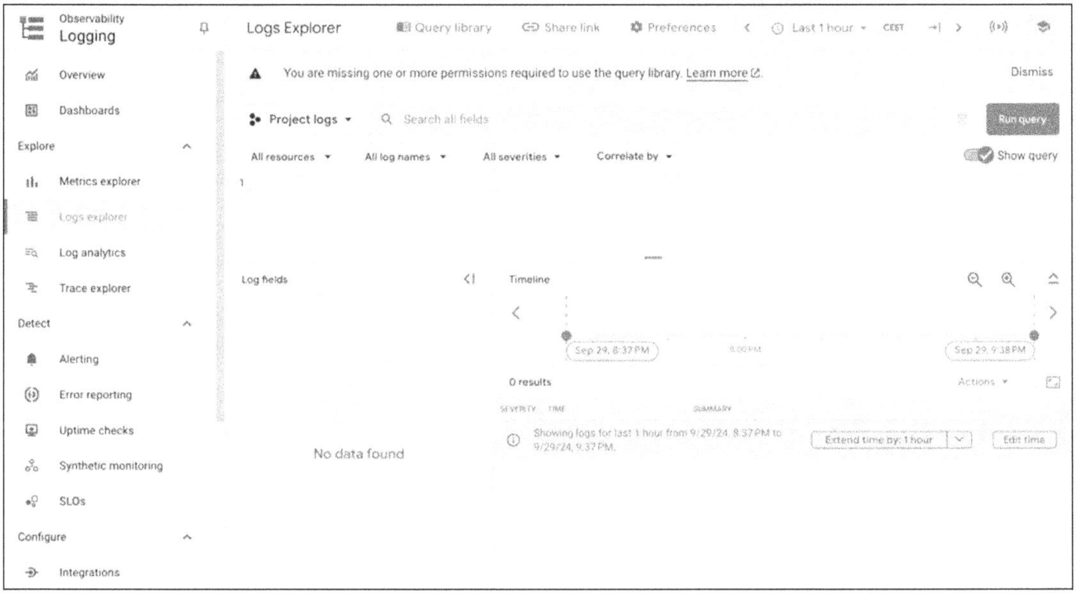

***Figure 7.6**: Logs Explorer*

Understanding **Logs Explorer** interface:

a. **Query builder**: You can use the query builder to filter logs based on various parameters like resource type, labels, severity, etc.

b. **Log entries**: Here you can view individual log entries with detailed information, including timestamps, severity levels, and message content.

2. **Filtering logs**:

   a. **By resource type**: Select Kubernetes Container to view container-specific logs.

   b. **By severity:** Filter logs based on severity levels (for instance, ERROR, WARNING, INFO).

   c. **By Pod or namespace:** Narrow down logs to specific Pods or namespaces for targeted troubleshooting.

3. **Analyzing logs**:

   - **Search functionality**: Use the search bar to find specific log messages or patterns.

   - **Log details**: Click on individual log entries to view detailed information, including stack traces and metadata.

The following screenshot shows the query pane:

Figure 7.7: Logs Explorer query pane

For detailed Kubenetes related queries, refer to Google official documentation **https://cloud.google.com/logging/docs/view/query-library#kubernetes-filters**.

Utilizing Monitoring and Logging features

In GKE, Cloud Monitoring and Cloud Logging offer powerful tools to ensure that applications and infrastructure are running smoothly. These tools help by:

- **Tracking key metrics** such as CPU utilization, memory usage, and Pod restarts.
- **Aggregating logs** from containers, nodes, and the GKE control plane to help troubleshoot issues.
- **Setting up alerts** to get notifications when performance thresholds are breached.

Here are some examples of how to utilize these features, mentioned in the following *Table 7.1*:

Feature	Description	Example use case
Cloud Monitoring	Tracks performance metrics from GKE clusters, including Pods and containers.	Monitor CPU usage across your GKE nodes to prevent performance issues.
Cloud Logging	Collects logs from applications and system components in GKE.	Capture application error logs from containers for debugging purposes.
Custom dashboards	Visualizes metrics in real-time using dashboards in Cloud Monitoring.	Create a dashboard to monitor Pod restarts and resource utilization.
Alerting policies	Sets up alerts for specific conditions (e.g., high CPU or memory usage) to notify the team.	Send an alert when memory usage exceeds 90% on a GKE node for more than 10 minutes.
Log-based metrics	Creates metrics from log data to trigger alerts or provide insights.	Set a log-based metric to alert when error logs are recorded more than 10 times in a minute.

Table 7.1: Monitoring and Logging features

Pricing overview for Google Cloud observability

Table 7.2 summarizes the pricing information for Cloud Logging, Cloud Monitoring, and Cloud Trace. It outlines the Free Tier allowances and the pricing beyond Free Tier for each product:

Product	Free Tier	Pricing beyond Free Tier
Cloud Logging	**Ingestion**: 50 GB/month per project	**Ingestion**: $0.50 per GB
	Storage: 30 days	**Storage**: $0.50 per GB per month
Cloud Monitoring	**Metrics ingestion**: 150 MB/month per project	**Metrics ingestion**: $0.30 per GB
	Custom metrics: 150 MB/month per project	**Custom metrics**: $0.30 per GB
Cloud Trace	**Trace data**: 100 MiB/month	**Trace data**: $0.50 per GiB

***Table 7.2**: Monitoring and Logging pricing*

Monitoring GKE clusters using Prometheus and Grafana

In *Chapter 4, Setting up your GKE Environment*, in the section *GKE management and automation tools*, we already mentioned that Prometheus and Grafana are powerful tools that, when combined, provide a robust monitoring solution tailored for Kubernetes environments. This chapter delves into leveraging Prometheus and Grafana to monitor your GKE clusters, create actionable alerts, and visualize critical metrics.

Introduction to Prometheus for GKE monitoring

Prometheus is an open-source systems monitoring and alerting toolkit. It has since become a standalone project and is maintained independently of any company. Prometheus is particularly well-suited for monitoring containerized applications and microservices architectures, making it an excellent choice for GKE environments.

Benefits of using Prometheus for GKE monitoring

The following features make Prometheus an excellent choice for GKE monitoring:

- **Kubernetes Native**: Prometheus seamlessly integrates with Kubernetes, leveraging its service discovery mechanisms to monitor Pods, nodes, and services dynamically.

- **Scalability**: It handles large volumes of metrics data efficiently, making it suitable for both small and large-scale deployments.
- **Flexibility**: It is highly configurable to meet diverse monitoring needs, from basic infrastructure metrics to complex application-specific metrics.
- **Community and ecosystem**: A vibrant community and a plethora of exporters extend Prometheus's capabilities, enabling monitoring of various applications and services.

Prometheus architecture

Prometheus architecture is designed to handle the challenges of monitoring dynamic, containerized environments while providing high availability and scalability. The architecture is based on a pull-based model, where Prometheus servers scrape metrics from configured targets at regular intervals.

Here is a breakdown of the key components in Prometheus architecture:

- **Prometheus server**: It scrapes and stores metrics data from monitored targets.
- **Exporters**: It exposes metrics from applications, services, and Kubernetes components. The common exporters include:
    - **kube-state-metrics**: This exporter exposes Kubernetes API object states.
    - **node_exporter**: This exporter provides hardware and OS metrics from nodes.
    - **cAdvisor**: This exporter collects container metrics.
- **Alertmanager**: It manages alerts sent by Prometheus server, handling deduplication, grouping, and routing to notification channels.
- **Grafana**: It visualizes metrics data stored in Prometheus, enabling the creation of interactive dashboards.

Practical overview of Prometheus in GKE

In a GKE cluster, Prometheus typically monitors various aspects, such as:

- **Cluster health**: CPU, memory, and disk usage of nodes and Pods.
- **Application performance**: Response times, error rates, and throughput of services.
- **Resource utilization**: Network traffic, storage I/O, and other resource metrics.
- **Custom metrics**: Application-specific metrics for business logic monitoring.

Thus, by systematically collecting and analyzing these metrics, Prometheus empowers administrators and developers to maintain optimal performance and swiftly address issues.

Creating alerts with Prometheus

Alerts are essential for proactive monitoring, enabling teams to respond promptly to potential issues before they escalate. Prometheus, combined with Alertmanager, offers a robust alerting mechanism tailored for dynamic Kubernetes environments.

Understanding Prometheus alerting

Prometheus uses alerting rules defined in its configuration to evaluate metric data and trigger alerts based on specified conditions. These alerts are then managed by Alertmanager, which handles notification delivery, silencing, and inhibition.

Setting up alerting rules

Alerting is a critical component of monitoring, as it enables you to proactively identify and respond to issues in your GKE environment before they impact performance or availability. In Prometheus, you can set up alerting rules to define conditions under which alerts should be triggered based on the metrics being collected. These conditions can be based on thresholds such as CPU usage, memory consumption, Pod status, or application-specific metrics.

Setting up alerting rules involves specifying the conditions and severity of the alerts and configuring the Alertmanager to handle these alerts and notify the appropriate team members. You can integrate alert notifications with various communication channels such as email, *Slack*, or *PagerDuty*, ensuring that the right people are notified when issues arise.

By setting up proper alerting rules, you can receive real-time notifications for critical issues, enabling you to respond quickly and maintain the health and stability of your GKE cluster. This proactive approach helps reduce downtime, prevent performance degradation, and improve the overall reliability of your cloud infrastructure.

- **Define alerting rules**: Alerting rules are written in YAML and specify conditions under which alerts should be triggered. These rules are placed in a separate YAML file, typically named **`alert_rules.yml`**.

  For example: High CPU utilization alert

```
groups:
  - name: GKE Alerts
    rules:
      - alert: HighCPUUtilization
        expr: sum(rate(container_cpu_usage_seconds_total{cluster="",
namespace="default"}[5m])) by (Pod) > 0.8
        for: 2m
        labels:
          severity: critical
```

```
        annotations:
          summary: "High CPU usage detected for Pod {{ $labels.Pod
}}"
          description: "CPU usage is above 80% for more than 2
minutes."
```

Explanation:

- **alert**: Name of the alert
- **expr**: The **Prometheus Query Language (PromQL)** expression evaluating the CPU usage
- **for**: Duration for which the condition must hold true before the alert is triggered
- **labels**: Metadata labels, such as severity
- **annotations**: Additional information about the alert, useful for notifications

- **Integrate alerting rules with Prometheus**: Ensure that Prometheus is configured to load the alerting rules. Update the `prometheus.yml` configuration file to include the rules file.

```
rule_files:
  - "alert_rules.yml"
```

- **Reload Prometheus configuration**: After updating the configuration, reload Prometheus to apply the new rules. This can be done by sending a **Signal Hang UP (SIGHUP)** signal or using the Prometheus API: `kubectl exec -n monitoring prometheus-server -- kill -HUP 1`

Note: Replace `prometheus-server` with the actual Prometheus Pod name.

Configuring Alertmanager

Alertmanager manages alerts sent by Prometheus, handling deduplication, grouping, and routing to various notification channels.

- **Define Alertmanager configuration**: Create or update the `alertmanager.yml` configuration file with your desired notification channels.

For example: Email notification

```
global:
  smtp_smarthost: 'smtp.gmail.com:587'
  smtp_from: 'alertmanager@example.com'
  smtp_auth_username: 'alertmanager@example.com'
  smtp_auth_password: 'yourpassword'

route:
```

```
    receiver: 'email-notifications'

receivers:
  - name: 'email-notifications'
    email_configs:
      - to: 'admin@example.com'
        send_resolved: true
```

Explanation:

- **global**: Defines global settings, such as SMTP server details
- **route**: Defines the default route for alerts
- **receivers**: Specifies the notification channels, such as email, Slack, PagerDuty, etc.

- **Deploy Alertmanager**: Ensure that Alertmanager is deployed in your GKE cluster and configured to use the updated `alertmanager.yml`. with the following commands:

```
kubectl apply -f alertmanager-configmap.yml
kubectl rollout restart deployment/alertmanager -n monitoring
```

Note: Replace `alertmanager-configmap.yml` and `alertmanager` with your actual configuration file and deployment names.

Testing alerts

After setting up your alerting rules, it is crucial to test them to verify that they trigger correctly under the expected conditions. Testing helps ensure that the alerts will be activated when there are performance issues or thresholds are crossed. One way to do this is by simulating high CPU usage to trigger a predefined alert and ensure that your monitoring system functions properly.

Here is how to test your High CPU Utilization alert in Prometheus:

1. **Simulate high CPU usage**:

   The following code deploys a test application that consumes CPU resources to trigger the HighCPUUtilization alert.

   ```
   kubectl run cpu-stresser --image=busybox --restart=Never -- /bin/sh
   -c "while true; do :; done"
   ```

2. **Verify alert triggering**:

   a. **Prometheus UI**: Access the Prometheus web interface and navigate to the Alerts section to see if the alert is firing.

   b. **Alertmanager notifications**: Check the configured notification channels (for example, email inbox) for alert notifications.

3. **Clean up test resources**: You can clean up test resources with the help of this command: `kubectl delete Pod cpu-stresser`

Note: Ensure that the alert resolves once the CPU usage returns to normal.

Best practices for alerting with Prometheus

Now let us look at a few best practices for alerting with Prometheus:

- **Define clear and actionable alerts**:
  - Avoid vague alert names; make them descriptive.
  - Provide actionable annotations to assist responders.
- **Set appropriate thresholds**:
  - Thresholds need to be based on historical data and performance requirements.
  - Use the for clause to prevent alert flapping due to transient spikes.
- **Group related alerts**:
  - Organize alerts logically to reduce noise and improve clarity.
- **Implement silencing and inhibition**:
  - Silence alerts during maintenance windows.
  - Prevent redundant alerts when higher-level alerts are firing.
- **Regularly review and refine alerts**:
  - Periodically assess the relevance and accuracy of your alerting rules.
  - Adjust thresholds and conditions as your infrastructure evolves.

Visualizing metrics with Grafana

Grafana is a leading open-source platform for monitoring and observability, renowned for its rich visualization capabilities and seamless integration with various data sources, including Prometheus. By leveraging Grafana, you can create interactive and insightful dashboards to visualize the metrics collected from your GKE clusters.

Setting up Grafana with Prometheus

In *Chapter 4, Setting up your GKE Environment*, in the section *GKE management and automation tools*, we already covered installation of Grafana. Follow these steps to configure it with Prometheus and start visualizing metrics.

1. **Access Grafana dashboard**:

    a. **Port forwarding**: If Grafana is deployed within the cluster and not exposed externally, use port forwarding to access it locally with this command: `kubectl port-forward deployment/grafana 3000:3000 -n monitoring`

Note: Replace grafana with your Grafana deployment name and monitoring with the appropriate namespace.

    b. **Login credentials**: The default login is typically:

        i. **Username**: admin

        ii. **Password**: admin (change upon first login for security)

2. **Add Prometheus as a data source**: To add Prometheus as a data source, we will have to follow these steps:

    a. **Navigate to configuration**:

        i. Click on the gear icon in the left sidebar.

        ii. Select data sources.

    b. **Add New data source**:

        i. Click Add data source.

        ii. Choose Prometheus from the list of available data sources.

    c. **Configure Prometheus data source**:

        i. **URL**: Enter the Prometheus server URL. If Prometheus is running within the cluster, it might be accessible via a service name, for example, **http://prometheus-server.monitoring.svc.cluster.local:9090**.

        ii. **Access**: Choose Server if Grafana is within the same cluster.

        iii. **Save and Test**: Click Save and Test, to verify the connection.

The following figure illustrates how to search for Prometheus as data source:

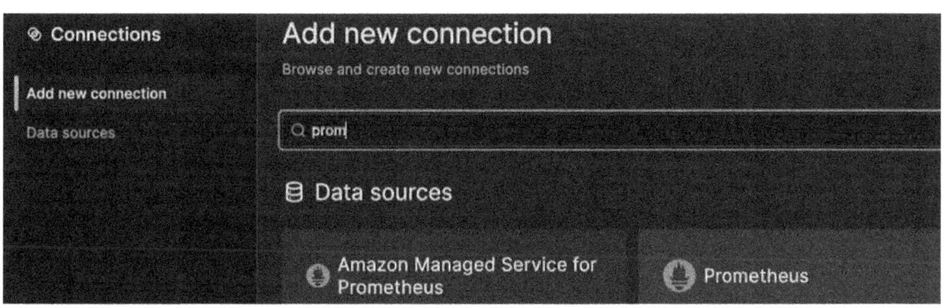

Figure 7.8: Search for Prometheus as data source in Grafana

3. **Import pre-built dashboards**: Grafana offers a vast library of pre-built dashboards for Kubernetes and Prometheus. Importing these dashboards can accelerate your monitoring setup. To import a pre-built dashboard, you can follow these steps:
   a. **Navigate to dashboards**:
      i. Click on the plus icon (+) in the left sidebar.
      ii. Select Import.
   b. **Choose a dashboard**:
      i. You can use Grafana's dashboard ID or upload a JSON file.
      ii. **Example**: For Kubernetes cluster monitoring, dashboard ID 1860 (Prometheus Kubernetes cluster monitoring) can be used.
   c. **Configure dashboard settings**:
      i. Select the Prometheus data source you added earlier.
      ii. Click Import to add the dashboard.
4. **Create custom dashboards**: While pre-built dashboards are useful, creating custom dashboards tailored to your specific needs provides deeper insights. To create a custom dashboard, you can follow these steps:
   a. **Start a new dashboard**:
      i. Click on the plus icon (+) and select Dashboard.
      ii. Click Add new panel.
   b. **Configure panels**:
      i. **Choose visualization type**: Select from options like Graph, Gauge, Table, etc.
      ii. **Define queries**: Use PromQL to query the desired metrics. For example:

```
promql
sum(rate(container_cpu_usage_seconds_total{cluster="my-
cluster", namespace="default"}[5m])) by (Pod)
```

   c. **Customize appearance**:
      i. Adjust titles, labels, colors, and other visualization settings for clarity.
   d. **Save the dashboard**:
      i. After adding all desired panels, click Save dashboard.
      ii. Provide a meaningful name, for example, Custom GKE Metrics.

Some example screenshots of dashboards are given in the following figure. You can also refer to official Grafana dashboards in this link **https://grafana.com/grafana/dashboards/18283-kubernetes-dashboard/**.

Creating insightful visualizations

Effective visualization transforms raw metrics into actionable insights. The following figure shows some key dashboards and panels to consider:

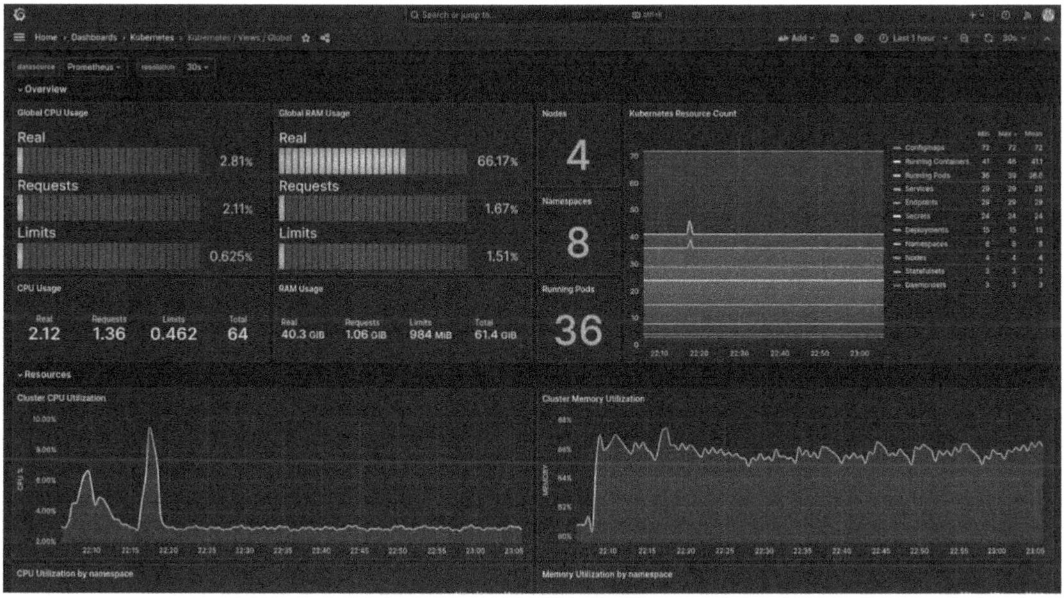

Figure 7.9: Sample cluster health dashboard in Grafana

Cluster health dashboard

This dashboard provides insights into the overall health of your Kubernetes cluster, focusing on both node and Pod performance. Sample dashboards using Grafana and Prometheus for GKE can measure a wide range of metrics, including cluster health, application performance, resource utilization, and custom business-specific metrics. These dashboards track key indicators such as CPU and memory usage, network traffic, Pod and node health, request rates, error rates, and feature usage. By visualizing these metrics, you can gain valuable insights into the performance and efficiency of your infrastructure and applications, enabling proactive management and optimization.

Enhancing dashboards with annotations and alerts

Enhancing dashboards with annotations and alerts provides valuable context to the visualized metrics, allowing teams to better understand system performance and track important events or changes in the environment. This can greatly improve the overall monitoring experience by adding additional information that helps in diagnosing issues and making informed decisions quickly.

Annotations

Now let us see how annotations enhance the dashboards:

Purpose: Annotations provide contextual information on graphs, such as deployments, incidents, or maintenance events.

Adding annotations: You can add annotations with the help of the following steps:

1. Click on a graph panel.
2. Select Edit | Annotations.
3. Define rules or manually add annotations with descriptions and timestamps.

Alerting within Grafana

While Prometheus handles alerting, Grafana also supports alerting on visualization panels. Now, let us see how to enhance the dashboards with alerts.

You can create the alerts with the following steps:

1. Within a panel, navigate to the Alert tab.
2. Define conditions based on query results.
3. Configure notification channels similar to Prometheus Alertmanager.

Best practices

Let us see a few best practices:

- Use Grafana alerts for visual anomalies or specific dashboard-focused alerts.
- Delegate system-wide alerts to Prometheus for centralized management.

Best practices for visualizing metrics with Grafana

To maximize the effectiveness of your Grafana dashboards, it is important to follow best practices that enhance both the performance and clarity of your visualizations. These practices help ensure that your dashboards are intuitive, efficient, and capable of providing valuable insights. Some of these are as follows:

- **Consistent labeling**: Ensure consistent use of labels in Prometheus metrics to facilitate easy querying and filtering in Grafana.
- **Optimized query performance**: Use efficient PromQL queries to prevent dashboard slowdowns, especially when dealing with large datasets.
- **Clear and descriptive panel titles**: Make it easy for users to understand what each panel represents without ambiguity.

- **Interactive dashboards**: Utilize Grafana's interactive features, such as variables and templating, to create dynamic and reusable dashboards.
- **Regular review and updates**: Periodically assess and update dashboards to align with evolving monitoring needs and infrastructure changes.

For more detailed information and advanced configurations, refer to the official Prometheus Documentation and Grafana Documentation:

- **https://prometheus.io/docs/visualization/grafana/**
- **https://grafana.com/docs/grafana/latest/dashboards/build-dashboards/best-practices/**

Logging best practices

Logging provides invaluable insights into the behavior and performance of your applications and infrastructure within GKE clusters. By systematically configuring and managing logs, and employing effective log analysis and troubleshooting techniques, you can proactively identify issues, optimize performance, and enhance security.

Configuring and managing logs in GKE

Proper configuration and management of logs are foundational to effective monitoring and troubleshooting. The following table outlines five essential use cases to ensure that your logging strategy in GKE is robust, scalable, and maintainable:

Use case	Description	Steps involved	Benefits
Centralizing application logs	Aggregate logs from multiple microservices into a single location for unified monitoring and analysis.	• Deploy Fluentd as a DaemonSet to collect logs from all Pods. • Configure Fluentd to forward logs to Cloud Logging. • Set up log routing based on namespaces or labels.	• Simplifies log management. • Enhances visibility across all services. • Facilitates comprehensive analysis.
Implementing structured logging	Use structured log formats (for example, JSON) to include metadata, making logs easier to parse and query.	• Modify application code to emit logs in JSON format. • Update logging configuration in Fluentd to parse JSON logs. • Verify log entries in Cloud Logging.	• Improves log readability. • Enables efficient filtering and searching. • Supports automated log processing.

Use case	Description	Steps involved	Benefits
Setting up log retention policies	Define how long logs are stored to balance between accessibility and cost management.	• Access Cloud Logging in the Google Cloud Console. • Navigate to Logs Router and create log sinks with specific retention settings. • Apply retention rules based on log types or severity.	• Controls storage costs. • Ensures compliance with data governance. • Maintains relevant log history.
Filtering out unnecessary logs	Exclude verbose or irrelevant logs to reduce noise and storage usage.	• Define exclusion filters in Cloud Logging's Logs Router. • Specify criteria (e.g., log severity, source) to exclude certain logs. • Apply and test the filters to ensure desired logs are excluded.	• Reduces storage costs. • Enhances focus on critical log data. • Improves log analysis efficiency.
Integrating third-party log management tools	Forward logs to external systems like Splunk or ELK Stack for advanced analytics and visualization.	• Configure Fluentd or another log forwarder to send logs to the third-party tool's endpoint. • Set up authentication and encryption for secure log transmission. • Verify log reception in the external system.	• Leverages specialized analytics capabilities. • Enhances data visualization options. • Facilitates integration with existing workflows.

Table 7.3: Logging strategy in GKE

Log analysis and troubleshooting techniques

Analyzing logs effectively is vital for identifying and resolving issues within your GKE clusters. The following table presents five practical use cases for log analysis and troubleshooting, demonstrating how to leverage logs to maintain and enhance cluster performance.

Use case	Description	Steps involved	Benefits
Identifying Pod failures	Detect and investigate Pods that are frequently restarting or failing.	• Access Logs Explorer in Google Cloud Console. • Filter logs by `resource.type="k8s_container"` and `severity="ERROR"`. • Identify patterns or common errors leading to Pod failures. • Trace back to the root cause (for example, application bugs, resource limits).	• Rapid identification of failing Pods. • Quick resolution of underlying issues. • Improved application reliability.
Monitoring application performance	Analyze response times and error rates to ensure applications are performing optimally.	• Query logs for response time metrics and error messages. • Visualize trends using Cloud Monitoring dashboards or Grafana. • Set up alerts for anomalous performance metrics. • Optimize code or infrastructure based on insights.	• Ensures applications meet performance standards. • Enhances user experience. • Proactively addresses performance bottlenecks.
Detecting security incidents	Identify suspicious activities or potential security breaches within the cluster.	• Filter logs for unauthorized access attempts, unusual API calls, or failed authentications. • Use Cloud Logging's security rules to highlight potential threats. • Integrate with security tools for automated threat detection. • Respond promptly to mitigate risks.	• Enhances cluster security. • Prevents data breaches. • Ensures compliance with security policies.
Analyzing resource utilization	Investigate high resource consumption issues impacting cluster performance.	• Access logs related to resource usage, such as CPU and memory metrics. • Correlate logs with Prometheus metrics to identify spikes. • Identify resource-hungry applications or misconfigurations. • Adjust resource allocations or optimize applications accordingly.	• Optimizes resource usage. • Reduces operational costs. • Prevents performance degradation due to resource exhaustion.
Root cause analysis (RCA) for incidents	Conduct comprehensive investigations to determine the underlying causes of incidents or outages.	• Aggregate relevant logs from affected services and infrastructure components. • Use log correlation techniques to connect related events. • Identify the sequence of events leading to the incident. • Document findings and implement preventive measures.	• Prevents issue recurrence. • Enhances understanding of system behavior. • Improves overall system resilience.

Table 7.4: Log analysis and troubleshooting in GKE

Conclusion

In this chapter, we delved into the comprehensive suite of tools and best practices essential for effective monitoring and logging within GKE environments. Beginning with an overview of the Google Cloud operations suite (formerly Stackdriver), we explored its robust monitoring and logging features that provide critical insights into cluster performance and application health. Leveraging these native tools ensures seamless integration and centralized management of your Kubernetes infrastructure.

Transitioning to Prometheus and Grafana, we examined how these open-source solutions enhance GKE monitoring by offering advanced metric collection, alerting capabilities, and dynamic visualization. Prometheus's powerful query language (PromQL) and Grafana's customizable dashboards empower administrators to create precise alerts and intuitive visual representations of complex metrics, facilitating proactive incident management and performance optimization.

Finally, we addressed logging best practices, emphasizing the importance of structured logging, centralized log management, and effective log analysis techniques. By configuring and managing logs meticulously, and employing strategic troubleshooting methods, teams can swiftly identify and resolve issues, ensuring the reliability and security of their applications.

Together, these practices and tools form a solid foundation for maintaining high-performing, resilient, and secure GKE clusters, enabling organizations to harness the full potential of their Kubernetes deployments.

Multiple choice questions

1. **What is the primary purpose of the Google Cloud operations suite in the context of GKE?**
    a. To deploy Kubernetes clusters automatically.
    b. To provide monitoring and logging capabilities for applications and infrastructure.
    c. To manage user permissions and access control.
    d. To offer machine learning services for data analysis.
2. **Which tool is primarily used for visualizing metrics collected by Prometheus in a GKE cluster?**
    a. Kibana
    b. Grafana
    c. Tableau
    d. Power BI

3. **What language does Prometheus use for querying metrics data?**
   a. SQL
   b. Python
   c. PromQL
   d. JavaScript
4. **In logging best practices for GKE, what is the advantage of implementing structured logging (e.g., JSON format)?**
   a. It reduces the size of log files.
   b. It makes logs easier to parse and query.
   c. It encrypts the log data for security.
   d. It automatically categorizes logs by severity.
5. **Which component of the Prometheus ecosystem is responsible for managing and routing alerts?**
   a. Alertmanager
   b. Prometheus Server
   c. Grafana
   d. kube-state-metrics

Answer key

1.	b.
2.	b.
3.	c.
4.	b.
5.	a.

CHAPTER 8
Security in GKE

Introduction

Security measures within GKE are paramount for protecting containerized applications against potential threats and ensuring compliance with industry standards. This chapter explores a comprehensive range of security considerations, from securing the GKE cluster itself to best practices in managing secrets and configurations, ultimately extending to the application layer.

Structure

This chapter will cover the following topics:

- Securing GKE clusters
- RBAC configuration
- Compliance best practices
- Managing sensitive data for compliance
- Managing secrets and configurations
- Securing applications in GKE
- Network security policies

Objectives

This chapter will explore a spectrum of security considerations, from securing the GKE cluster itself to best practices in managing secrets and configurations, ultimately extending to the application layer. You will understand the importance of security in GKE environments. As you will progress you will learn how to implement cluster-wide security measures and explore compliance best practices and the use of *Kyverno* policies. By the end of this chapter, you will master secrets management and configuration security and gain insights into securing applications within GKE.

For more detailed and official guidance, refer to the official documentation **https://cloud.google.com/kubernetes-engine/docs/concepts/security-overview**.

Securing GKE clusters

Securing GKE clusters is a critical aspect of managing and operating containerized environments. It involves a comprehensive approach to protect applications, data, and infrastructure from unauthorized access and vulnerabilities. This guide focuses on two primary areas: implementing cluster-wide security measures and configuring **role-based access control** (**RBAC**). By following best practices in these areas, organizations can significantly enhance the security posture of their GKE clusters.

Implementing cluster-wide security measures

Securing your GKE clusters is the first step towards a robust security posture for your cloud-native applications. This section covers essential security measures and best practices for protecting your clusters.

Node security

Nodes, the worker machines in a Kubernetes cluster, must be secured to protect your infrastructure and applications. Implement the following practices to enhance node security:

- **Regular updates**: Keep the nodes updated with the latest security patches. Enable automatic upgrades in GKE to ensure nodes are always running the latest version. You can make use of maintenance windows and exclusions to avoid any disruptions.
- **Restricted access**: Limit SSH access to nodes. Use Google Cloud's IAM to control who can interact with your GKE clusters.
- **Security groups**: Utilize Google Cloud security groups to restrict inbound and outbound traffic to nodes based on the principle of least privilege.

- **Actionable step**: Enable Workload Identity to provide a secure way for your GKE applications to access Google Cloud resources. Following are the steps to enable Workload Identity in your GKE cluster:
- **Enable workload identity on the cluster**: Navigate to the Google Cloud Console, select your GKE cluster, and under the Security section, enable Workload Identity.
- **Update existing node pool**: For existing clusters, update the node pool to use Workload Identity with the command:

```
gcloud container node-pools update NODE_POOL_NAME --cluster=CLUSTER_
NAME --workload-metadata=GKE_METADATA
```

- **Create a new node pool with workload identity**: If you prefer creating a new node pool with Workload Identity enabled, use the following command:

```
gcloud container node-pools create NODE_POOL_NAME --cluster=CLUSTER_
NAME --workload-metadata=GKE_METADATA
```

- **Configure IAM service account for workloads**: Create a Google Cloud IAM service account for your workload if you have not already.
- **Bind Kubernetes service account to Google Cloud IAM service account**: Use the command below:

  `gcloud iam service-accounts add-iam-policy-binding` command to bind the Kubernetes service account to the Google Cloud IAM service account.

- **Annotate Kubernetes service account**: Annotate the Kubernetes service account with the email of the Google Cloud IAM service account using this command:

```
kubectl annotate serviceaccount KSA_NAME iam.gke.io/gcp service-
account=GSA_NAME@PROJECT_ID.iam.gserviceaccount.com
```

By following these steps, you enable Workload Identity for your GKE cluster, enhancing the security of your applications by securely managing access to Google Cloud resources.

Use Container-Optimized OS

Google's **Container-Optimized OS (COS)** is designed specifically for running Docker containers securely and efficiently. It comes with several security features mentioned as follows:

- **Immutable filesystem**: Ensures system integrity by preventing modifications to the system.
- **Automatic updates**: Keeps the OS patched with the latest security fixes.
- **Least privilege**: Runs containers with minimal permissions to reduce the attack surface.

- **Recommendation**: For most GKE deployments, select COS as the node operating system to leverage these built-in security features.

Enable network policies

Network policies are Kubernetes resources that control the traffic flow between Pods within a GKE cluster. They provide a basic level of security at the IP address or port level.

- **Default deny**: Implement a default deny policy to block all traffic to Pods that do not match any rule.
- **Whitelist traffic**: Explicitly allow traffic between specific Pods or namespaces based on your application's needs.

Example:

```
apiVersion: networking.k8s.io/v1
kind: NetworkPolicy
metadata:
  name: default-deny
spec:
  podSelector: {}
  policyTypes:
  - Ingress
```

This policy denies all inbound traffic to all Pods. You can then create additional policies to allow specific traffic.

The following *Figure 8.1* contains a flowchart demonstrating the process of securing a GKE cluster, including node security measures, the choice of operating system, and the implementation of network policies:

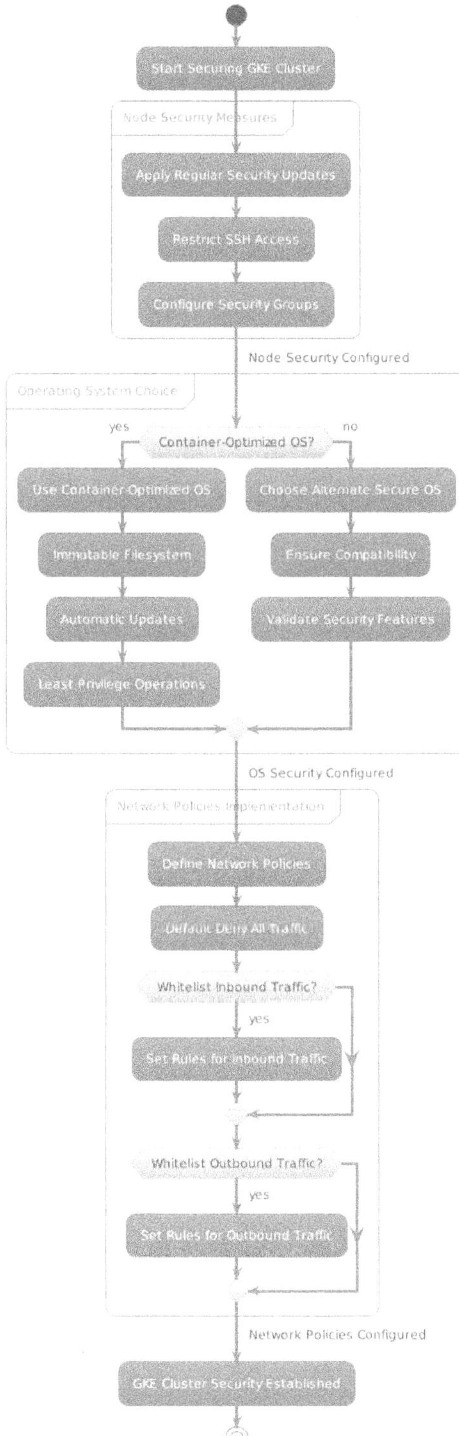

***Figure 8.1**: Flowchart depicting process of securing a GKE cluster*

RBAC configuration

RBAC in GKE is a powerful mechanism for managing access to resources. It allows you to regulate what actions users and systems can perform.

Understanding RBAC

RBAC uses Roles and RoleBindings (or ClusterRoles and ClusterRoleBindings for cluster-wide resources) to associate users with permissions. Let us see what Roles and RoleBindings do:

- **Roles/ClusterRoles**: They define a set of permissions to access resources like Pods, Deployments, or Services.
- **RoleBindings/ClusterRoleBindings**: They assign roles to users or groups within a specific namespace or across the entire cluster.

Implementing RBAC

To implement RBAC, you will have to implement the following steps:

1. **Define roles**: Determine the necessary permissions for each type of user (for instance, developers, administrators, and so on) and define Roles or ClusterRoles.
2. **Assign roles to users**: Use RoleBindings or ClusterRoleBindings to grant the defined roles to users or service accounts.

   Let us look at an example:

   ```
   kind: Role
   apiVersion: rbac.authorization.k8s.io/v1
   metadata:
     namespace: default
     name: pod-reader
   rules:
   - apiGroups: [""]
     resources: ["pods"]
     verbs: ["get", "watch", "list"]
   ```

   This preceding `Role` allows reading `pods` in the `default namespace`.

   ```
   kind: RoleBinding
   apiVersion: rbac.authorization.k8s.io/v1
   metadata:
     name: read-pods
     namespace: default
   subjects:
   ```

```
  - kind: User
    name: jane
    apiGroup: rbac.authorization.k8s.io
roleRef:
  kind: Role
  name: pod-reader
  apiGroup: rbac.authorization.k8s.io
```

This preceding **RoleBinding** grants **jane** the **pod-reader** role in the **default namespace**.

Now, let us look at *Table 8.1* which lists few examples of RBAC roles and their permissions in GKE:

Role name	Permissions	Scope
Admin	Full access to all resources. Can create, modify, and delete resources.	Cluster
Developer	Create, update, and delete deployments, Pods, and services.	Namespace
Viewer	Read-only access to view resources but cannot modify them.	Namespace
Network Admin	Manage network policies and Ingress rules.	Namespace
Secrets Manager	Create, update, and delete secrets.	Namespace
Storage Admin	Manage storage classes, PVCs, and PVs.	Cluster
Service Account Admin	Manage service accounts, including creating and assigning roles.	Namespace/ Cluster
Pod Security Policy Enforcer	Apply Pod Security Policies to control Pod creations and updates based on security criteria.	Cluster
Cluster Health Monitor	Read access to all monitoring and logging features for cluster health analysis.	Cluster
Application Deployer	Deploy applications using Helm or Kustomize, manage rollouts, rollbacks, and updates.	Namespace

***Table 8.1**: Examples of RBAC roles and their permissions in GKE*

Implementing RBAC effectively allows you to control who can do what within your GKE clusters, significantly enhancing your security posture.

Best practices for RBAC configuration

To make the most out of RBAC in GKE, consider the following best practices:

- **Principle of least privilege**: Assign roles that grant only the minimum necessary permissions to perform a task. This minimizes potential damage in case of compromised accounts or errors.
- **Audit regularly**: Periodically review your RBAC policies and role assignments to ensure they are still appropriate for your users' current roles and responsibilities.
- **Use namespace-specific roles when possible**: Limiting permissions to a specific namespace reduces the risk of affecting resources in other parts of your cluster.
- **Secure service accounts**: Service accounts are often overlooked. Ensure they have minimal permissions, especially if they are used with automated processes or applications.

Tools and resources for managing RBAC

Several tools and resources can help manage RBAC in GKE more effectively:

- **kubectl for RBAC management**: Use `kubectl` commands to create, view, and edit roles and role bindings.
- **GKE Workload Identity**: Use Workload Identity to securely bind Kubernetes service accounts to Google Cloud service accounts, providing a more secure way to access Google Cloud resources.
- **Policy auditor for GKE**: Utilize tools like policy auditor to analyze and audit your RBAC settings against best practices and compliance requirements.
- **Action item**: Regularly audit your RBAC configurations using command line tools or third-party solutions to ensure they align with security best practices and compliance requirements.

Common RBAC scenarios and solutions

Let us look at some common scenarios where RBAC plays a critical role in securing your GKE clusters:

- **Scenario**: A developer needs temporary access to debug Pods in a specific namespace.

  Solution: Create a role with read-only access to Pods in the namespace and bind it to the developer's user account with a RoleBinding. Remove the RoleBinding once access is no longer needed.

- **Scenario**: An external CI/CD tool needs access to deploy applications in your cluster.

  Solution: Create a Service Account within the namespace where deployments will occur. Bind a role to this Service Account with the necessary permissions for deployment actions. Configure your CI/CD tool to use this Service Account.

- **Scenario**: Compliance requirements dictate strict access control and auditing of all actions within the cluster.

  Solution: Implement RBAC with detailed roles and bindings, ensuring that all user actions are scoped to their responsibilities. Enable audit logging on your GKE cluster to capture all API interactions for auditing purposes.

- **Scenario**: You need to integrate your GKE cluster with an external identity provider (e.g., Google Identity, LDAP, etc.) for centralized user management.

  Solution: Configure your cluster to use an external identity provider with GKE's support for IAP or integrate with Google Cloud IAM. By configuring federated identity sources, you can authenticate and authorize users from an external directory, simplifying user management and enhancing security.

Compliance best practices

Ensuring your GKE clusters meet compliance requirements is crucial for operating in regulated industries or simply for maintaining high security and governance standards. This section delves into best practices for achieving and maintaining compliance within your GKE environments.

Policy engines: OPA vs. Kyverno

When choosing a policy engine for Kubernetes, it is important to consider factors such as flexibility, ease of use, and integration with your existing workflows. Here is a comparison of two popular options:

- **Open Policy Agent** (**OPA**) is a flexible policy engine that allows fine-grained control over Kubernetes policies, but it requires learning the Rego language and can be complex to set up.
- **Kyverno** is a Kubernetes-native policy engine that simplifies policy enforcement by using YAML-based definitions, making it easier to integrate into Kubernetes environments and CI/CD pipelines.

In this book, we have chosen Kyverno for its seamless integration with Kubernetes, simple YAML-based policy definitions, and focus on Kubernetes-specific use cases. It provides an easy and efficient way to manage policies without the complexity of other engines like OPA.

Introduction to Kyverno policies

Kyverno is a Kubernetes-native policy engine that enables you to manage, automate, and enforce policies across your clusters. It simplifies compliance by allowing you to specify policies as Kubernetes resources, making it easier to integrate them into your CI/CD pipeline.

Implementing Kyverno in GKE

Below, we outline the steps to deploy and utilize Kyverno for enforcing cluster-wide policies.

1. **Install Kyverno**: Deploy Kyverno to your GKE cluster using Helm or Argo CD.

   For example, using Helm to install Kyverno on your GKE cluster with this command: `helm repo add kyverno https://kyverno.github.io/kyverno/ helm install kyverno kyverno/kyverno --namespace kyverno --create-namespace`

2. **Define policies**: Create policies according to your compliance requirements. Policies can enforce configurations, validate resource changes, or mutate resources to adjust them to a compliant state.

3. **Test policies**: Before enforcing policies, test them in a non-production environment or in audit mode to ensure they work as expected without impacting existing workloads.

   Let us look at an example policy:

```
apiVersion: kyverno.io/v1
kind: ClusterPolicy
metadata:
  name: require-labels
spec:
  rules:
    - name: check-for-labels
      match:
        resources:
          kinds:
            - Pod
      validate:
        message: "Missing required labels: app"
        pattern:
          metadata:
            labels:
              app: "?*"
```

This preceding policy ensures that all Pods have an app label.

Implementing GKE security controls for compliance

Achieving compliance requires a comprehensive approach, including implementing GKE's built-in security controls and integrating external tools where necessary.

Compliance standards

Familiarity with compliance standards like **Payment Card Industry Data Security Standard (PCI-DSS)**, **Health Insurance Portability and Accountability Act (HIPAA)**, and **General Data Protection Regulation (GDPR)** is essential. Each has specific requirements that impact how you configure and manage your GKE clusters.

Table 8.2 tabulates a few GKE features and their compliance standards:

Feature	Compliance standard	Description
Audit Logging	All	Logs all administrative actions, providing an audit trail for compliance.
Binary Authorization	PCI-DSS, HIPAA	Ensures only trusted container images are deployed.
Shielded GKE Nodes	GDPR	Provides verifiable integrity to prevent Rootkits and Bootkits.

***Table 8.2**: GKE features and compliance standards*

Key steps for implementing compliance

Let us look at few key steps for implementing compliance:

1. **Assessment**: Identify the compliance standards relevant to your organization.
2. **Policy definition**: Use tools like Kyverno to define policies that enforce the necessary controls.
3. **Automate enforcement**: Automate policy enforcement using CI/CD pipelines to ensure all deployments comply.
4. **Regular audits**: Conduct regular audits and reviews to ensure ongoing compliance.
5. **Remediation**: In case of policy violations, set up automated remediation actions in Kyverno to correct non-compliant resources and bring them back into compliance.

Figure 8.2 shows a flowchart showing steps from compliance assessment to enforcement and audit, highlighting tools and GKE features used at each step:

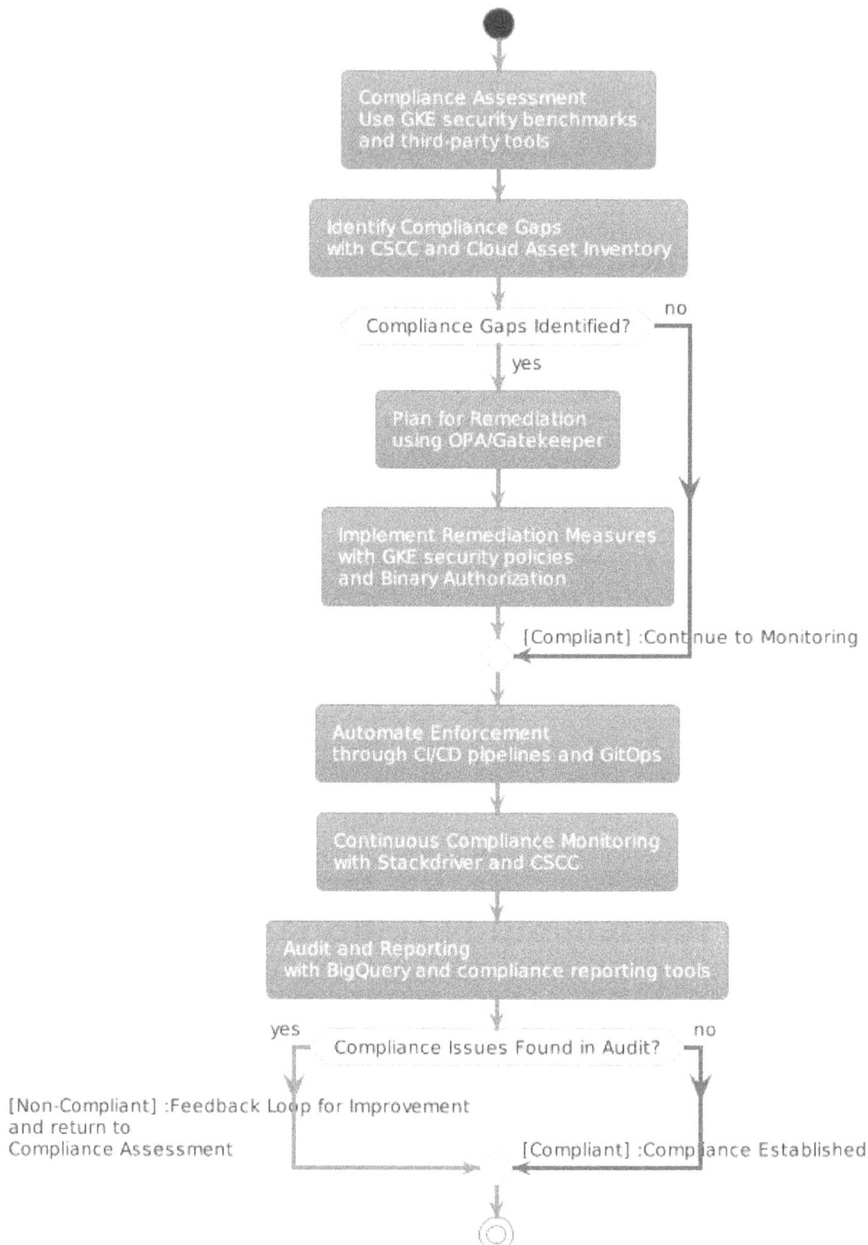

***Figure 8.2**: Steps from compliance assessment to enforcement and audit*

Managing sensitive data for compliance

Sensitive information management is critical for compliance. Kubernetes Secrets and external key management systems play a vital role.

Kubernetes Secrets management in GKE

To ensure secure handling of sensitive data, it is essential to follow best practices for secrets management in GKE.

Here are a few best practices for secrets management in GKE:

- Encrypt secrets at rest and in transit.
- Limit access to secrets using RBAC.
- Rotate secrets regularly.

Let us look at an example of directory structure for managing Secrets:

```
my-application/
├── k8s/
│   ├── secrets/
│   │   └── db-credentials.yaml
│   └── deployments/
│       └── web-app.yaml
└── src/
```

This directory structure organizes the application as follows:

- **my-application/**: The main project folder.
- **k8s/**: Contains Kubernetes configurations.
- **secrets/**: Stores sensitive data like **`db-credentials.yaml`**.
- **deployments/**: Holds deployment files like **`web-app.yaml`**.
- **src/**: Contains the application's source code.

This setup keeps Kubernetes configurations, Secrets, and code separate for better management.

External Secrets and key management systems

Integrate GKE with Google Cloud Secret Manager or HashiCorp Vault for enhanced security and management of Secrets.

Figure 8.3 shows the flow from application request to Secret retrieval:

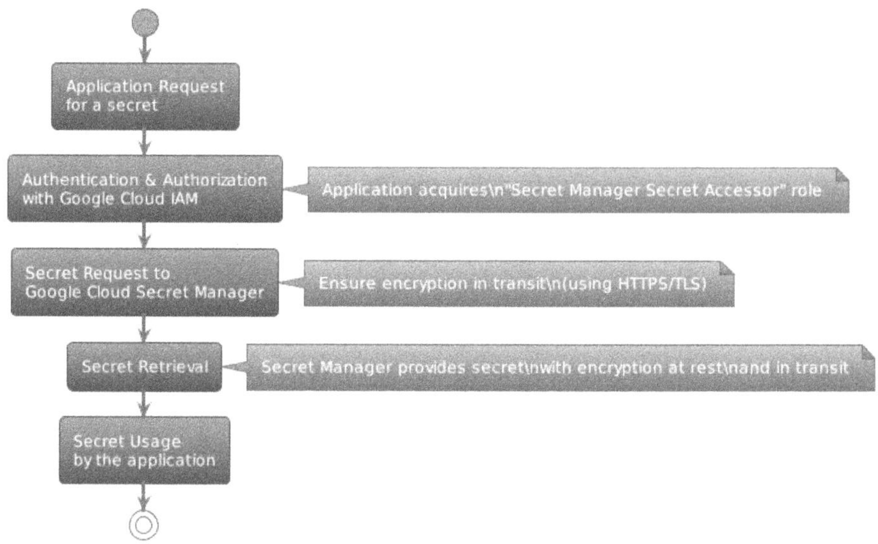

Figure 8.3: *Integration of GKE with Google Cloud Secret Manager*

The flowchart illustrates the process from an application request to the retrieval of a secret. It outlines the steps involved, starting with the application sending a request for sensitive information, followed by the Kubernetes system securely fetching the secret, and finally providing it to the application for use. This flow ensures that sensitive data is handled securely throughout the process.

Google Cloud Secret Manager

Google Cloud Secret Manager provides a centralized and secure service to manage, access, and audit secrets across Google Cloud.

Integration steps: Here are the steps to integrate Google Cloud Secret Manager with GKE:

1. Enable Secret Manager API in your Google Cloud project using the below CLI command:

   ```
   gcloud services enable secretmanager.googleapis.com
   ```

2. Create Secrets in Secret Manager and set permissions for GKE to access.

3. **CLI commands for Secret creation**: To create a Kubernetes secret, use the following CLI command:

   ```
   kubectl create secret generic db-credentials --from-
   literal=username=your-username --from-literal=password=your-password
   --dry-run=client -o yaml > k8s/secrets/db-credentials.yaml
   ```

   This command creates a secret with **`db-credentials`** in the **`secrets/`** directory, which contains the username and password.

4. **IAM Policy examples for access control**: To ensure GKE has permissions to access Google Cloud Secret Manager, you can assign the **`secretmanager.secretAccessor`** role to the GKE service account:

```
bindings:
  - role: roles/secretmanager.secretAccessor
    members:
      - serviceAccount: your-service-account@your-project.iam.
gserviceaccount.com
```

   This IAM policy allows GKE service accounts to access secrets stored in Google Cloud Secret Manager.

5. **Secret versioning examples:** Google Cloud Secret Manager allows versioning of secrets. Here is how you can manage secret versions:

   a. **Create a new version of a secret**:

```
echo -n "new-password" | gcloud secrets versions add db-
credentials --data-file=-
```

   This command creates a new version of the **`db-credentials secret`** in Google Cloud Secret Manager.

   b. **Access a specific version of a secret**:

```
gcloud secrets versions access 1 --secret=db-credentials
```

   This command retrieves version 1 of the **`db-credentials secret`**.

   c. **Roll back to a previous version**:

```
gcloud secrets versions access 1 --secret=db-credentials > db-
credentials.yaml
```

   This will export version 1 of the secret to a file that can be used for your application.

6. Access secrets from GKE Pods using workload identity to authenticate to secret manager.

   The following are the steps to access Secrets from GKE Pods using workload identity:

   a. First, enable Workload Identity on GKE Cluster:

```
gcloud container clusters update CLUSTER_NAME --workload-
pool=YOUR_PROJECT_ID.svc.id.goog
```

   b. Then create Google Cloud IAM service account:

```
gcloud iam service-accounts create my-service-account --display-
name="Service Account for GKE Access"
```

c. Next, grant IAM service account permissions:

```
gcloud projects add-iam-policy-binding YOUR_PROJECT_ID \
      --member="serviceAccount:my-service-account@YOUR_PROJECT_
ID.iam.gserviceaccount.com" \
  --role="roles/secretmanager.secretAccessor"
```

d. Then, bind Kubernetes service account to IAM service account:

```
kubectl create serviceaccount my-k8s-service-account
gcloud iam service-accounts add-iam-policy-binding my-service-
account@YOUR_PROJECT_ID.iam.gserviceaccount.com \
  --member="serviceAccount:YOUR_PROJECT_ID.svc.id.goog[default/
my-k8s-service-account]" \
  --role="roles/iam.workloadIdentityUser"
```

e. Annotate Kubernetes service account:

```
kubectl annotate serviceaccount my-k8s-service-account \
        iam.gke.io/gcp-service-account=my-service-account@YOUR_
PROJECT_ID.iam.gserviceaccount.com
```

f. Deploy Pod using Kubernetes service account:

```
apiVersion: v1
kind: Pod
metadata:
  name: secret-access-pod
spec:
  serviceAccountName: my-k8s-service-account
  containers:
    - name: secret-access-container
      image: busybox
      command: [ "sleep", "3600" ]
```

g. Access Secrets inside the Pod:

```
kubectl exec -it secret-access-pod -- /bin/sh
gcloud secrets versions access latest --secret="db-credentials"
```

This allows the Pod to securely access secrets from Google Cloud Secret Manager using Workload Identity.

HashiCorp Vault

HashiCorp Vault offers secrets management, data encryption, and identity-based access.

Integration steps: Let us look the integration steps:

- Deploy Vault on GKE or use Vault's managed service.

- Configure authentication between Vault and GKE using Kubernetes authentication method.
- Access secrets from Vault within GKE Pods using vault's API or SDKs.

Common scenarios and solutions

Now let us look at few common scenarios and how can those be solved:

- **Scenario**: An application needs to access a database password stored securely.

  Solution: Store the password in Google Cloud Secret Manager. Configure the application's Kubernetes deployment to use Workload Identity to authenticate to Secret Manager and retrieve the secret at runtime.

- **Scenario**: A team requires centralized management of SSH keys for accessing multiple services.

  Solution: Use HashiCorp Vault to store SSH keys and configure services to authenticate and fetch keys dynamically, ensuring keys can be rotated and managed centrally.

By following these practices for managing secrets and configurations in GKE, organizations can significantly reduce the risk of sensitive data exposure and streamline secret management processes, ensuring applications remain secure and compliant.

Managing secrets and configurations

Efficient management of secrets and configurations is essential for protecting sensitive data such as passwords, API keys, and certificates. This section explores strategies for securing secrets in GKE and utilizing external management systems for heightened security for applications.

Best practices for secrets management

Let us look at few best practices for secrets management:

- **Encrypt secrets at rest**: Ensure that secrets are encrypted in etcd using Kubernetes' built-in encryption or an external KMS.
- **Limit access with RBAC**: Define RBAC policies to restrict who can create, access, or modify secrets.
- **Use namespaces wisely**: Organize secrets in namespaces to limit access scope and reduce the risk of accidental exposure.
- **Regular rotation**: Regularly rotate secrets to minimize the impact of potential leaks.

Figure 8.4 illustrates the lifecycle of a secret from creation, through encryption and access control, to rotation:

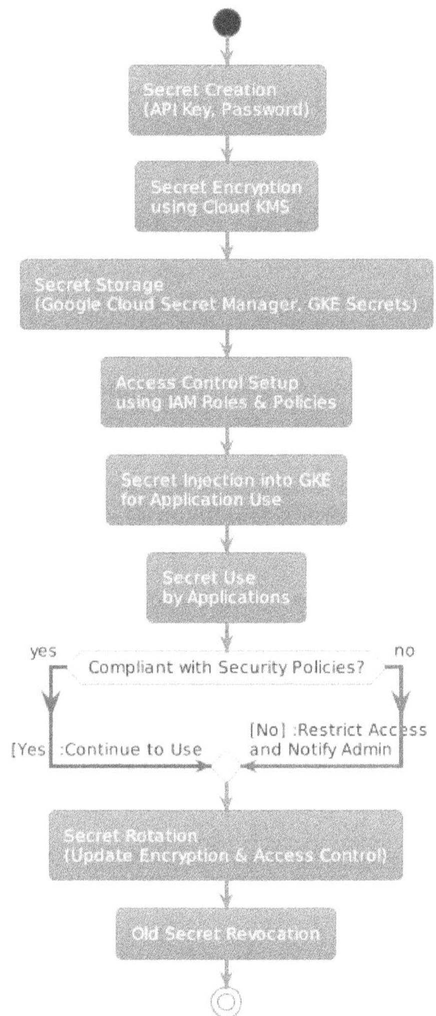

***Figure 8.4**: Secrets management workflow in GKE*

Implementing secrets in GKE

To securely manage sensitive information in your GKE clusters, it is essential to follow a structured process.

Let us look at a step-by-step guide to implement secrets in GKE:

1. **Creating a secret**: Use **`kubectl`** to create a secret from a file or literal value using this command: **`kubectl create secret generic db-secret --from-literal=username='dbuser' --from-literal=password='dbpass'`**

2. **Encrypting secrets at rest**: Configure Kubernetes to use **Key Management Service (KMS)** for encrypting secrets stored in etcd.
3. **Accessing secrets in Pods**: Modify Pod specifications to include secret volumes or environment variables You can use the following code:

```
apiVersion: v1
kind: Pod
metadata:
  name: mypod
spec:
  containers:
  - name: mypod
       image: myimage
       env:
       - name: USERNAME
       valueFrom:
       secretKeyRef:
              name: db-secret
              key: username
```

   This code defines a Kubernetes Pod named **`mypod`** with a container that uses the image **`myimage`**. It also includes an environment variable USERNAME, which gets its value from a Kubernetes secret called **`db-secret`**. The **`secretKeyRef`** specifies that the value of the username key in the **`db-secret`** should be used for the USERNAME environment variable in the container. This ensures that sensitive data, like database credentials, is securely injected into the container.
4. **Rotating secrets**: Regularly update secrets and adjust Pod specifications to reference new secrets.

   Table 8.3 enlists few commands used in secret management in **`kubectl`**:

Command	Description
`kubectl create secret`	Create a new secret.
`kubectl get secrets`	List all secrets in a namespace.
`kubectl describe secret [name]`	Show details of a specific secret.
`kubectl delete secret [name]`	Delete a secret.

Table 8.3: Secrets management commands in kubectl

Securing applications in GKE

Securing applications in GKE is crucial for maintaining the integrity and confidentiality of the application data and ensuring the resilience of the applications against cyber threats. This section explores container security best practices and the implementation of application security policies within GKE.

Container security best practices

Container security involves securing the containers' build, ship, and run phases. Here, we focus on practices that ensure the security of container images and their runtime environment.

Secure container images

Here are some key best practices to consider:

- **Use minimal base images**: Start with the smallest possible base image (e.g., *Alpine Linux*) to minimize the attack surface.
- **Scan for vulnerabilities**: Regularly use tools like *Clair*, *Trivy*, or *Google Container Analysis* to scan images for known vulnerabilities.
- **Implement image signing and verification**: Use tools like *Docker Content Trust* or *Sigstore* to sign your images and verify their integrity upon deployment.

Table 8.4 enlists various tools for container image security:

Tool	Purpose	Description
Clair	Vulnerability scanning	Open-source project for the static analysis of vulnerabilities in app containers.
Trivy	Vulnerability scanning	A simple and comprehensive vulnerability scanner for containers and other artifacts, suitable for CI.
Sigstore	Image signing and verification	A set of tools for signing and verifying container images.
Google Container Analysis	Vulnerability scanning	Integrated vulnerability scanning for containers hosted in Google Container Registry.

***Table 8.4**: Tools for container image security*

Secure container runtime

Securing the container runtime is essential for protecting your workloads in Kubernetes. To ensure your containers run securely, follow these best practices:

- **Implement least privilege**: Run containers as a non-root user whenever possible.
- **Use network policies**: Restrict communication between Pods using GKE network policies to only what is necessary.

- **Enable runtime security**: Utilize GKE's built-in security features like seccomp, AppArmor, or third-party tools like Falco to monitor and enforce runtime security.

Figure 8.5 illustrates the stages from image creation, scanning, signing, to runtime security enforcement with examples of tools and policies applied at each stage:

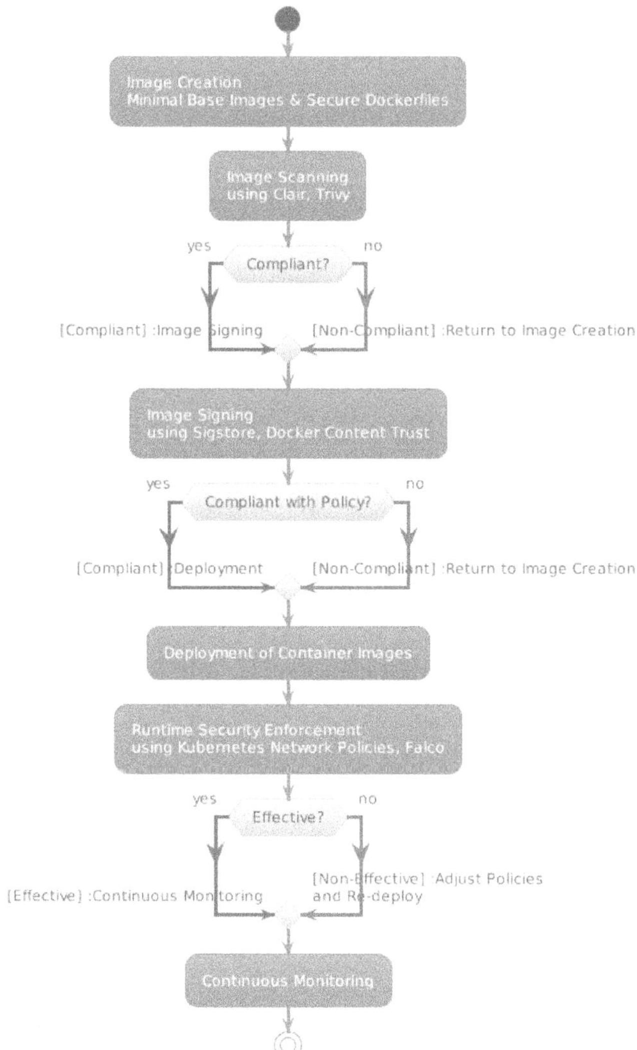

***Figure 8.5:** Container security lifecycle*

Implementing application security policies

Application security policies in GKE are defined and enforced through Kubernetes mechanisms like **Pod Security Policies** (**PSP**), network policies, and by integrating security tools.

Pod Security Policies

PSPs allow you to define a set of conditions that Pods must meet to run in your cluster. Although PSPs are deprecated in Kubernetes 1.21 and will be removed in version 1.25, alternatives like OPA Gatekeeper or Kyverno can be used to enforce similar policies.

Kyverno policy enforcement

To maintain security and compliance in your Kubernetes environment, enforcing policies with Kyverno is crucial. Here is how you can effectively implement Kyverno policies:

- **Define policies**: Create policies for security best practices like requiring non-root users, disallowing privileged containers, etc.
- **Apply and enforce policies**: Apply policies cluster-wide or to specific namespaces and enforce them as required, audit, or warn.

  Example policy (non-root users):

```
apiVersion: kyverno.io/v1
kind: ClusterPolicy
metadata:
  name: require-non-root-users
spec:
  validationFailureAction: enforce
  rules:
  - name: check-for-non-root-users
      match:
      resources:
      kinds:
      - Pod
      validate:
      message: "Running as root is not allowed. Please use a non-
root user."
      pattern:
      spec:
      securityContext:
            runAsNonRoot: true
```

Network policies

Network policies in GKE enable you to control the flow of traffic between Pods, enhancing the security posture by isolating application components.

- **Define network policies**: Specify Ingress and egress rules based on Pod selectors and ports to control traffic flow.

- **Apply network policies**: Apply the defined policies to the relevant namespaces or Pods.

  Example network policy (Ingress):

```
apiVersion: networking.k8s.io/v1
kind: NetworkPolicy
metadata:
  name: allow-nginx
spec:
  podSelector:
       matchLabels:
       app: nginx
  Ingress:
  - from:
       - podSelector:
       matchLabels:
       app: web-client
       ports:
       - protocol: TCP
       port: 80
```

Figure 8.6 depicts the relationship between policy types (PSP replacements, network policies), enforcement mechanisms (Kyverno, OPA), and tools for runtime security:

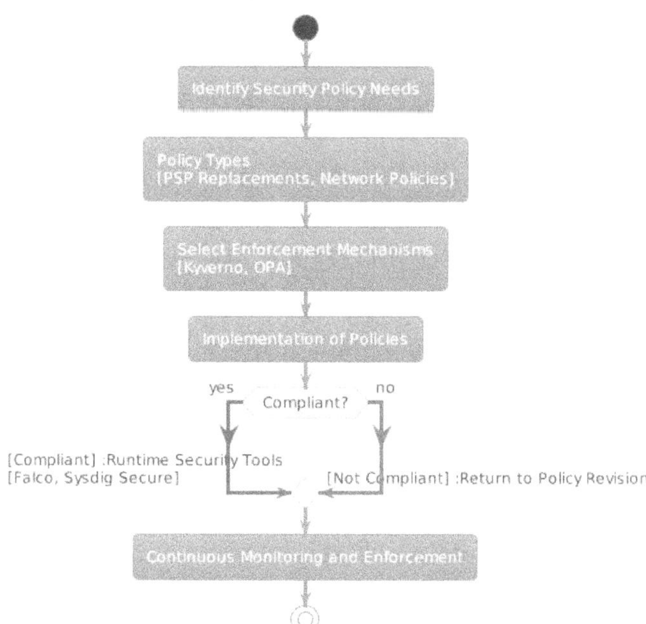

***Figure 8.6**: Application security policy enforcement in GKE*

Common scenarios and solutions

Now let us look at few common scenarios and how can those be solved:

- **Scenario**: A finance application requires strict compliance with PCI-DSS, including the need to run containers as non-root and ensure encryption of data in transit.

  Solution: Implement a Kyverno policy to enforce containers to run as non-root users. Use GKE network policies to restrict traffic only to authorized services and ensure all communication is over TLS. Integrate with an external secrets manager to handle TLS certificates securely.

- **Scenario**: An e-commerce platform needs to isolate its frontend and backend services to reduce the risk of lateral movement in case of a compromise.

  Solution: Define network policies that strictly allow Ingress traffic to the backend only from the frontend Pods. Additionally, enforce egress controls from the backend to external services only as necessary for its operation.

- **Scenario**: A healthcare application dealing with **Protected Health Information** (**PHI**) must enforce strict access controls and auditing to comply with HIPAA.

  Solution: Use GKE's audit logging features to capture all access and modifications to Kubernetes resources. Implement Kyverno policies to enforce the principle of least privilege, ensuring that containers and service accounts have only the permissions necessary for their function. Additionally, integrate Kubernetes Secrets with a Key Management System to ensure the encryption of PHI both at rest and in transit.

Tools and practices for enhanced security

To further enhance the security of applications running in GKE, consider integrating additional tools and practices, such as:

- **Container runtime security**: Utilize tools like Sysdig Falco or Aqua Security to monitor container runtime behavior and detect anomalies.

- **Static code analysis**: Implement **Static Application Security Testing** (**SAST**) tools in the CI/CD pipeline to catch security issues early in the development process.

- **Dependency scanning**: Use tools like Snyk or Dependabot to scan dependencies for known vulnerabilities and apply updates or patches automatically.

Security monitoring and response

Establish a monitoring and response framework to detect security incidents and respond promptly:

- **Logging and monitoring**: Utilize Google Cloud's operations suite (formerly Stackdriver) for comprehensive logging and monitoring of GKE clusters and applications.
- **Incident response plan**: Develop and rehearse an incident response plan tailored to your GKE environment, detailing steps for containment, eradication, and recovery from security incidents.

Continuous security assessment

Adopt a continuous security assessment approach to keep up with new threats:

- **Regular audits**: Conduct periodic security audits of your GKE clusters and applications to identify and remediate potential vulnerabilities.
- **Penetration testing**: Perform regular penetration testing to simulate attacks on your environment and identify weaknesses.

Network security policies

Effective network security is foundational for safeguarding applications in GKE. This section covers the essentials of network policies in GKE, focusing on their role in controlling traffic flow and ensuring secure communication between services.

Introduction to network policies in GKE

Network policies in Kubernetes are rules that govern how Pods can communicate with each other and with other network endpoints. In GKE, network policies enable administrators to enforce a default deny firewall policy in a namespace, ensuring that only allowed traffic can reach the Pods.

Key concepts

Here are the key concepts which will be covered in this section:

- **Ingress and egress**: Ingress rules control incoming traffic to Pods, while egress rules manage outgoing traffic.
- **Pod selectors**: These are used to specify the Pods to which the policy applies based on their labels.
- **Policy scope**: Policies can be applied at the namespace level, affecting all Pods within, or targeted to specific Pods through selectors.

Figure 8.7 illustrates the flow of allowed and blocked traffic based on defined network policies:

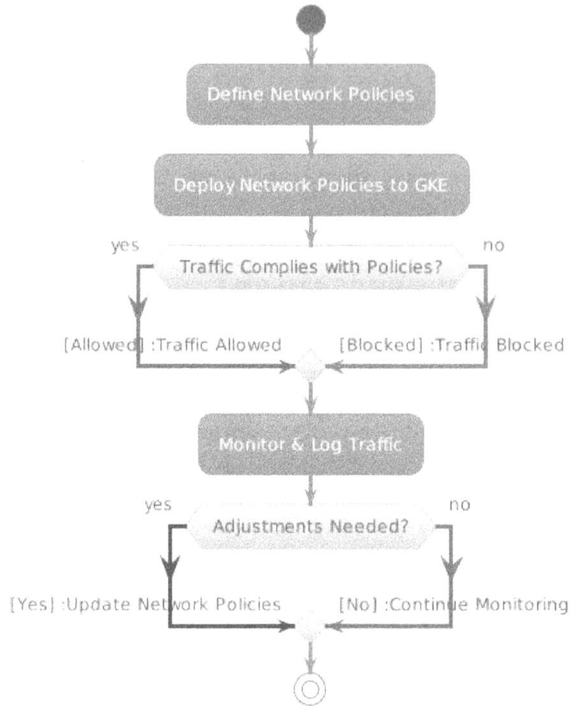

***Figure 8.7**: Network policy enforcement in GKE*

Implementing network security policies for traffic control

Creating and enforcing network policies involves defining the rules that specify allowed traffic flows between Pods within a GKE cluster.

Steps to implement network policies

To ensure secure and controlled communication within your GKE cluster, follow these essential steps for implementing network policies:

1. **Enable network policy logging**: Ensure that network policy logging is enabled in your GKE cluster to monitor and audit policy enforcement.
    a. Define network policies.
    b. Identify the services that need to communicate with each other.
2. Determine the minimal necessary traffic flows to allow for operational functionality.
3. **Create and apply network policies**: Use `kubectl` to create network policy objects based on your defined rules.

4. **Test and validate policies**: Verify that the policies work as expected by testing communication between Pods.

Example: Restricting traffic between frontend and backend

Suppose you have a frontend and a backend service, and you want to ensure that only the frontend can communicate with the backend.

Network policy definition:

```
apiVersion: networking.k8s.io/v1
kind: NetworkPolicy
metadata:
  name: backend-policy
  namespace: prod
spec:
  podSelector:
       matchLabels:
       app: backend
  Ingress:
  - from:
       - podSelector:
       matchLabels:
       app: frontend
       ports:
       - protocol: TCP
       port: 80
```

This policy allows TCP traffic on port 80 to the backend Pods from the frontend Pods only.

Common scenarios and solutions

Scenario 1: Isolate a sensitive application to prevent unauthorized access

A company has a sensitive application that processes personal data. It was exposed to unauthorized users due to improper access controls, resulting in a data leak.

Solution:

Create a network policy that denies all Ingress traffic to the application Pods except from authorized services.

Real-world example: In 2020, a breach occurred when an e-commerce platform exposed an internal financial application to unauthorized users. Attackers gained access and exfiltrated sensitive customer data. If a proper network policy had been in place, restricting access to only trusted services, this breach could have been prevented.

Scenario 2: Restrict internet access for certain Pods to mitigate data exfiltration risks

A company's internal database Pods accidentally sent sensitive customer information to external servers due to a misconfigured outbound connection. This incident was caused by lack of restrictions on internet access.

Solution:

Implement an egress policy that blocks all traffic to external IP addresses for specific Pods that do not require internet access.

Real-world example: In 2017, an organization's internal Kubernetes Pods, which housed confidential data, unintentionally sent data to an external server. The lack of an egress policy allowed this. By configuring egress restrictions to block traffic to unauthorized external IPs, this data exfiltration could have been avoided, keeping the sensitive data secure.

These examples highlight how improper configuration led to real-world security incidents, and how the right policies—like network and egress policies—could have prevented them from happening.

Tools and resources

To effectively manage network policies in Kubernetes, several tools and resources can help streamline policy creation, enforcement, and monitoring:

- **kubectl**: Primary command line tool for creating and managing network policies.
- **Calico**: A popular network policy engine that can be used with GKE for advanced policy management.
- **Terraform**: Infrastructure as code tool that can define and deploy network policies as part of your GKE cluster configuration.

Figure 8.8 shows allowed and blocked paths of communication between Pods in a namespace after applying network policies:

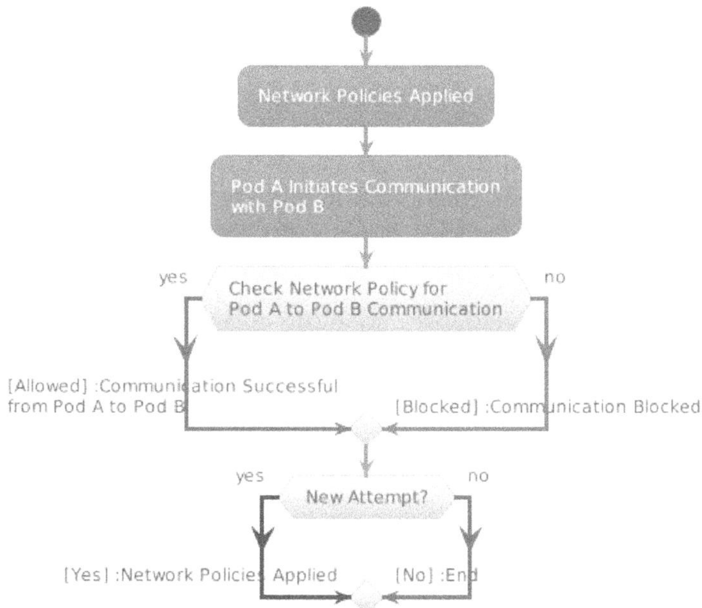

Figure 8.8: *Pod communication workflow*

Monitoring and auditing

Effective monitoring and auditing are key to maintaining the integrity and security of your network policies. Here are some tools and strategies to help track and ensure the proper enforcement of your policies:

- **Stackdriver**: Use Google Cloud's operations suite for logging and monitoring network policy enforcement.
- **Policy auditor**: Tools like Calico Enterprise provide visibility into network traffic and policy effectiveness, helping to audit compliance with security policies.

Continuous improvement

To ensure your system remains secure and compliant, it is important to regularly review and update your policies. As your applications evolve, so should your network policies to accommodate new communication patterns and services.

- **Review and update policies regularly**: As your applications evolve, so too should your network policies to accommodate new communication patterns and services.
- **Automate policy enforcement**: Integrate network policy definition and deployment into your CI/CD pipeline to ensure policies are consistently enforced across all environments.

Conclusion

In conclusion, this chapter has provided a comprehensive overview of security practices within GKE, highlighting their vital role in safeguarding containerized applications. By implementing cluster-wide security measures, configuring RBAC, adhering to compliance best practices, managing secrets and configurations effectively, securing applications, and implementing network security policies, organizations can fortify their GKE environments against threats and ensure compliance with industry standards.

Looking ahead, maintaining vigilance, adapting to evolving threats, and fostering a culture of security awareness will be crucial. By embracing a holistic approach and staying proactive in security measures, organizations can navigate the dynamic landscape of cloud-native environments with confidence, ensuring the integrity, confidentiality, and availability of their applications and data in GKE clusters.

Multiple choice questions

1. **Which aspect of GKE security involves the implementation of RBAC for fine-grained access management?**
    a. Managing Secrets and configurations
    b. Securing applications in GKE
    c. Implementing cluster-wide security measures
    d. Introduction to network policies in GKE
2. **What tool is introduced in the compliance best practices section for enforcing policies and ensuring GKE security controls align with regulatory standards?**
    a. Helm
    b. Kyverno
    c. Kustomize
    d. ArgoCD
3. **Which practice within GKE involves the secure management of sensitive information such as passwords, API tokens, and encryption keys?**
    a. Network security policies
    b. Securing applications in GKE
    c. Managing secrets and configurations
    d. Implementing GKE security controls for compliance

4. **What is a key benefit of implementing container security best practices in GKE?**
    a. Ensuring compliance with industry standards
    b. Simplifying deployment processes
    c. Reducing resource utilization
    d. Enhancing network performance
5. **Which tool introduced in the network security policies section allows organizations to define rules for controlling traffic between Pods in a GKE cluster?**
    a. Helm
    b. Kustomize
    c. ArgoCD
    d. Network Policies

Answer key

1.	c.
2.	b.
3.	c.
4.	a.
5.	d.

CHAPTER 9
Troubleshooting and Best Practices

Introduction

As you venture into the world of containerized applications, you will face complex issues that require good problem-solving skills and proactive optimization. This chapter explores GKE to help you handle challenges and improve your GKE clusters. We will guide you through common GKE problems with practical solutions and share valuable tips and tricks to boost the performance, reliability, and resilience of your GKE deployments. Whether you are new to GKE or an experienced Kubernetes user, this chapter is your guide to mastering GKE operations. It covers troubleshooting techniques and best practices for optimizing your GKE environment, helping you navigate the complexities of containerized environments effectively.

Structure

In this chapter, we will discuss the following topics:

- Troubleshooting common GKE issues
- GKE best practices and optimization tips
- Backup and disaster recovery strategies

Objectives

This chapter outlines the best practices and optimization tips to enhance the performance, reliability, and resilience of your GKE clusters. You will learn effective troubleshooting techniques for common GKE issues and understand best practices and optimization tips for GKE clusters. Furthermore, you will develop backup and disaster recovery strategies to ensure high availability.

Troubleshooting common GKE issues

Effective troubleshooting begins with a systematic approach to diagnosing issues at both the Pod and node levels. By recognizing common failure patterns and understanding the underlying causes, you can quickly restore stability to your GKE environment. Let us dive into the key challenges and their solutions to help you maintain a resilient and high-performing cluster.

Identifying and resolving Pod and node-level issues

Pod and node-related issues can impact application performance and cluster stability. Pods are the smallest deployable units, and nodes are the infrastructure running them. Understanding how to identify and resolve these issues is essential for ensuring smooth operation in GKE. This section provides methods, commands, and resolution steps for addressing common Pod and node-level problems.

Issue 1: Pod out of resources

Alert: `Container <container_name>` in `pod <pod_name>` crashed with `exit code <exit_code>` (insufficient memory / CPU): Pods running out of CPU or memory resources, causing performance degradation.

Generic steps:

1. Use `kubectl top pods` to check resource utilization for specific Pods.
2. Analyze Pod logs with `kubectl logs <pod-name>` for resource exhaustion errors.

Resolution:

- Modify the Pod's resource requests and limits in its definition.

```
apiVersion: v1
kind: Pod
metadata:
  name: web-server
spec:
```

```
    containers:
    - name: web-server
      image: nginx
      resources:
        requests:
          cpu: "500m"
          memory: "256Mi"
        limits:
          cpu: "1"
          memory: "512Mi"
```

- Define **Horizontal Pod Autoscaling** (**HPA**) to scale the number of replicas based on CPU usage.

```
apiVersion: autoscaling/v2
kind: HorizontalPodAutoscaler
metadata:
  name: web-server-hpa
spec:
  scaleTargetRef:
    apiVersion: apps/v1
    kind: Deployment
    name: web-server
  minReplicas: 1
  maxReplicas: 10
  metrics:
  - type: Resource
    resource:
      name: cpu
      target:
        type: Utilization
        averageUtilization: 80
```

- Consider **Vertical Pod Autoscaling** (**VPA**) to automatically adjust individual Pod resources based on demand.

```
apiVersion: autoscaling.k8s.io/v1
kind: VerticalPodAutoscaler
metadata:
  name: example-vpa
spec:
  targetRef:
apiVersion: "apps/v1"
```

```
kind: Deployment
name: example-deployment
  updatePolicy:
updateMode: "Auto"
```

Issue 2: Pod CrashLoopBackOff

Alert: `Pod <pod_name>` repeatedly crashing and restarting (`CrashLoopBackOff`): Pods repeatedly crash and restart, indicating application issues.

Generic steps:

1. Check Pod status with `kubectl get pods`.
2. Inspect Pod logs for error messages using `kubectl logs <pod-name>`.
3. Use describe command to inspect events using `kubectl describe pod <pod_name>`.
4. Access the Pod (if needed) `using kubectl exec -it <pod_name> -- /bin/bash`.

   This command can be used to get a shell inside the Pod for deeper debugging.

Resolution:

- Review Pod configuration and fix application errors identified in logs.
- Update dependencies with package managers like `apt-get` or `yum`.

  Remember that a `CrashLoopBackOff` can be due to various factors. Consider checking:

  - Resource constraints (CPU, memory)
  - Misconfigured readiness or liveness probes
  - Issues with external dependencies or services

Issue 3: Pod pending

Alert: `Pod <pod_name>` stuck in pending state, unable to start: Pods stuck in a pending state, unable to start.

Generic steps:

1. List pending Pods with `kubectl get pods --field-selector=status.phase=Pending`.

Resolution:

- Check for resource constraints with `kubectl describe pod <pod_name>`.
- Ensure proper node availability and networking.

The following figure shows the GKE Pod issue resolution workflow provides a step-by-step approach to systematically analyze and address common issues, ensuring the stability and performance of your cluster:

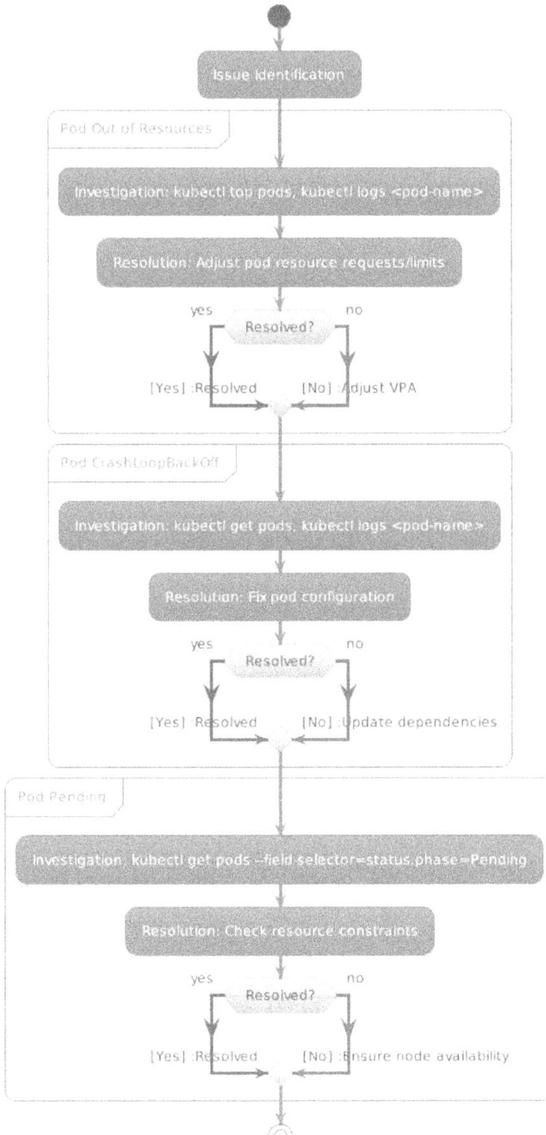

***Figure 9.1**: GKE Pod issue resolution workflow*

Issue 4: Node not ready

Alert: `Node <node_name>` is in not ready state due to `kubelet` issue. Please check `kubelet` logs on the node for more details.

Generic steps:

1. List nodes and their status with **kubectl get nodes**.
2. Monitor node logs for issues with **gcloud** compute instances **get-serial-port-output <node_name>**.

Resolution:

- Access the node using SSH and check **kubelet** logs with **journalctl -u kubelet**.
- Review system logs **dmesg** for potential hardware or software issues.
- Troubleshoot node connectivity and issues.
- Monitor system logs and events for node problems with these commands:
  - **gcloud logging read "resource.type=gce_instance and resource.labels.instance_id=<instance_id>"**
  - **kubectl get events --sort-by='.metadata.creationTimestamp'**

Issue 5: Pod ImagePullBackOff

Alert: **Pod <pod_name>** failed to pull **image <image_name>** from registry. Authentication error or image unavailability suspected.

Generic step:

1. Inspect Pod status with the following commands:

```
kubectl get pods
kubectl describe pod <pod_name>
```

Resolution:

- Check image availability and authentication within the registry.
- Correct image name and registry access details in the Pod definition.

Issue 6: Node taints and tolerations conflict

Alert: **Pod <pod_name>** unable to schedule on **node <node_name>** due to taint and toleration conflict.

Generic step:

1. List taints and tolerations on nodes with this command: **kubectl describe node <node-name> | grep Taints**

Resolution:

- Adjust Pod tolerations to match node taints or remove taints from nodes as needed.

```
apiVersion: v1
kind: Pod
metadata:
  name: mypod
spec:
  containers:
  - name: mycontainer
    image: myimage
  tolerations:
  - key: "key1"
    operator: "Equal"
    value: "value1"
    effect: "NoSchedule"
  - key: "key2"
    effect: "Exists"
    operator: "Exists"
```

This configuration allows **mypod** to be scheduled on nodes with taints that either have **key1=value1:NoSchedule** or **key2** with any value and effect.

- Ensure compatibility between Pod requirements and node configurations.

```
apiVersion: v1
kind: Pod
metadata:
  name: mypod
spec:
  containers:
  - name: mycontainer
      image: myimage
  nodeSelector:
      disktype: ssd
```

This configuration ensures that **mypod** will only be scheduled on nodes labeled with **disktype: ssd**.

Issue 7: Persistent Volume access issues

Alert: **Pod <pod_name>** unable to mount **persistent volume <pv_name>**. Access mode mismatch or storage class issue suspected.

Generic step:

1. Check PV and PVC status with **kubectl get pv** and **kubectl get pvc**.

Resolution:

- Review PV and PVC configurations.
- Verify storage class and access modes.

The following figure shows the GKE Node issue resolution workflow provides a step-by-step approach to systematically analyze common issues related to the nodes in a cluster:

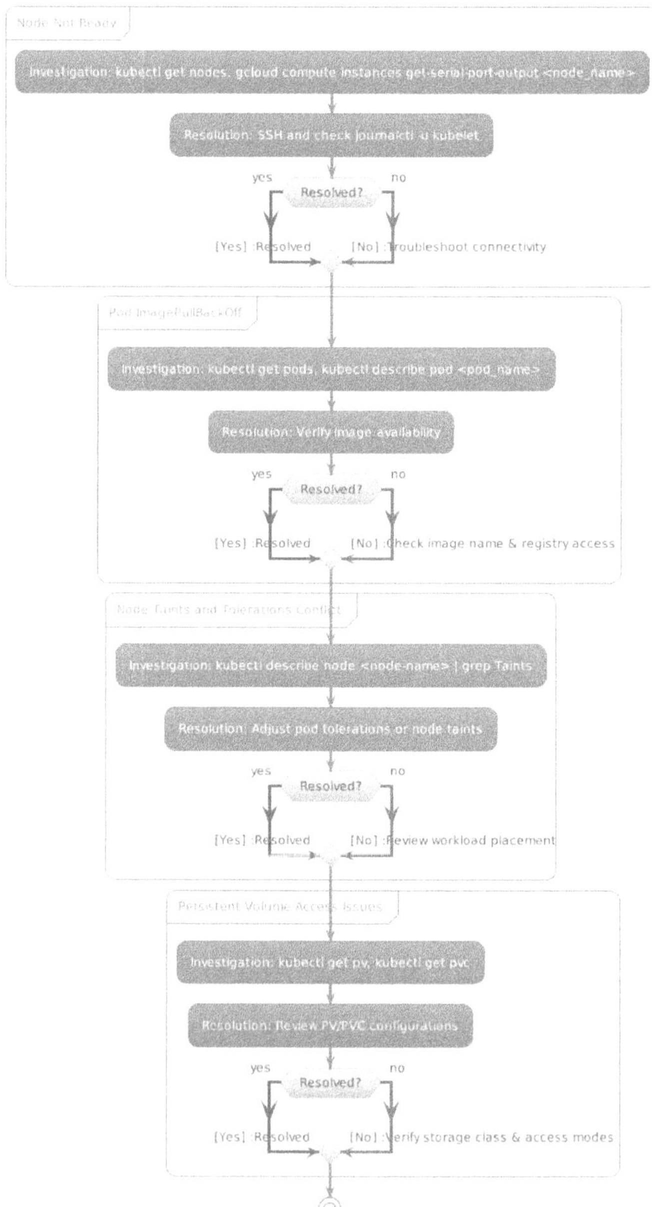

Figure 9.2: GKE node issue resolution workflow

Debugging networking problems in GKE

Navigating the intricate networking landscape of GKE is essential for ensuring seamless communication between Pods and external resources. In this section, we delve into the world of troubleshooting networking problems in GKE. Networking issues can be challenging, impacting the availability and performance of your applications. Understanding how to identify and resolve these problems is crucial for maintaining a robust and reliable GKE environment.

We will explore few common challenges related to networking and provide practical solutions to keep our GKE workloads communicating effectively. By mastering the art of troubleshooting networking issues, you will be well-equipped to ensure uninterrupted connectivity for your applications and provide an exceptional user experience.

Issue 1: Pod cannot access external resources

Alert: Pods in `cluster <cluster_name>` are unable to reach the external resources on the internet. Egress traffic might be blocked.

Generic steps:

1. Run `kubectl run -it --rm test-pod --image=busybox -- sh ping google.com` or `kubectl run -it --rm test-pod --image=busybox -- sh -c 'ping google.com'` in your cluster to test connectivity.
2. Verify node egress configurations with `gcloud compute firewall-rules list`.
3. Check firewall rules for outbound traffic restrictions with `gcloud compute firewall-rules describe <rule_name>`.

Resolution:

- Ensure that your GKE nodes have proper egress configurations to allow outbound traffic. `gcloud compute instances list`.
- Review firewall rules to make sure they allow outbound traffic from your Pods: `gcloud compute firewall-rules update [RULE_NAME] --allow tcp:80,tcp:443`.

Issue 2: Pod-to-Pod communication failures

Alert: Pods in `namespace <namespace_name>` unable to communicate with each other. Network policies or firewall rules might be blocking communication.

Generic steps:

1. Deploy two Pods in the same namespace and attempt to establish a connection between them with this command: **`kubectl exec -it pod-1 -- /bin/sh wget -O - http://pod-2`**
2. Review Kubernetes network policies with **`kubectl get networkpolicies -n <namespace_name>`**.
3. Examine firewall rules with **`gcloud compute firewall-rules list`**.

Resolution:

- Verify that Kubernetes network policies or firewall rules are not blocking communication between Pods with this command: **`kubectl describe networkpolicies -n [NAMESPACE_NAME]`**
- Ensure that the Pods have proper labels and selectors to enable communication with this command: **`kubectl label pods [POD_NAME] key=value`**

Issue 3: Ingress controller not routing traffic

Alert: Traffic not reaching **`service <service_name>`** through **`Ingress <Ingress_name>`**. Configuration or backend service issue suspected.

Generic steps:

1. Inspect Ingress: **`kubectl get Ingress`** and **`kubectl describe Ingress <Ingress_name>`**
2. Check service endpoints: **`kubectl get svc`**

Resolution:

- Check the Ingress configuration and service selectors, and make sure DNS resolves to the correct IP address.
- Review the backend services associated with the Ingress and their readiness.

The following figure shows the GKE network issue resolution workflow provides a step-by-step approach to systematically analyze common issues related to the Pods in the cluster and associated network related services:

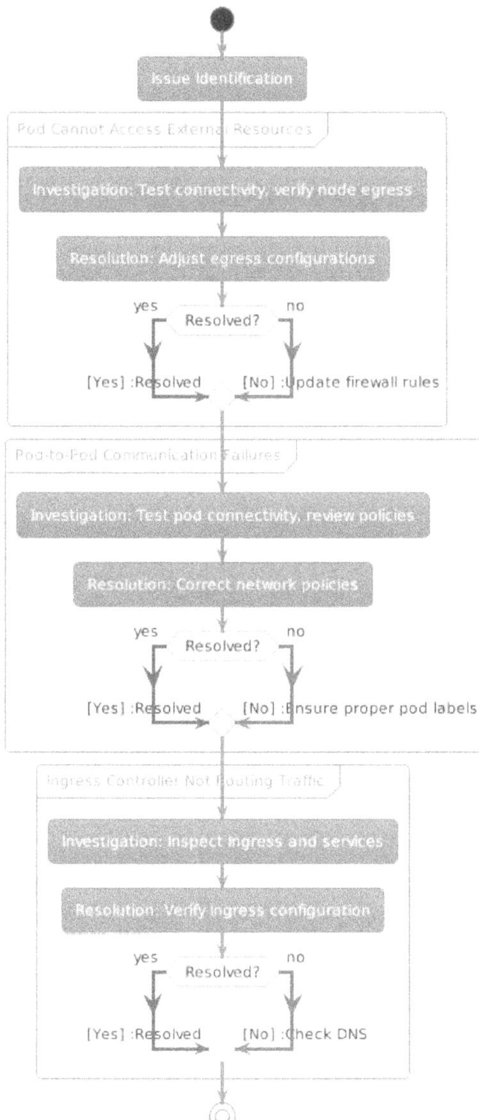

***Figure 9.3**: GKE network issue resolution workflow*

Issue 4: DNS resolution problems

Alert: Pods in **`cluster <cluster_name>`** experiencing DNS resolution failures. DNS configuration issue suspected.

Generic steps:

1. Create a Pod and check DNS resolution with this command: **`kubectl run -it --rm test-pod --image=busybox --restart=Never -- sh -c 'nslookup google.com'`**

2. Verify CoreDNS or custom DNS setup with this command: **`kubectl get pods -n kube-system`**

Resolution:

- Ensure CoreDNS or custom DNS configuration functions correctly: **`kubectl get pods -n kube-system | grep coredns`**
- Check DNS policies (if used) for proper name resolution: **`kubectl describe pod [POD_NAME] -n [NAMESPACE]`**

Issue 5: Service load balancing not working

Alert: Traffic not evenly distributed among Pods in **`service <service_name>`**. Load balancing issue suspected.

Generic steps:

1. Examine service endpoints and network policy settings: **`kubectl get svc`** and **`kubectl describe svc <service_name>`**

Resolution:

- Verify service selectors, endpoint readiness, and Pod availability.
- Consider adjusting the load balancing algorithm, such as session affinity, if **applicable.**

```
apiVersion: v1
kind: Service
metadata:
  name: [SERVICE_NAME]
spec:
  sessionAffinity: ClientIP
```

Issue 6: Ingress SSL/TLS certificate errors

Alert: SSL/TLS certificates in **`Ingress <Ingress_name>`** causing issues. Certificate or private key issue suspected.

Generic steps:

1. Inspect Ingress resource and certificate configuration:

```
kubectl get Ingress
kubectl describe Ingress <Ingress_name>
```

2. Verify certificate existence and access permissions with:

```
gcloud secrets list
gcloud secrets describe <secret_name>
```

Resolution:

- Ensure certificates are referenced correctly, and private keys are accessible.

```
apiVersion: networking.k8s.io/v1
kind: Ingress
metadata:
  name: [Ingress_NAME]
spec:
  tls:
  - hosts:
    - [HOSTNAME]
    secretName: [TLS_SECRET_NAME]
```

- Verify that the certificate files and paths are correctly configured in the Ingress resource.

```
kubectl describe Ingress [Ingress_NAME]
```

Issue 7: Unauthorized access to Services

Alert: Unauthorized access detected to **`service <service_name>`**. RBAC misconfiguration suspected.

Generic step: Audit Kubernetes RBAC settings:

```
kubectl get clusterrolebindings
kubectl describe clusterrolebinding <cluster-role-binding-name>
```

Resolution:

- Review and adjust RBAC policies to restrict unauthorized access.

```
kubectl get roles,clusterroles --all-namespaces
kubectl edit clusterrole [CLUSTER_ROLE_NAME]
```

- Regularly audit and update RBAC roles and bindings for security compliance.

```
kubectl get rolebindings,clusterrolebindings --all-namespaces
```

The following figure is some further GKE service-related resolution workflow providing a step-by-step approach to systematically analyze common issues related to the services in the cluster:

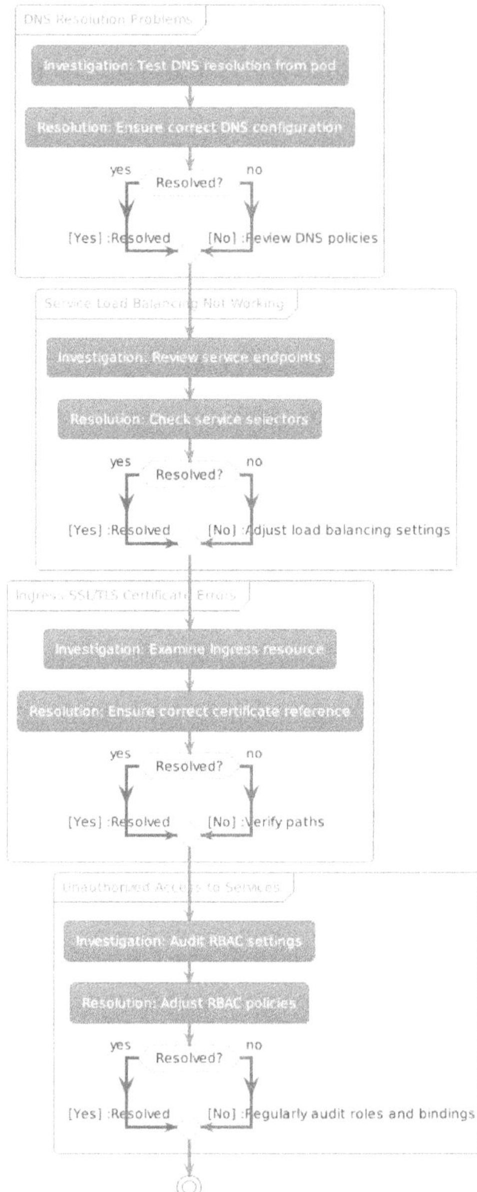

***Figure 9.4**: GKE services related resolution workflow*

Analyzing resource utilization for performance bottlenecks

In the dynamic world of GKE, optimizing resource utilization is essential to ensure the peak performance of your containerized workloads. However, identifying and addressing performance bottlenecks can be a complex task. In this section, we embark on a journey to analyze resource utilization within GKE clusters, shedding light on key aspects that impact performance.

Analyzing resource utilization for performance bottlenecks equips you with the knowledge and techniques needed to identify and mitigate performance bottlenecks effectively. By mastering the art of resource analysis, you will be better prepared to optimize your GKE workloads, ensuring optimal performance and resource efficiency.

Issue 1: CPU and memory resource starvation

Alert: Pods in **`namespace <namespace_name>`** experiencing CPU resource exhaustion. Performance degradation likely.

Generic steps:

1. Monitor Pod CPU utilization with this command: **`kubectl top pods`**
2. Check Pod resource requests and limits with this command: **`kubectl describe pod <pod_name>`**
3. Analyse node CPU metrics with this command: **`kubectl top nodes`**

Resolution:

- Adjust Pod CPU requests and limits based on application requirements.

```
apiVersion: v1
kind: Pod
metadata:
  name: example-pod
spec:
  containers:
  - name: example-container
      image: example-image
      resources:
      requests:
      cpu: "250m"
      memory: "256Mi"
      limits:
      cpu: "500m"
memory: "512Mi"
```

- Consider HPA to dynamically allocate more CPU resources as needed (command or YAML already provided above in the *Issue 1* of section *Identifying and resolving Pod and node-level issues*).

- Implement VPA to automatically adjust memory resources as needed (command or YAML already provided above in the *Issue 1* of section *Identifying and resolving Pod and node-level issues*).
- Investigate potential bottlenecks or inefficient CPU usage and memory leaks or inefficient memory usage within applications.

Issue 2: Disk I/O bottlenecks

Alert: High disk I/O latency detected for Pods in `namespace <namespace_name>`. Application performance may be impacted.

Generic steps:

1. Utilize monitoring tools like Prometheus with Grafana, or Kubernetes metrics-server, to analyze Pod disk I/O metrics.
2. Check storage class and provisioner configurations for Pods using these commands: `kubectl get sc` or `kubectl describe sc <storage_class_name>`.
3. Monitor node-level disk I/O metrics using external monitoring tools or cloud provider-specific metrics dashboards.

Resolution:

- Optimize application disk I/O patterns to reduce unnecessary read/write operations.
- Consider faster storage options like SSDs for critical workloads with high I/O needs.

```
apiVersion: storage.k8s.io/v1
kind: StorageClass
metadata:
  name: fast-storage
provisioner: kubernetes.io/gce-pd
parameters:
  type: pd-ssd
```

- Review and adjust storage class configurations for optimal performance.

```
apiVersion: v1
kind: PersistentVolumeClaim
metadata:
  name: example-pvc
spec:
  accessModes:
  - ReadWriteOnce
```

```
resources:
    requests:
    storage: 10Gi
storageClassName: fast-storage
```

Issue 3: High Pod restart rate

Alert: Excessive Pod restarts observed in **`deployment <deployment_name>`**. Investigate for potential stability issues.

Generic steps:

1. Check Pod restart counts and events with this command:

   ```
   Kubectl get pods --field-selector=status.phase=Running -o custom-columns=NAME:.metadata.name,RESTARTS:.status.containerStatuses[0].restartCount
   ```

2. Analyze Pod logs for error messages or crash signals with this command: **`kubectl logs <pod_name>`**
3. Review resource requests and limits for the Pods.

Resolution:

- Investigate root causes of Pod crashes in logs and events.
- Adjust resource requests and limits to provide more stability to Pods.
- Consider implementing liveness and readiness probes for healthy Pod restarts.

```
apiVersion: v1
kind: Pod
metadata:
  name: liveness-readiness-pod
spec:
  containers:
  - name: mycontainer
    image: example-image
    livenessProbe:
      httpGet:
        path: /healthz
        port: 8080
      initialDelaySeconds: 3
      periodSeconds: 3
    readinessProbe:
      httpGet:
        path: /ready
```

```
      port: 8080
    initialDelaySeconds: 3
    periodSeconds: 3
```

The following figure shows the step-by-step workflow, which helps in analyzing and resolving resource utilization issues in GKE, focusing on common bottlenecks within the cluster:

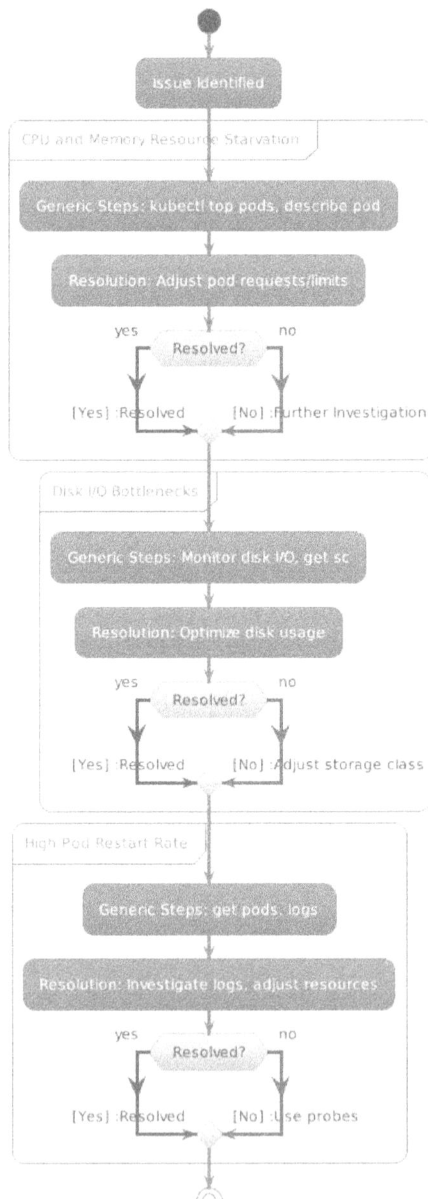

***Figure 9.5:** GKE resource troubleshooting workflow*

Issue 4: Node overloading

Alert: **Node <node_name>** exceeding CPU/memory/disk utilization thresholds. High risk of Pod evictions and performance degradation.

Generic steps:

1. Monitor node resource utilization with **kubectl top nodes**.
2. Analyze Pod distribution across nodes with **kubectl get pods -o wide**.
3. Check for CPU/Memory/Disk pressure events with **kubectl describe node <node_name> | grep "Pressure"**.

Resolution:

Implement node auto-scaler to automatically add nodes when utilization is high with: **gcloud container clusters update example-cluster --enable-autoscaling --min-nodes 1 --max-nodes 10 --node-pool default-pool**

- Adjust Pod scheduling with affinity/anti-affinity rules for balanced distribution.

```
apiVersion: apps/v1
kind: Deployment
metadata:
  name: example-deployment
spec:
  selector:
    matchLabels:
      app: example
  template:
    metadata:
      labels:
        app: example
    spec:
      containers:
      - name: example-container
        image: example-image
      affinity:
        podAntiAffinity:
          preferredDuringSchedulingIgnoredDuringExecution:
          - weight: 100
            podAffinityTerm:
              labelSelector:
                matchExpressions:
                - key: app
                  operator: In
```

```
                values:
                - example
            topologyKey: kubernetes.io/hostname
```

It defines a K8s Deployment named **example-deployment** with a single container running an **example-image**. Additionally, it specifies a Pod anti-affinity rule that prefers not to schedule Pods with the same label **app: example** on the same node, enhancing availability and resilience by spreading workload across nodes.

- Investigate and address bottlenecks causing high resource consumption on overloaded nodes.

Issue 5: Inefficient queries or processing

Alert: Pods in **deployment <deployment_name>** experiencing high CPU/Memory usage. Potential application inefficiency detected.

Generic steps:

1. Analyze Pod logs for errors or excessive resource consumption with **kubectl logs <pod_name> -c <container_name>**.
2. Profile application queries and resource utilization with tools like Jaeger or Prometheus.
3. Review database queries and implement optimization strategies like caching or indexing.

Resolution:

- Optimize application code and database queries for resource efficiency.
- Analyze and address any identified inefficiencies causing excessive resource consumption.
- Consider container resource limits to prevent runaway processes.

```
apiVersion: v1
kind: Pod
metadata:
  name: example-pod
spec:
  containers:
  - name: example-container
    image: example-image
    resources:
      limits:
        cpu: "1"
        memory: "1Gi"
```

Issue 6: Excessive Pod replicas

Alert: `Deployment <deployment_name>` running excessive replicas (>X) exceeding available resources.

Generic steps:

1. Check desired and current replica count for the deployment with this command: `kubectl get deployment <deployment_name> -o=jsonpath='{.spec.replicas} {.status.replicas}'`
2. Analyze resource utilization across Pods and nodes with this command: `kubectl top pods", "kubectl top nodes"`

Resolution:

Adjust desired replica count for the deployment based on actual resource needs with this command: `kubectl scale deployment example-deployment --replicas=3`

- Implement HPA to dynamically adjust replicas based on resource utilization (command or YAML already provided above).
- Consider `ResourceQuota` to limit the number of Pods per namespace or project.

```
apiVersion: v1
kind: ResourceQuota
metadata:
  name: example-quota
  namespace: example-namespace
spec:
  hard:
       pods: "10"
       requests.cpu: "4"
       requests.memory: 5Gi
       limits.cpu: "8"
       limits.memory: 10Gi
```

This `ResourceQuota` limits the namespace `example-namespace` to a maximum of 10 Pods, with specific CPU and memory request and limit thresholds.

Issue 7: Unoptimized workload distribution

Alert: Cluster experiencing imbalanced Pod distribution across nodes. Resource constraints or performance issues possible.

Generic steps:

1. Review Pod distribution across nodes with `kubectl get pods -o wide`.

2. Analyze node resource utilization with **kubectl top nodes**.
3. Check Pod affinity/anti-affinity rules for Pod placement with **kubectl get pod <pod_name> -o jsonpath='{.spec.affinity}'**.

Resolution:

- Implement Pod scheduling rules with affinity/anti-affinity for targeted placement.
- Consider Pod disruption budgets to limit disruptions during rebalancing processes.

```
apiVersion: policy/v1
kind: PodDisruptionBudget
metadata:
  name: example-pdb
spec:
  minAvailable: 2
  selector:
       matchLabels:
         app: example-app
```

This PDB ensures that at least two instances of Pods with the label app: **example-app** are always available during voluntary disruptions.

Use tools like Cluster Autoscaler to automatically balance workloads across nodes. When we create a new GKE cluster or a node pool, we can enable the Cluster Autoscaler as follows: **gcloud container clusters create [CLUSTER_NAME] --zone [COMPUTE_ZONE] --num-nodes [MIN_NODES] --enable-autoscaling --min-nodes [MIN_NODES] --max-nodes [MAX_NODES] --node-labels=[KEY]=[VALUE]**

For an existing cluster, you can update the node pool to enable autoscaling with this command: **gcloud container clusters update [CLUSTER_NAME] --zone [COMPUTE_ZONE] --enable-autoscaling --min-nodes [MIN_NODES] --max-nodes [MAX_NODES] --node-pool [NODE_POOL_NAME]**

Here is a step-by-step workflow for resolving GKE performance-related issues, designed to help analyze and address common bottlenecks in the cluster:

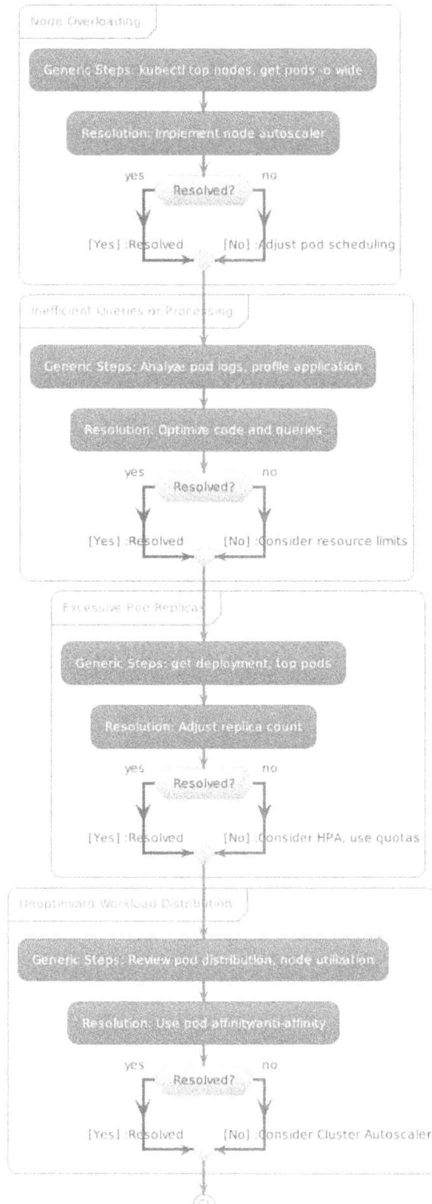

***Figure 9.6**: GKE performance troubleshooting workflow*

GKE best practices and optimization tips

To ensure the best performance, efficiency, and scalability of your workloads in GKE, adopting the best practices and optimization strategies is key. This section explores essential guidelines for enhancing your GKE environment and improving resource management.

Implementing best practices for resource management

Implementing best practices for resource management in GKE is crucial for optimizing the performance, efficiency, and cost-effectiveness of your containerized workloads. In this section of the chapter, we will delve into the essential strategies and guidelines for allocating, managing, and compute resources effectively within your GKE clusters. Whether it is CPU, memory, or storage, understanding how to define and control these resources according to your application's requirements is fundamental to achieving a well-balanced and highly available environment. By following these best practices, you will not only ensure optimal resource utilization but also enhance the reliability and scalability of your GKE workloads, ultimately leading to a smoother and more cost-efficient Kubernetes experience.

Resource requests and limits

Define appropriate requests and limits for each Pod in the resources field of your Pod YAMLs. This helps Kubernetes understand Pod resource needs and allocate resources efficiently (command or YAML already provided above in the *Issue 1* of section *Identifying and resolving Pod and node-level issues*).

Horizontal Pod Autoscaling

Implement HPA for dynamic scaling based on resource utilization. Define resource-based thresholds for autoscaling (e.g., CPU usage) using the **`kubectl autoscale`** command (command or YAML provided in *Identifying and resolving Pod and node-level issues*).

Vertical Pod Autoscaling

Use VPA for fine-grained resource adjustments within Pods. VPA automatically adjusts CPU and memory requests based on observed needs (command or YAML provided in *Identifying and resolving Pod and node-level issues*).

Evaluate if your workload characteristics necessitate VPA. Consider the trade-offs of using both HPA and VPA simultaneously, as they serve different purposes.

Node management

Enable node auto-repair to replace unhealthy nodes automatically. Set up a node pool with auto-repair enabled using the **`gcloud container`** command: **`gcloud container clusters update [CLUSTER_NAME] --enable-autorepair --zone [ZONE]`**

Enable node auto-upgrade for automatic node software updates. Use node pool settings to enable auto-upgrade with this command: **`gcloud container clusters update [CLUSTER_NAME] --enable-autoupgrade --zone [ZONE]`**

Network policies and security

Implement network policies to control Pod communication. Define policies based on namespaces, labels, and Pods for granular control:

```
apiVersion: networking.k8s.io/v1
kind: NetworkPolicy
metadata:
  name: example-network-policy
spec:
  podSelector:
    matchLabels:
      role: db
  policyTypes:
  - Ingress
  - Egress
  Ingress:
  - from:
    - ipBlock:
        cidr: 172.17.0.0/16
        except:
        - 172.17.1.0/24
    ports:
    - protocol: TCP
      port: 6379
```

Use PSPs to enforce security standards. Define PSPs and bind them to service accounts or namespaces for enhanced security:

```
apiVersion: policy/v1beta1
kind: PodSecurityPolicy
metadata:
  name: example-psp
spec:
  privileged: false
  seLinux:
    rule: RunAsAny
  supplementalGroups:
    rule: RunAsAny
  runAsUser:
    rule: RunAsAny
  fsGroup:
    rule: RunAsAny
  volumes:
  - '*'
```

Consider a private cluster for improved security. Restrict external access and configure authorized networks and routes.

Pod distribution and scaling

Use **PodTopologySpread** to ensure even Pod distribution across nodes. Set **topologySpreadConstraints** to control Pod placement:

```
apiVersion: v1
kind: Pod
metadata:
  name: mypod
spec:
  containers:
  - name: mycontainer
      image: myimage
  topologySpreadConstraints:
  - maxSkew: 1
      topologyKey: kubernetes.io/hostname
      whenUnsatisfiable: ScheduleAnyway
      labelSelector:
      matchLabels:
      app: myapp
```

Enable Cluster Autoscaler to automatically adjust node count based on resource utilization. Use node pool auto-upgrade settings for effective scaling (command or YAML provided in node management).

Advanced strategies

Now let us look at a few advanced strategies:

- Explore multi-cluster Ingress for global load balancing. Deploy an Ingress resource across multiple clusters and configure a global DNS entry.
- Consider GKE autopilot for fully managed, serverless clusters. Simplify resource management and scaling with autopilot clusters and node pools.
- Implement cluster shared VPC for resource sharing across projects. Configure network peering and routing for enhanced resource utilization.
- Use workload identity for secure authentication with Google services. Link service accounts to GKE workloads for secure access.
- Set resource quotas to limit resource consumption per namespace. Define quotas for various resources like Pods, CPU, and memory.

Monitoring and disaster recovery

Implement regular monitoring with tools like Prometheus, Grafana, or Stackdriver. Set up alerts for resource utilization thresholds and create custom dashboards for visualization.

Have a backup and disaster recovery plan in place. Utilize GKE features like PV snapshots for data persistence and create and test disaster recovery plans.

Further exploration

Explore additional best practices in the GKE documentation, including:

- **Pod Security Policies (PSPs)**
- Node pools for isolation
- Node version management
- **Persistent Volume (PV)** scalers
- Secrets management
- ConfigMap management
- Health checks and Readiness Probes
- StatefulSets
- Pod anti-affinity rules
- **CustomResourceDefinitions (CRDs)**
- **PodDisruptionBudgets (PDBs)**
- Node labels and annotations
- Pod priority and preemption
- Use of Helm charts
- Pod-node affinity rules
- Service mesh integration
- Resource quotas for Pods
- Node taints and tolerations
- Advanced logging and monitoring

By following these best practices and exploring advanced strategies, you can ensure your GKE clusters are efficient, cost-effective, and meet your application's demands effectively.

Optimizing workload deployments in GKE

Efficiently deploying and managing workloads in GKE is essential to ensure cost-effectiveness and performance. This section of the chapter focuses on optimizing workload deployments, exploring best practices and strategies to enhance the deployment process in GKE.

Optimizing workload deployments in GKE equips you with the knowledge and techniques needed to streamline the deployment of containerized applications. By mastering the art of workload optimization, you will be able to deploy applications more efficiently, reduce costs, and ensure optimal performance.

Methodologies and best practices

This section delves into various methods and best practices for streamlining workload deployments within GKE. Each strategy is presented with detailed explanations, actionable steps, and examples to empower you with efficient and effective deployment practices.

Managing deployments effectively

To ensure smooth scaling and minimal downtime, it is essential to manage deployments efficiently. By utilizing Kubernetes deployment controllers, you can gain better control over application updates, scaling, and availability. Here's how to optimize your deployment strategy:

- **Leverage deployment controllers**: Migrate from Pods to Deployments for superior manageability and scaling. Define desired replica counts and rolling updates within your deployment YAML for controlled scaling and minimal service disruption.

```
apiVersion: apps/v1
kind: Deployment
metadata:
  name: nginx-deployment
spec:
  replicas: 3
  selector:
      matchLabels:
      app: nginx
  template:
      metadata:
      labels:
      app: nginx
      spec:
      containers:
      - name: nginx
      image: nginx:1.14.2
      ports:
      - containerPort: 80
```

- **Seamless rolling updates**: Implement rolling updates to minimize downtime during deployments. Utilize `kubectl set image` or update the Deployment YAML to seamlessly transition between versions.
- **Blue-green deployments**: Blue-green deployments set up two parallel environments—one live (blue) and one for staging updates (green)—so you can smoothly switch traffic using Ingress or Service routing, minimizing downtime and enabling quick rollback if issues occur; meanwhile, for rolling updates, monitor progress with `kubectl rollout status deployment/<deployment_name>` and revert changes with `kubectl rollout undo deployment/<deployment_name>` if necessary.

  Additionally, during rolling updates, you can monitor progress with `kubectl rollout status deployment/<deployment_name>`, ensuring a smooth, controlled transition between versions.
- **Canary deployments**: Incrementally roll out new versions to a subset of users using Istio or traffic splitting with a Service Mesh. This allows for gradual validation and reduces risk exposure.

Controlling Pod placement and prioritization

Effective Pod placement ensures optimal resource usage and application performance. By using affinity rules and node selectors, you can control where Pods are scheduled based on specific requirements:

- **Pod affinity and anti-affinity rules**: Control Pod placement using node affinity rules with labels and topology constraints. This ensures co-location or separation of specific Pods based on your application needs (command or YAML provided in analyzing and addressing performance bottlenecks).
- **Node selector**: Specify nodes for Pod placement using labels within the Pod YAML. This ensures Pods land on desired nodes based on available resources or specific node characteristics.

```
apiVersion: v1
kind: Pod
metadata:
  name: mypod
spec:
  containers:
  - name: mycontainer
      image: nginx
  nodeSelector:
      disktype: ssd
```

This YAML is used to create a Pod that will only be scheduled on nodes with the label **disktype: ssd**. It ensures that the Pod is placed on a node with SSD storage for performance reasons.

- **Pod priority and preemption**: Prioritize critical Pods and preempt lower priority Pods if necessary, by setting the **priorityClassName** in the Pod YAML. This guarantees resource allocation for essential services.

```
apiVersion: v1
kind: Pod
metadata:
  name: high-priority-pod
spec:
  containers:
  - name: high-priority-container
      image: nginx
  priorityClassName: high-priority
```

This configuration sets a priority class for a Pod, allowing it to have higher scheduling priority over lower-priority Pods. This can lead to preemption, where lower-priority Pods are evicted to make room for higher-priority Pods if resources are scarce.

Configuration management and security

Proper configuration management is crucial for maintaining security and flexibility in your applications. Here is how to securely manage and use configuration data and secrets in your GKE environment:

- **Utilize** ConfigMaps **and secrets**: Store configuration data and secrets separately from application code. Mount them as volumes or environment variables in Pods for secure and manageable configuration.

```
apiVersion: v1
kind: ConfigMap
metadata:
  name: example-configmap
data:
  # Property-like keys; each key maps to a simple value
  database_url: jdbc:mysql://mydatabase.example.com:3306/mydatabase
  database_user: user_example

  # File-like keys
  config.json: |
      {
      "key": "value",
```

```
        "jsonKey": {
              "subKey": "subValue"
        }
        }
```

This **ConfigMap** named **example-configmap** contains three entries: two simple key-value pairs (**database_url** and **database_user**) and one multi-line string that represents a JSON configuration (**config.json**). Applications can reference this **ConfigMap** to configure themselves without hardcoding configuration data.

```
apiVersion: v1
kind: Secret
metadata:
  name: example-secret
  annotations:
      # Annotation to indicate the secret management tool or policy, if any.
      kubernetes.io/description: "Sensitive database credentials"
type: Opaque
data:
  # Secrets should be base64 encoded.
  # These values should be generated securely and stored securely before being applied.
  # Use external secret management tools when possible.
  password: cGFzc3dvcmRTZWNyZXQ= # Example: echo -n 'passwordSecret' | base64
  token: dG9rZW5TZWNyZXQ=       # Example: echo -n 'tokenSecret' | base64
```

This secret YAML script defines a Kubernetes secret named **example-secret** intended to securely store sensitive information, specifically a **password** and a **token**. Both values are base64 encoded to conform to the data format expected by Kubernetes secrets. The **annotations** field includes a description to provide context about the secret, indicating it contains sensitive database credentials.

- **Enforce security with PSP**: Define and enforce security policies for Pod creation using PSPs. Bind them to service accounts for granular security control.

  Check Pod security context:

  ```
  kubectl get pod <pod-name> -o jsonpath='{.spec.containers[*].securityContext}'.
  ```

  Implement **PodSecurityPolicies** for cluster-wide security enforcement:

  ```
  apiVersion: policy/v1beta1
  kind: PodSecurityPolicy
  ```

```
metadata:
  name: restricted
spec:
  privileged: false
  runAsUser:
      rule: MustRunAsNonRoot
```

- **Implement health checks**: Ensure Pod health with readiness and liveness probes. Define **readinessProbe** and **livenessProbe** in your Pod YAML for reliable service availability (command or YAML provided in analyzing and addressing performance bottlenecks).
- **Container image scanning**: Integrate container image scanning tools like Trivy into your CI/CD pipeline to identify and address vulnerabilities in your container images.

Advanced optimizations and workflow management

For enhanced resource management and efficient scaling, advanced tools and optimizations are key. Here is how to leverage event-driven autoscaling for better resource utilization in your GKE environment:

- **Resource efficiency tools**: Utilize tools like **Kubernetes Event-Driven Autoscaling (KEDA)** for event-driven autoscaling that dynamically adjusts resource allocation based on workload events, optimizing resource utilization. First, ensure KEDA is installed in your GKE cluster. You can install KEDA using Helm:

  ```
  helm repo add kedacore https://kedacore.github.io/charts
  helm repo update
  helm install keda kedacore/keda --namespace keda --create-namespace
  ```

  Here is an example of a KEDA **ScaledObject** YAML that autoscales a deployment based on the length of a Google Cloud Pub/Sub subscription:

  ```
  apiVersion: keda.sh/v1alpha1
  kind: ScaledObject
  metadata:
    name: pubsub-scaledobject
    namespace: default
  spec:
    scaleTargetRef:
        name: your-deployment-name
    pollingInterval: 30  # Optional. Default: 30 seconds
    cooldownPeriod:  300 # Optional. Default: 300 seconds
    minReplicaCount: 0   # Optional. Default: 0
    maxReplicaCount: 100 # Optional. Default: 100
  ```

```
  triggers:
  - type: gcp-pubsub
      metadata:
      subscriptionSize: "5"
      subscriptionName: "your-subscription-name"
      credentialsFromEnv: GOOGLE_APPLICATION_CREDENTIALS_JSON
```

- **Ensure balanced Pod distribution**: Employ node labels and affinities to achieve an even distribution of Pods across nodes, balancing resource usage and improving cluster performance.

  First, label your nodes based on any criteria important for your application's distribution, such as zone, instance type, or any custom label: **`kubectl label nodes <node-name> zone=us-central1-a`**

  Here is an example of a deployment that uses Pod affinity to ensure that Pods are scheduled on nodes in a specific zone:

```
apiVersion: apps/v1
kind: Deployment
metadata:
  name: balanced-deployment
spec:
  replicas: 3
  selector:
      matchLabels:
      app: balanced-app
  template:
      metadata:
      labels:
      app: balanced-app
      spec:
      containers:
      - name: nginx
      image: nginx
      affinity:
      nodeAffinity:
      requiredDuringSchedulingIgnoredDuringExecution:
            nodeSelectorTerms:
            - matchExpressions:
            - key: zone
            operator: In
            values:
            - us-central1-a
```

- **Monitoring with tools like Prometheus and Grafana**: Create custom dashboards and alerting rules for proactive performance monitoring and issue identification.
- **Fine-tuning resource requests and limits**: Regularly review and adjust resource requests and limits based on observed metrics and performance data to optimize resource allocation and prevent under- or over-provisioning (command or YAML provided in *Identifying and resolving Pod and node-level issues*).

Package and deploy with Helm

Helm simplifies the packaging and deployment of applications in Kubernetes, streamlining management and scaling. Here is how to use Helm for efficient application packaging, deployment, and release management in your GKE cluster:

- **Leverage Helm for packaging**: Structure your applications into reusable Helm charts with modular components and clear configuration management through value files.
- **Install and initialize Helm**: Install Helm locally or integrate it into your CI/CD pipeline. Initialize Helm in your GKE cluster using **`helm init`**.
- **Package and deploy applications**: Package your Helm charts and deploy them to your cluster using **`helm install`**. Manage releases and configurations through Helm commands.
- **Manage releases**: Upgrade, rollback, or delete Helm releases as needed for efficient version control and rollback capabilities.

For detailed information on Helm, refer to the section Helm charts for GKE applications in *Chapter 5, Deploying Applications on GKE*.

Implementing GitOps for automated deployments:

GitOps enables automated, declarative deployment workflows using Git as the source of truth. By integrating tools like Argo CD or Flux CD, you can simplify and automate the deployment process. Here is how to implement GitOps in your GKE cluster:

- **Choose between Argo CD and Flux CD**: Both tools achieve GitOps deployments. Choosing one depends on your preference and project requirements.
- **Install and configure the chosen tool**: Follow the provided steps for installing and configuring Argo CD or Flux CD in your GKE cluster.
- **Set up repositories**: Connect your Git repository to the chosen tool for version control and automatic deployment.
- **Define applications**: Create applications within the chosen tool to represent your workloads, specifying the target namespace and sync policy.

- **GitOps workflow**: Push changes to your Git repository, and the chosen tool automatically detects and synchronizes them to your cluster. Monitor the application status using the tool's UI.

Remember:

This is a starting point, and specific implementation details may vary depending on your needs. Always consult official GKE documentation for in-depth guidance and advanced troubleshooting.

By following these best practices and exploring advanced strategies, you can ensure efficient, reliable, and scalable workload deployments in your GKE clusters.

Backup and disaster recovery strategies

Implementing robust backup and disaster recovery strategies is essential for protecting GKE clusters and ensuring business continuity. Here is how to design reliable backup solutions that safeguard your applications and data while minimizing downtime and ensuring quick recovery from incidents:

Comprehensive backup strategies

To ensure the safety and availability of your data, implementing a comprehensive data protection strategy for GKE is essential. Here is how to leverage various tools and techniques to safeguard your persistent data and streamline recovery processes:

- **GKE PD snapshots**: Regularly capture snapshots of PDs to safeguard data. Utilize GCP Console or `gcloud` commands for scheduling and managing snapshot lifecycles.
- **Velero backup and restore**: Deploy Velero for efficient cluster-wide data protection, enabling scheduled backups and policy-driven retention to ensure comprehensive data recovery capabilities.
- **Kasten K10 data management platform**: Leverage Kasten K10 for Kubernetes-native data management, offering streamlined backup processes and data mobility solutions tailored for GKE environments.

Application and database resilience

Ensuring resilience at both the application and database levels is essential for maintaining data integrity and minimizing downtime. Here is how to implement targeted backup solutions to protect critical application and database data effectively:

- **Stash for application-level backup**: Implement Stash to provide granular backup solutions for applications, ensuring critical data is protected at the application layer.

- **Database-specific backup solutions**: Utilize database-specific tools, such as Cloud SQL automated backups, to secure database environments, ensuring data integrity and quick recovery.

Configuration and volume backup

Backing up configurations and PVs ensures the stability and recoverability of your GKE environment. Here is how to use GitOps and backup tools to safeguard configurations and persistent data effectively:

- **GitOps for configuration backup**: Adopt GitOps methodologies with tools like Argo CD to manage and synchronize Kubernetes configurations, enhancing infrastructure as code practices.
- **PV backups**: Secure PVs using tools like Velero or Stash, establishing robust data retention policies to protect against data loss.

Disaster recovery planning and readiness

Certain applications and workloads require tailored backup strategies to meet their unique data protection needs. Additionally, a well-defined disaster recovery plan helps ensure business continuity. Here Is how to implement specialized backup solutions and plan for effective disaster recovery:

- **Application-specific backup strategies**: Tailor backup solutions to specific applications, such as Elasticsearch, to address unique data protection needs and ensure application resilience.
- **Disaster recovery planning**: Develop a comprehensive disaster recovery plan, detailing backup procedures, **Recovery Time Objectives** (**RTO**), and **Recovery Point Objectives** (**RPO**) to ensure business continuity.

Adopting a multi-faceted approach to data protection and disaster recovery in GKE not only ensures the safety of critical data but also enhances the overall resilience of cloud-native applications. From leveraging PD snapshots and employing Kubernetes-native data management platforms like Kasten K10, to implementing application-specific backup strategies and comprehensive disaster recovery planning, these practices provide a robust framework for data integrity. By integrating these methodologies into your GKE deployments, you can safeguard against data loss, minimize downtime, and maintain operational continuity, ensuring that your data remains secure and readily available when needed.

Comprehensive data protection and recovery

Data backup and restoration plan: Regularly perform data backups and establish streamlined restoration processes using tools like Velero, ensuring data integrity and availability.

Velero is a tool to back up and restore Kubernetes cluster resources and PVs. It can be used to back-up your entire cluster data and state and restore in case of loss. Velero requires a GCP storage bucket to store backups.

Installing Velero with GCP provider:

```
velero install --provider gcp
  --plugins velero/velero-plugin-for-gcp:v1.2.0 \
  --bucket <BUCKET_NAME> \
  --secret-file <YOUR_CREDENTIALS_FILE>
```

Backing up cluster data: `velero backup create <BACKUP_NAME>`

Restoring from backup: `velero restore create --from-backup <BACKUP_NAME>`

Ensuring cluster availability and performance

Cluster scaling and redundancy plan: Leverage GKE Cluster Autoscaler and multi-zone clusters to maintain service availability and performance, even under varying loads and potential zone failures (command or YAML provided in analyzing and addressing performance bottlenecks).

Validating disaster recovery readiness

Disaster recovery testing plan: Conduct regular **disaster recovery (DR)** drills to validate the effectiveness of your DR strategies, ensuring your team is prepared for real-world scenarios.

Service continuity measures

Failover and load balancing plan: Implement GCP Load Balancers and Cloud CDN to ensure seamless failover and efficient global distribution, minimizing downtime during disruptions.

Application resilience

Application-level redundancy plan: Deploy applications across multiple zones or regions using Kubernetes StatefulSets and affinity rules, enhancing application durability and availability.

Proactive monitoring and response

Monitoring and alerting plan: Set up comprehensive monitoring with Prometheus and Grafana, coupled with custom alerts, to enable rapid detection and response to issues.

Securing data and infrastructure

Data encryption and security plan: Secure sensitive data with GCP encryption at rest and enforce access controls using RBAC policies, safeguarding your environment against unauthorized access.

Effective incident communication

Disaster communication plan: Develop a clear communication strategy for disaster scenarios, including contact lists and incident response teams, to ensure coordinated response efforts.

Geographic risk mitigation

Geographic distribution plan: Minimize regional risks by deploying resources across multiple geographic regions, utilizing GCP Multi-Regional Storage for resilient data storage.

Configuration management and control

Configuration backup and versioning plan: Adopt GitOps practices for efficient configuration backup and versioning, ensuring **infrastructure as code** (**IaC**) principles are maintained for disaster recovery purposes.

Adopting a layered approach to disaster recovery in GKE environments not only safeguards against data loss and service interruptions but also ensures that your cloud-native applications remain resilient in the face of disruptions. From data backup and application redundancy to proactive monitoring and geographic distribution, these strategies provide a comprehensive framework for maintaining continuous operations. Implementing these disaster recovery plans empowers organizations to navigate unforeseen challenges confidently, ensuring business continuity and the protection of critical digital assets in GKE deployments.

Conclusion

By adopting these strategies, you can significantly mitigate the risk of data loss and enhance the high availability of your applications within GKE clusters. From automated backups and multi-regional deployments to sophisticated scaling and redundancy mechanisms, each practice contributes to building a robust and resilient cloud-native environment. As you implement these methodologies, you will not only protect your critical data and applications but also ensure that your GKE deployments are optimized for both performance and reliability, ready to meet the demands of your users and business operations.

Multiple choice questions

1. **What is the primary purpose of implementing resource management best practices in GKE?**
   a. To increase the number of running Pods
   b. To optimize performance, efficiency, and cost-effectiveness
   c. To prevent Kubernetes from scheduling workloads
   d. To eliminate the need for autoscaling
2. **Which tool can be used for Kubernetes-native data management, including backup and recovery, in GKE?**
   a. Prometheus
   b. Kasten K10
   c. Terraform
   d. Grafana
3. **What is the key advantage of using GitOps methodologies for configuration backup in GKE?**
   a. It eliminates the need for Persistent Volumes
   b. It provides automated synchronization and version control for cluster configurations
   c. It replaces Kubernetes' built-in backup mechanisms
   d. It increases storage capacity in GKE clusters
4. **How can you ensure application resilience in GKE using backup strategies?**
   a. Relying only on manual snapshots for recovery
   b. Using Stash for application-level backups and Cloud SQL automated backups for databases
   c. Avoiding database backups to save storage costs
   d. Limiting the number of backup tools used
5. **Which best practice helps optimize Pod placement and resource efficiency in GKE?**
   a. Deploying all Pods on a single node for better performance
   b. Using Pod affinity and anti-affinity rules to control Pod scheduling
   c. Disabling autoscaling to maintain static resource allocation
   d. Avoiding node selectors to keep deployments flexible

Answer key

1.	b.
2.	b.
3.	b.
4.	b.
5.	b.

Join our book's Discord space

Join the book's Discord Workspace for Latest updates, Offers, Tech happenings around the world, New Release and Sessions with the Authors:

https://discord.bpbonline.com

CHAPTER 10
Advanced Topics in GKE

Introduction

Diving deeper into GKE, this chapter explores advanced topics that push the boundaries of what is possible with container orchestration. As applications grow in complexity and scale, the need for sophisticated management strategies becomes paramount. This part of the book sheds light on advanced features within GKE, designed to meet the needs of complex, high-demand applications. Whether you are looking to optimize your deployments across multiple clusters, automate scaling based on real-time demands, or harness the power of service meshes for enhanced networking capabilities, the topics will guide you through the advanced landscapes of GKE, equipping you with the knowledge to fully leverage the platform's capabilities. This chapter is curated to provide insights into the more complex functionalities of GKE, with each section outlined to enhance your understanding and application of these advanced features.

Structure

The following topics will be covered in this chapter:

- Multi-cluster Ingress in GKE
- Cluster Autoscaler in GKE
- Service mesh and Istio
- Cost optimization in GKE

Objectives

This chapter explores the cutting-edge realms of GKE, providing deeper insights into advanced container orchestration. These topics are crucial for scaling, optimizing, and securing Kubernetes workloads in enterprise settings.

You will learn how to set up and optimize Multi-cluster Ingress for global traffic management and improved application reach, implement and manage Cluster Autoscaler to ensure efficient resource utilization and cost-effectiveness. Moreover, you will understand the architecture and benefits of Service Mesh and Istio for enhanced networking, security, and observability within GKE, and explore strategies and tools for cost optimization while running applications on GKE.

Multi-cluster Ingress in GKE

Managing Ingress traffic across multiple clusters can introduce significant operational complexity, especially when dealing with diverse workloads, regional preferences, and varying availability requirements. Multi-cluster Ingress in GKE streamlines this process by providing a centralized solution that minimizes the need for custom configurations while ensuring efficient traffic distribution. This section focuses on the technical aspects of implementing multi-cluster Ingress to optimize your Kubernetes deployments.

Introduction to multi-cluster Ingress

With the globalization of applications and the need for high availability, scalability, and low latency across geographically dispersed user bases, managing Ingress traffic across multiple Kubernetes clusters has become crucial. GKE addresses this need with multi-cluster Ingress, a feature that enables unified traffic management across multiple clusters, ensuring users are directed to the closest or most optimal cluster hosting the application.

Real-world example: A global e-commerce platform or an international TV streaming service benefits from multi-cluster Ingress by ensuring that users around the world experience low-latency access to their services. By deploying clusters in multiple regions and using global HTTP(S) load balancing, these platforms can dynamically route traffic to the nearest available cluster, reducing downtime and improving user experience.

Key concepts

Here are a few key concepts that will be covered in this section:

- **Global HTTP(S) load balancing**: Leverages Google Cloud's global HTTP(S) load balancer to intelligently route traffic across multiple clusters.
- **Cross-region redundancy**: Enhances application availability by spanning clusters across different regions.

- **Centralized management**: Offers a single point of control for managing Ingress resources across clusters.

Figure 10.1 depicts how traffic from various global locations is routed to the nearest or best-performing cluster:

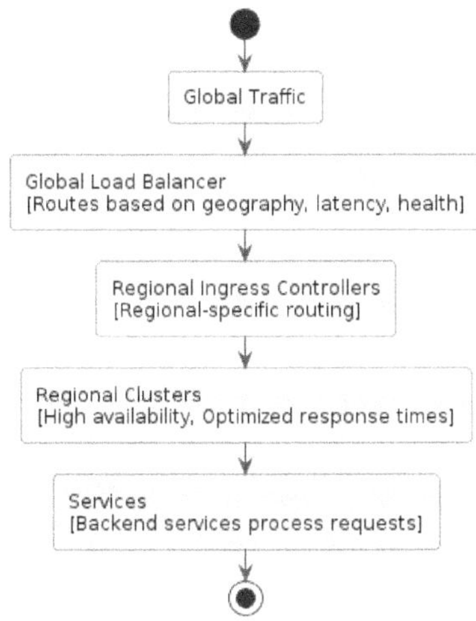

***Figure 10.1**: Multi-cluster Ingress traffic flow*

This flowchart illustrates the steps involved in managing multi-cluster Ingress traffic, focusing on the role of the Global Load Balancer and the distribution of traffic across regional clusters:

1. **Global traffic**: Represents users or clients from various global locations initiating requests to access the application.
2. **Global load balancer**: Acts as the central point for incoming traffic, making routing decisions based on geography, latency, health checks, and custom routing policies to ensure optimal user experience.
3. **Regional Ingress controllers**: Within each regional cluster, dedicated Ingress controllers manage regional-specific traffic routing, applying rules defined in Ingress resources to direct traffic to the appropriate backend services.
4. **Regional clusters**: Ensures high availability and optimized response times by distributing the application logic across multiple Kubernetes clusters located in different regions. This setup provides geographically closer endpoints for global users.
5. **Services**: Backend services deployed within each regional cluster process the incoming requests, representing the actual functionalities users interact with.

This figure effectively showcases the architecture behind multi-cluster Ingress traffic management, emphasizing how traffic is intelligently directed to ensure efficient and reliable access to services across geographical boundaries.

Use cases for multi-cluster deployments

Multi-cluster Ingress is particularly beneficial in scenarios requiring global reach, disaster recovery, and traffic optimization. Let us look at these scenarios as follows:

- **Global reach**: For services with a global customer base, ensuring low latency and high availability.
- **Disaster recovery**: Automatic traffic rerouting in case of a regional outage, maintaining service continuity.
- **Resource optimization**: Balancing workloads across clusters to optimize resource utilization and performance.

Configuring multi-cluster Ingress

Setting up multi-cluster Ingress in GKE involves integrating multiple clusters and ensuring seamless traffic management across regions. The process requires careful preparation and adherence to specific configuration steps to ensure that traffic is routed efficiently, and applications remain highly available. This section covers the configuration steps and also the prerequisites as outlined below.

Pre-requisites

Here are few pre-requisites which will be required to configure multi-cluster Ingress:

- Multiple GKE clusters deployed across different regions.
- The application deployed and exposed as a service in each cluster.
- Google Cloud SDK (**`gcloud`**) and **`kubectl`** configured for your GCP project.

Configuration steps

Now let us look at the configuration steps:

1. **Enable multi-cluster Ingress**: First, ensure the multi-cluster Ingress API and associated GKE features are enabled in your GCP project with this command: **`gcloud services enable multiclusterIngress.googleapis.com`**
2. **Deploy multi-cluster Ingress resource**: Define a MultiClusterIngress YAML configuration that specifies the global routing rules:

```
apiVersion: networking.gke.io/v1
kind: MultiClusterIngress
metadata:
  name: global-Ingress
  namespace: default
```

```
spec:
  template:
    spec:
      rules:
      - host: myapp.example.com
        http:
          paths:
          - path: /
            pathType: Prefix
            backend:
              service:
                name: my-service
                port:
                  number: 80
```

Deploy this configuration across the clusters where the application is hosted.

3. **Verify the Ingress status**: After deployment, verify the status of the MultiClusterIngress to ensure it is active and routing traffic as expected with this command: **`kubectl describe multiclusterIngress global-Ingress`**

Monitoring and diagnostics

Effective monitoring and diagnostics are critical to ensuring the reliability and performance of your multi-cluster Ingress setup. This section highlights key practices and tools to help maintain optimal performance and address potential challenges in your multi-cluster Ingress deployment.

- **Monitoring traffic distribution**: Use Google Cloud Monitoring to observe traffic distribution across clusters and identify potential bottlenecks.
- **Logging and analysis**: Enable logging for Ingress traffic to analyze patterns, performance, and troubleshoot issues.

Figure 10.2 illustrates the setup for monitoring and logging Ingress traffic across clusters:

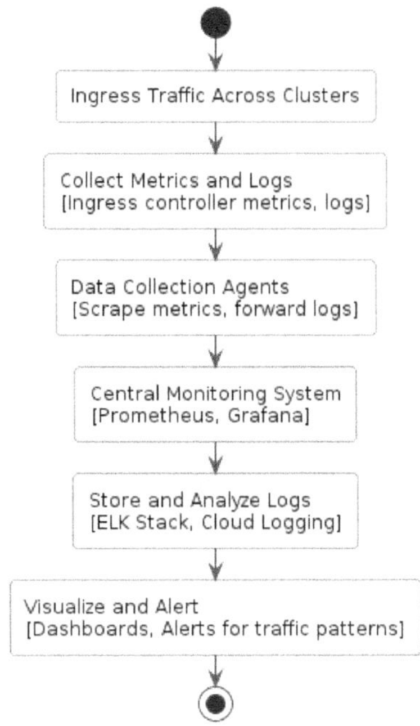

***Figure 10.2**: Monitoring multi-cluster Ingress*

The flowchart in *Figure 10.2* highlights the following steps:

1. **Ingress traffic across clusters**: Represents the initial point where users from various locations access the application, generating Ingress traffic entering multiple clusters.

2. **Collect metrics and logs**: Key performance metrics and logs are captured by each cluster's Ingress controller, detailing request rates, errors, response times, latency, and other relevant data.

3. **Data collection agents**: Deployed within each cluster or utilizing existing infrastructure, these agents scrape metrics from the Ingress controllers and forward logs to a centralized system.

4. **Central monitoring system**: Utilizes tools like Prometheus for storing and managing the metrics and Grafana for creating dashboards to visualize traffic patterns and identify issues.

5. **Store and analyze logs**: Systems such as the ELK stack or Cloud Logging consolidate and analyze logs from all clusters, enabling detailed examination of request details, user behaviors, and potential anomalies.

6. **Visualize and alert**: Dashboards in Grafana provide real-time insights into Ingress traffic, with alerts set up to notify administrators of significant issues based on predefined thresholds.

This visualization effectively outlines the infrastructure and processes involved in monitoring multi-cluster Ingress traffic, ensuring comprehensive oversight and proactive management of network performance and security.

Advanced use cases and solutions

Now let us look at few advanced use cases and their solutions:

- **Scenario**: Achieving zero downtime during regional failures.

  Solution: Implement multi-cluster Ingress with health checks and automatic failover to reroute traffic away from affected regions without interrupting the service.

- **Scenario**: Dynamic scaling for global events.

  Solution: Leverage multi-cluster Ingress in conjunction with Cluster Autoscaler to dynamically scale resources in clusters based on demand spikes during global events.

YAML configuration for health checks

Health checks play a vital role in ensuring that only healthy application instances receive traffic, maintaining the reliability and performance of your multi-cluster Ingress setup. By configuring health checks within your YAML definition, you enable GKE to monitor the health of your services continuously and route traffic accordingly. The **`healthChecks`** field in the YAML configuration specifies parameters like the health check path and port, allowing GKE to probe the application endpoints effectively.

The following is an example of a YAML configuration that integrates health checks:

```
spec:
  backend:
    service:
      name: my-service
      port:
        number: 80
  healthChecks:
    - path: /healthz
```

In this configuration:

- **`path: /healthz`** specifies the endpoint where GKE will perform health probes to verify the application's status.
- **`port: 8080`** defines the port to which the health check requests will be sent.

By implementing these health checks, you ensure traffic is routed only to healthy instances, preventing potential disruptions and improving the user experience. This mechanism is particularly important in a multi-cluster environment, where the health of services can vary across regions or clusters.

Cluster Autoscaler in GKE

The Cluster Autoscaler in GKE dynamically scales the cluster's node pools, ensuring optimal resource utilization while maintaining application performance. This capability allows clusters to grow or shrink automatically, aligning with workload requirements and cost-saving strategies. In this section, we will explore the functionality, benefits, and implementation of the Cluster Autoscaler to help you effectively manage your GKE deployments.

Overview of Cluster Autoscaling in GKE

Effective resource management is crucial for optimizing performance and cost-efficiency in cloud environments. GKE addresses this with the Cluster Autoscaler, a tool designed to automatically adjust the size of a cluster based on the demands of the workloads and the constraints of the specific policies set by administrators.

Key concepts

Here are few key concepts which will be covered in this section:

- **Node management**: Automatically adds or removes nodes in a cluster based on the needs of your applications.
- **Resource efficiency**: Ensures that nodes are efficiently utilized, reducing costs by eliminating unneeded resources.
- **Scalability**: Enhances the ability of a cluster to handle increased load without manual intervention.

Figure 10.3 shows the process of scaling up and down in response to demand fluctuations:

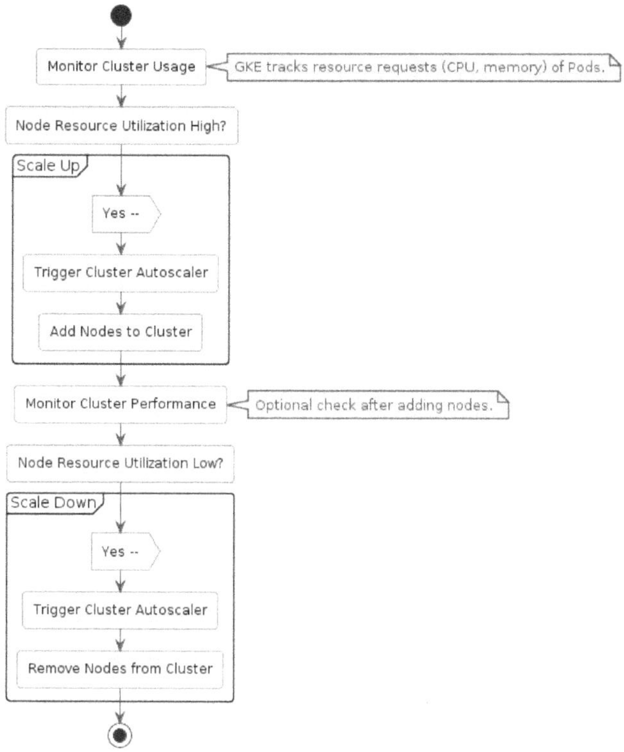

***Figure 10.3**: Cluster Autoscaler workflow in GKE*

The flow chart in *Figure 10.3* illustrates the following steps:

1. **Monitor cluster usage**: GKE tracks the resource requests (CPU, memory) of Pods across the nodes to gauge cluster usage.
2. **Node resource utilization high?**: The Autoscaler assesses if the cumulative resource requests exceed the threshold that warrants scaling up.
3. **Yes**: Triggers the Cluster Autoscaler to add nodes, expanding cluster capacity to accommodate increased demands.
4. **Monitor cluster performance**: Optionally checks the impact on cluster performance post-scaling to ensure service stability and efficiency.
5. **Node resource utilization low?**: Evaluates whether resources are underutilized, indicating a potential for scaling down.
6. **Yes**: Activates the Cluster Autoscaler to remove nodes, optimizing resource allocation and reducing unnecessary costs.

The flowchart in *Figure 10.3* effectively showcases the dynamic nature of the Cluster Autoscaler in GKE, highlighting how it responds to workload fluctuations to maintain optimal performance and cost efficiency.

Configuring Cluster Autoscaler in GKE

The configuration of the Cluster Autoscaler involves setting appropriate parameters when creating or updating a GKE cluster.

Steps to enable Cluster Autoscaler

The following are the steps to enable Cluster Autoscaler:

1. **Create a GKE cluster with autoscaling enabled**: Use the Google Cloud Console or the **gcloud** command line tool to create a cluster with autoscaling configured for its node pools:

   ```
   gcloud container clusters create "my-cluster" \
    --zone “us-central1-a” \
    --num-nodes “1” \
    --enable-autoscaling --min-nodes "1" --max-nodes "10"
   ```

2. **Configure autoscaling parameters**: Define policies regarding the minimum and maximum number of nodes in the cluster, and other parameters such as cooldown periods and resource limits.

3. **Deploy workloads**: Deploy your applications on the cluster, ensuring that resource requests and limits are properly defined in the deployment configurations to guide the Autoscaler's decisions.

   ```
   apiVersion: apps/v1
   kind: Deployment
   metadata:
     name: my-application
   spec:
     replicas: 3
     selector:
         matchLabels:
         app: my-application
     template:
         metadata:
         labels:
         app: my-application
         spec:
         containers:
         - name: my-application
         image: my-image
         resources:
         requests:
   ```

```
            cpu: "250m"
            memory: "512Mi"
        limits:
            cpu: "500m"
            memory: "1Gi"
```

Monitoring and metrics for autoscaling

Effectively monitoring the autoscaling process is crucial for understanding how resources are being utilized and ensuring that scaling actions align with workload demands.

Tools and techniques for monitoring

Monitoring the autoscaling process is essential to ensure that your cluster's scaling behaviour aligns with workload demands and operational goals. By observing resource utilization and tracking scaling events, you can identify patterns, optimize configurations, and address potential issues proactively. Effective monitoring provides visibility into the efficiency of your autoscaling setup and helps maintain a balance between performance and cost.

In this section, we will explore the tools and techniques that enable you to monitor the autoscaling process effectively, ensuring your clusters operate smoothly and adapt to workload changes as expected.

- **Google Cloud monitoring**: Provides detailed insights into cluster performance, including CPU and memory utilization, which can help administrators understand the behavior of the Autoscaler.
- **Logging and event tracking**: Use Google Cloud Logging to track scale-up and scale-down events within the cluster.

Figure 10.4 depicts key metrics and events that administrators should monitor:

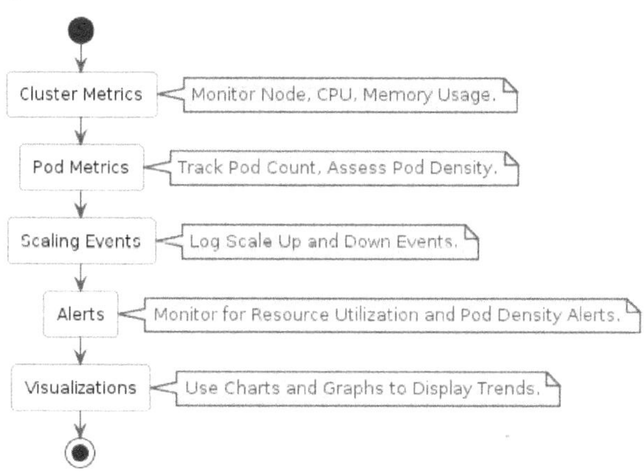

***Figure 10.4**: Autoscaling monitoring dashboard*

The flowchart in *Figure 10.4* visualizes the key components of an autoscaling monitoring dashboard:

1. **Cluster metrics**: Monitoring node count, CPU, and memory usage to understand current scale and identify potential scaling events.
2. **Pod metrics**: Tracking the total number of active Pods in the cluster to assess Pod density and efficiency.
3. **Scaling events**: Logging scale up and down events to understand responses to changing resource demands.
4. **Alerts**: Monitoring alerts triggered by resource utilization or Pod density reaching predefined thresholds.
5. **Visualizations**: Utilizing charts and graphs to display trends and relationships between metrics, enhancing understanding of the impact of scaling actions.

This dashboard is crucial for managing resource efficiency and ensuring the cluster meets the workload demands effectively.

Metrics to monitor

Let us now look at the metrics which need to be monitored:

- **CPU and memory utilization**: Tracks how much CPU and memory are being used by nodes and Pods.
- **Pod count**: Observes the number of Pods in different states (pending, running, failed) to assess the capacity needs.
- **Autoscaling events**: Monitors when and why the Autoscaler added or removed nodes.

Table 10.1 shows all the key metrics for monitoring cluster autoscaling:

Metric	Description	Importance
CPU utilization	Percentage of CPU resources used by all nodes in the cluster	High
Memory utilization	Amount of memory used by workloads on each node	High
Scaling events	Instances of node addition or removal by the Autoscaler	Critical

***Table 10.1**: Key metrics for monitoring Cluster Autoscaling*

Scenarios and solutions

Now let us look at few use cases and their solutions:

- **Scenario**: A sudden spike in web traffic causes Pod deployment failures due to insufficient resources.

  Solution: Configure Cluster Autoscaler with a higher maximum node limit and ensure Pod resource requests are set accurately to allow the Autoscaler to scale the cluster effectively.

- **Scenario**: Over-provisioning of nodes leads to higher operational costs.

  Solution: Adjust the Autoscaler's minimum node count and fine-tune resource requests and limits to better match the workload demands, optimizing resource usage and cost.

By understanding the advanced capabilities of the Cluster Autoscaler in GKE and leveraging effective monitoring strategies, administrators can ensure that their clusters are both reactive to changing demands and cost-efficient. This dynamic balancing act between performance and cost is key to managing a robust, scalable Kubernetes environment.

Service mesh and Istio

As microservices architectures grow in complexity, managing interactions between services becomes increasingly challenging. A service mesh, such as Istio, addresses these challenges by providing a unified layer for controlling and securing service-to-service communication. Istio extends Kubernetes capabilities, enabling developers and operators to efficiently manage traffic, enhance security, and gain deeper insights into application performance.

This section will explore some of these features to streamline operations in distributed systems, empowering teams to build resilient and scalable microservices-based applications.

Overview of service mesh architecture

A service mesh is a dedicated infrastructure layer for handling service-to-service communication in microservices architectures, making it easier to manage service interactions across a distributed environment. Istio, one of the most popular service mesh frameworks, provides advanced traffic management, enhanced security, observability, and reliability across microservices.

Key concepts

Here are the key concepts which will be covered in this section:

- **Traffic management**: Istio provides fine-grained controls to direct and control traffic flow within a microservices architecture without modifying application code.

- **Security**: Enhances security across services with strong identity-based authentication and authorization.
- **Observability**: Offers detailed insights into the behavior of services through tracing, telemetry, and logging.

Figure 10.5 shows how Istio integrates with Kubernetes Pods to manage traffic, enforce policies, and gather metrics:

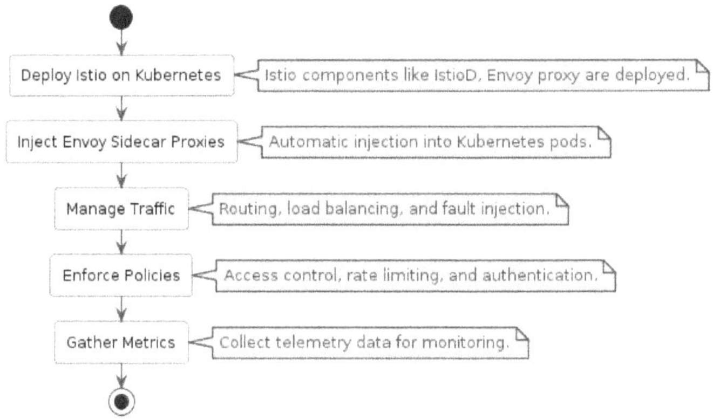

***Figure 10.5**: Service mesh architecture with Istio*

The flowchart in *Figure 10.5* details the following key processes:

1. **Deploy Istio on Kubernetes**: Istio components like **Istio Daemon (istiod)** and Envoy proxy are deployed across the cluster.
2. **Inject envoy sidecar proxies**: Automatic injection of Envoy proxies into Kubernetes Pods, enabling detailed traffic management and policy enforcement.
3. **Manage traffic**: Istio handles routing, load balancing, and fault injection to optimize and control Pod-to-Pod traffic.
4. **Enforce policies**: Implementation of access control, rate limiting, and authentication to secure and manage the service mesh.
5. **Gather metrics**: Collection of telemetry data, which is crucial for monitoring the health and performance of services within the mesh.

This architecture enables comprehensive management and control over network traffic and policy enforcement in Kubernetes environments, enhancing both security and operational efficiency.

Integrating Istio with GKE clusters

Deploying Istio within a GKE cluster transforms it into a robust environment capable of managing complex microservices with ease.

Pre-requisites

Here are few pre-requisites which will be required to integrate Istio with GKE clusters:

- An active GKE cluster.
- **kubectl** and **istioctl** (Istio command line tool) installed and configured to communicate with your GKE cluster.

Steps to deploy Istio in GKE

Now let us look at the deployment steps:

1. **Install Istio on GKE**: Enable the Istio add-on for GKE or manually install Istio using **istioctl**.
    a. Enable Istio on GKE via Google Cloud Console or using **gcloud** this command: **gcloud container clusters update "my-cluster" --update-addons=Istio=ENABLED**
    b. You can manually install Istio as well using **istioctl**: **istioctl install --set profile=default**
2. **Configure Istio's control plane components**: Customize the Istio installation to suit your specific requirements, such as enabling **auto-mTLS**, configuring gateways, and setting up Istio's telemetry features.

```
apiVersion: install.istio.io/v1alpha1  # Istio API version
kind: IstioOperator  # Istio setup resource
spec:
  profile: default  # Default installation profile
  meshConfig:
    enableAutoMtls: true  # Enable mTLS
  components:
    egressGateways:
      - name: istio-egressgateway  # Egress gateway
        enabled: true  # Enable egress
    IngressGateways:
      - name: istio-Ingressgateway  # Ingress gateway
        enabled: true  # Enable Ingress
```

3. **Deploy workloads**: Annotate your application namespaces to automatically inject Istio sidecars when deploying Pods with this command: **kubectl label namespace default istio-injection=enabled**
4. **Deploy an Istio gateway and VirtualService**: Define an Istio **Gateway** and **VirtualService** to manage Ingress traffic for your applications.

```
apiVersion: networking.istio.io/v1alpha3
kind: Gateway
metadata:
  name: my-gateway
spec:
  selector:
      istio: Ingressgateway
  servers:
  - port:
      number: 80
      name: http
      protocol: HTTP
      hosts:
      - "example.com"
---
apiVersion: networking.istio.io/v1alpha3
kind: VirtualService
metadata:
  name: my-service
spec:
  hosts:
  - "example.com"
  gateways:
  - my-gateway
  http:
  - route:
      - destination:
      host: my-service
      port:
      number: 80
```

Deployment and configuration strategies for Istio in GKE

Continuing from the initial setup and monitoring of Istio within GKE, let us explore more detailed deployment strategies and configuration options that can enhance your service mesh's capabilities and security.

Advanced traffic management

Istio's sophisticated traffic routing rules allow you to control traffic flow with high granularity, which is crucial for testing new features, A/B testing, and blue-green deployments.

Configuring traffic rules

Now let us see how to configure traffic rules:

1. **Set up fine-grained routing rules**: Use Istio's **VirtualService** to direct traffic based on request attributes such as headers or cookies.

   ```
   apiVersion: networking.istio.io/v1alpha3
   kind: VirtualService
   metadata:
     name: my-service
   spec:
     hosts:
     - "my-service"
     http:
     - match:
         - headers:
         user-type:
         exact: tester
         route:
         - destination:
         host: my-service
         subset: v2
     - route:
         - destination:
         host: my-service
         subset: v1
   ```

   This configuration routes users with a **user-type** header of **tester** to version 2 of the service, while all others receive version 1.

2. **Implement retry and timeout policies**: Enhance service reliability with automatic retries and timeouts for calls between services.

   ```
   apiVersion: networking.istio.io/v1alpha3
   kind: VirtualService
   metadata:
     name: my-service
   spec:
     hosts:
     - my-service
     http:
     - route:
         - destination:
         host: my-service
   ```

```
subset: v1
timeout: 5s
retries:
attempts: 3
perTryTimeout: 2s
```

Security enhancements with Istio

Securing communication within the service mesh is a critical aspect that Istio addresses with robust security policies and authentication mechanisms.

Mutual TLS authentication

Now let us look at mutual TLS authentication:

1. **Enable mTLS in the service mesh**: Ensure that all communications between services are secured with TLS, providing confidentiality, integrity, and authentication.

```
apiVersion: security.istio.io/v1beta1
kind: PeerAuthentication
metadata:
  name: default
  namespace: istio-system
spec:
  mtls:
      mode: STRICT
```

This policy enforces `mTLS` for all services in the mesh, ensuring that traffic is encrypted and authenticated.

In *Figure 10.6* we can see a flowchart showing the sequence of applying security configurations, starting from `mTLS` settings, applying authorization policies, and ensuring encrypted traffic with `DestinationRules`:

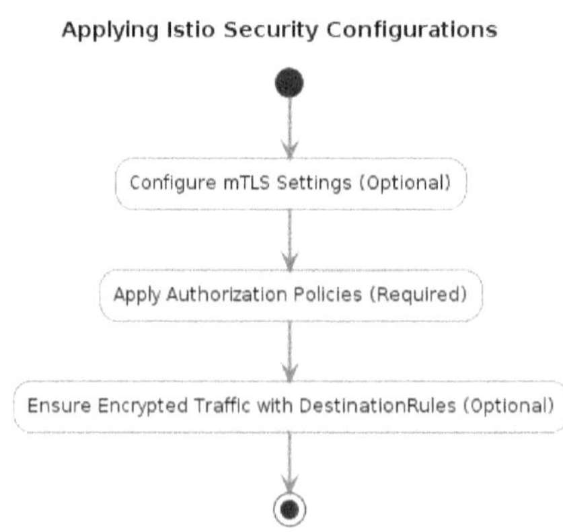

***Figure 10.6**: Sequence of applying Istio security configurations*

The flowchart in *Figure 10.6* details the following key processes:

1. **Configure mTLS settings (optional)**:
    a. **Process**: Set up **mutual TLS** (**mTLS**) across the service mesh to enable secure, authenticated service-to-service communication. This involves automatically configuring TLS certificates and keys on Envoy proxies.
    b. **Importance**: mTLS lays the foundational trust between services, enhancing security by allowing only authenticated services to communicate, though it is optional and does not enforce encryption by default.
2. **Apply authorization policies (required)**:
    a. **Process**: Administrators use YAML files to define Authorization Policies that specify which users or services can access which resources under certain conditions. This involves setting subjects, objects, and actions for fine-grained access control.
    b. **Importance**: Essential for enforcing detailed security policies, controlling access, and preventing unauthorized access or breaches within the service mesh. This step is mandatory for defining access control.
3. **Ensure encrypted traffic with DestinationRules (optional)**:
    a. **Process**: Employ DestinationRules to dictate traffic policies for specific destinations within the service mesh, typically including encryption settings (like requiring TLS) and load balancing configurations.
    b. **Importance**: Further secures specific traffic flows by enforcing encryption, ensuring data integrity and confidentiality over the network. This step is optional but crucial for securing data in transit to targeted services.

This flowchart illustrates a sequence where mTLS establishes a trust layer, Authorization Policies enforce access control, and DestinationRules optionally bolster traffic security. Each step builds upon the previous step to enhance the overall security posture within the Kubernetes environment managed by Istio.

Authorization policies

Control access with fine-grained policies: Define who can access what services within your mesh based on identities, namespaces, and other attributes.

```
apiVersion: security.istio.io/v1beta1
kind: AuthorizationPolicy
metadata:
  name: productpage-viewer
  namespace: default
spec:
```

```
selector:
    matchLabels:
    app: productpage
action: ALLOW
rules:
- from:
    - source:
    principals: ["cluster.local/ns/default/sa/bookinfo-productpage"]
    to:
    - operation:
    methods: ["GET"]
```

This policy allows the **bookinfo-productpage** service account to make GET requests to the **productpage** service.

Table 10.2 contains few security features and their configurations:

Feature	Configuration	Description
mTLS	PeerAuthentication	Ensures secure service-to-service communication within the mesh.
Access control	AuthorizationPolicy	Defines fine-grained access rules for services based on identities and metadata.
Traffic encryption	DestinationRule	Enforces encrypted traffic between specific services.

***Table 10.2**: Security features and their configurations in Istio*

Monitoring and metrics with Istio

Istio provides comprehensive tools to observe and understand traffic within your service mesh, enhancing both basic telemetry and advanced monitoring capabilities. This integration helps in detailed tracking and analysis of service mesh health and performance.

Tools for monitoring and visualization

There are various tools available for monitoring and visualization, let us look at some of them:

- **Kiali**: Visualizes the service mesh topology, allowing users to observe traffic flow and analyze configurations. Kiali helps in understanding the complex interactions within your service mesh.
- **Jaeger and Zipkin**: These tools offer distributed tracing capabilities that help identify request flows and latencies within the service mesh, crucial for diagnosing problems related to service communication.

- **Prometheus**: Integrates with Istio to collect detailed metrics which are essential for monitoring the performance and health of services.
- **Grafana**: It is used alongside Prometheus to provide visual dashboards for better insight into the metrics collected.

Implementing monitoring tools

Now, let us see how to implement these tools:

1. **Set up Istio to export metrics to Prometheus with this command**: `kubectl apply -f https://raw.githubusercontent.com/istio/istio/release-1.12/samples/addons/prometheus.yaml`
2. **Deploy Grafana for Istio metrics visualization with this command**: `kubectl apply -f https://raw.githubusercontent.com/istio/istio/release-1.12/samples/addons/grafana.yaml`
3. **Access Kiali dashboard for service mesh visualization with this command**: `istioctl dashboard kiali`

Enhanced logging strategy

Implement structured logging with **`Fluentd`** to enhance the traceability of interactions across services within the service mesh. This setup ensures that all log data is captured and organized effectively.

Use cases and scenario-based optimization

Here are a few use cases and their optimization solutions:

- **Canary deployments for safe rollouts**:
    - **Scenario**: Gradually introducing a new version of a service into production.
    - **Solution**: Use Istio's traffic management features to configure a canary deployment, directing a small percentage of traffic to the new version and monitoring its performance. Gradually increase traffic as confidence in the new version grows.
- **Service resiliency under high load**:
    - **Scenario**: Services failing sporadically under high load.
    - **Solution**: Configure circuit breakers and outlier detection in Istio to prevent cascading failures and maintain system stability.
- **Handling high traffic volumes**:
    - **Scenario**: Managing sudden spikes in traffic during peak hours.

  - **Solution**: Implement rate limiting and quota management in Istio to control traffic flow and prevent service overload.

- **Compliance and auditing**:
  - **Scenario**: Ensuring compliance with industry regulations concerning data handling and user privacy.
  - **Solution**: Utilize Istio's detailed logging and auditing tools to track data access and transfer across services, ensuring alignment with compliance requirements.

Figure 10.7 illustrates how traffic data is collected and visualized through tools like Kiali, Jaeger, and Prometheus, and how it integrates with advanced monitoring setups like Grafana:

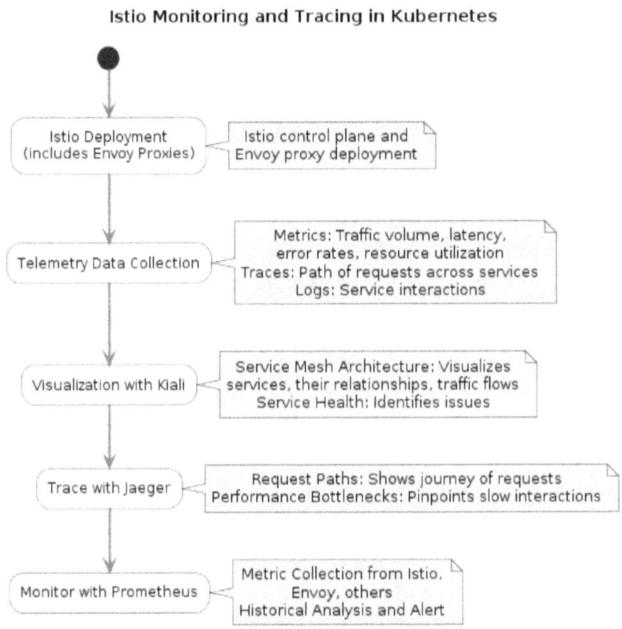

***Figure 10.7**: Istio monitoring and tracing*

The visualization of the Istio monitoring and tracing flowchart, structured to emphasize key processes in managing and observing a Kubernetes service mesh, focuses on the following main stages:

1. **Istio deployment**:
   a. **Key process**: Deployment of Istio components like Istiod (Istio's control plane) and Envoy sidecar proxies across the Kubernetes cluster.
   b. **Importance**: This sets up the fundamental framework for traffic management, security, and observability within the service mesh.

2. **Telemetry data collection**:

   a. **Key process**: Automatic collection of telemetry data from Envoy proxies, which includes metrics on traffic volume, latency, error rates, and resource utilization, along with traces showing the path of requests across services and logs detailing service interactions.

   b. **Importance**: This data collection is crucial for monitoring the performance and health of the services within the mesh and for debugging issues.

3. **Visualization with Kiali**:

   a. **Key process**: Kiali uses the collected telemetry data to provide a graphical representation of the service mesh architecture and the health of services, showing relationships and traffic flows between services.

   b. **Importance**: This helps in visualizing the entire mesh structure, identifying potential issues like unhealthy services or overloaded connections, and understanding the real-time operational state.

4. **Trace with Jaeger**:

   a. **Key process**: Jaeger processes trace data to provide insights into the complete journey of requests as they travel across different services within the mesh, helping to pinpoint performance bottlenecks.

   b. **Importance**: Enables detailed request tracing and performance analysis, which is critical for optimizing service interactions and improving overall efficiency.

5. **Monitor with Prometheus**:

   a. **Key process**: Prometheus scrapes metrics from Istio, Envoy, and potentially other sources within the cluster, storing these metrics for historical analysis and alerting.

   b. **Importance**: Acts as the central repository for all monitoring data, enabling historical performance tracking and the basis for alerting on anomalies or operational thresholds being breached.

6. **Integrate with Grafana**:

   a. **Key process**: Grafana integrates with Prometheus to create visual dashboards that monitor service mesh health and performance, correlate metrics from different sources, and define alerts based on predefined thresholds.

   b. **Importance**: Provides powerful visualization tools for easy monitoring and proactive management of the service mesh, ensuring quick response to potential issues.

These processes collectively enhance the ability to manage, troubleshoot, and optimize a service mesh, ensuring its health, performance, and security through detailed data analysis and robust visualization tools.

By leveraging these advanced monitoring tools and techniques alongside Istio, organizations can not only monitor their service mesh more effectively but also enhance their ability to respond to dynamic conditions and ensure compliance with regulatory standards. These capabilities are critical for maintaining a robust, secure, and highly available service infrastructure in complex microservices environments.

Cost optimization in GKE

Optimizing costs in GKE is crucial for ensuring efficient resource utilization and avoiding unnecessary cloud spending. This section delves into various strategies and best practices to help you manage your GKE costs effectively.

Strategies for cost-effective GKE deployments

Deploying and managing Kubernetes clusters in GKE can become costly without proper optimization strategies. By focusing on rightsizing resources, you can avoid overprovisioning and ensure that your workloads only use what they need, minimizing unnecessary expenses. This section covers key strategies for optimizing GKE deployments, focusing on resource management practices that maximize efficiency, such as accurately defining resource requests and limits, and selecting the appropriate machine types to meet workload demands. These practices help maintain performance while keeping costs under control.

Table 10.3 indicates the potential cost reduction:

Resource type	Optimization strategy	Potential cost reduction
Pod resource allocation	Matching resource requests and limits using Kubernetes HPA	Up to 20% by preventing over-provisioning and idle resources
Compute instances	Choosing the right machine type, utilizing preemptible VMs and spot VMs	Up to 80% with preemptible VMs and spot instances
Pod resource adjustment	Utilizing VPA for auto-adjusting Pod resources	Up to 50% by optimizing Pod resource consumption
Resource usage analysis	Analyzing historical resource usage with Stackdriver Monitoring	Up to 30% by rightsizing based on usage patterns
Pod scheduling	Using node selectors, node affinity / anti-affinity, and dedicated node pools	Up to 25% by optimizing node utilization

***Table 10.3**: Optimization strategies for GKE*

Leveraging Kubernetes features

Kubernetes provides a wide range of features designed to optimize resource usage, ensure high availability, and improve scalability. By making the most of these features, you can streamline your workloads and minimize costs, while maintaining performance. The following are some key features to leverage for enhanced efficiency:

- **Horizontal Pod Autoscaler (HPA)**: Implement HPA to automatically scale the number of Pods in a deployment based on predefined metrics like CPU or memory usage. This ensures your workloads have adequate resources during peak times while scaling down during low traffic periods, optimizing resource usage and cost.

- **Cluster Autoscaler**: Utilize Cluster Autoscaler to automatically adjust the number of nodes in your GKE cluster based on the overall resource demands of your workloads. This ensures you have enough nodes to handle your workload while not running unnecessary nodes that incur costs.

- **Blue-green deployments**: Implement blue-green deployments for zero-downtime updates. This approach involves deploying a new version of your application alongside the existing one and then switching traffic over once the new version is ready. This minimizes resource usage during deployments.

- **Readiness and liveness probes**: Utilize Kubernetes readiness and liveness probes to ensure only healthy Pods receive traffic. Readiness probes determine if a Pod is ready to serve requests, while liveness probes monitor Pod health and restart unhealthy Pods. This prevents resource wastage on unhealthy Pods.

- **Pod Disruption Budget (PDB)**: Implement PDB to define acceptable Pod disruption levels during scaling events. This helps maintain application availability while allowing the cluster to optimize resource utilization by potentially evicting less critical Pods.

- **GKE network policies**: Utilizing network policies to control traffic flow at the IP address or port level can help prevent unwanted traffic, reducing potential costs associated with data transfer and improving security.

Storage optimization

Optimizing storage in Kubernetes is essential for reducing costs while ensuring the availability and performance of your applications. By selecting the right storage options and implementing efficient data management practices, you can maximize resource utilization and minimize waste. Here are some strategies for optimizing storage in your Kubernetes environment:

- **Storage classes**: Highlight different storage classes in GKE, such as standard, premium (SSD), and cold storage. Choose the appropriate class based on access frequency and performance requirements, which can significantly impact cost.
- **Storage lifecycle policies**: Implement automated policies to downgrade or delete data that is infrequently accessed. For instance, transitioning older data to colder storage or automatically deleting unused volumes can lead to substantial savings.
- **Deduplication and compression**: Utilize data deduplication and compression techniques to reduce the storage footprint. This is especially effective for organizations with large volumes of redundant data.

You can refer to the *GCP storage and database products* section in *Chapter 2, Overview of Google Cloud Platform* for a detailed comparison of various storage options.

Network optimization

Optimizing network performance and cost in GKE is crucial for delivering fast, reliable applications while managing expenses. By fine-tuning traffic management, load balancing, and content delivery, you can ensure that your network resources are used efficiently and securely. Here are some key practices for optimizing your Kubernetes network:

- **Efficient use of network policies**: Implement GKE network policies to control and limit Pod-to-Pod communication within your Kubernetes cluster, reducing unnecessary network traffic and enhancing security.
- **Choose the right network service tier**: Decide between Google Cloud's standard and premium network service tiers. Premium offers optimized performance through Google's global network, while standard may reduce costs with slightly lower performance, suitable for less critical applications.
- **Implement Google Cloud CDN for GKE**: Use Google Cloud CDN to cache static content from your GKE applications closer to users, significantly reducing latency and network load, which can help in lowering costs.
- **Optimization of load balancing**: Deploy Google Cloud load balancing to efficiently distribute client requests across multiple server instances. This not only ensures high availability and fault tolerance but also optimizes cost by improving the usage efficiency of underlying resources.
- **Traffic management with global and regional load balancing**: Utilize global load balancing when you have users in different geographic locations to route traffic to the nearest regional endpoint, reducing latency and inter-region data transfer costs. For localized traffic, regional load balancing can be more cost-effective.
- **Monitoring and logging network traffic**: Leverage Google Cloud's operations suite to monitor, log, and analyze network traffic patterns. Insights gained can be used to further optimize traffic flows and identify redundant or wasteful practices that can be curtailed to save costs.

Table 10.4 tabulates various optimization strategies for GKE storage and network layers:

Resource type	Optimization strategy	Potential cost reduction
Storage	• Using storage classes based on access frequency and performance requirements (standard, SSD, cold storage) • Implement storage lifecycle policies • Data deduplication and compression to reduce storage footprint	Up to 60%
Network	• Implement network policies to limit unnecessary traffic and enhance security • Choose the right network service tier (Standard vs Premium) for cost vs performance balance • Use GCP CDN for caching static content • Optimize load balancing for efficient distribution • Utilize global and regional load balancing to reduce latency and data transfer costs • Monitor and log network traffic to identify and reduce wasteful practices	Up to 50%

***Table 10.4**: Optimization strategies*

GKE application or service-specific controls

Managing costs across different Google Cloud services requires a focused approach tailored to each service's usage patterns. By fine-tuning settings and optimizing configurations, you can achieve cost-effective performance while avoiding unexpected charges. Here are key strategies for controlling costs in GKE and related Google Cloud services:

1. **BigQuery cost management**

    a. **BigQuery maximum bytes billed setting**: Use the maximum bytes billed setting to cap the amount of data processed by a query in BigQuery, preventing unexpected high charges. Encourage setting cost controls at the project or dataset level to manage expenses proactively.

    b. **Partitioning and clustering**: Optimize query costs and performance by partitioning and clustering tables. Partitioning tables by date or other fields can reduce the amount of data scanned by queries, and clustering sorts data based on the contents of one or more columns, which can lead to more efficient data retrieval.

    c. **Efficient streaming inserts**: For real-time data analysis in BigQuery, optimize streaming inserts to minimize costs associated with high-volume data ingestion. Batching data before sending it to BigQuery can reduce the number of API calls and associated costs.

d. **Flex slots**: Utilize BigQuery's Flex Slots for flexible, short-term capacity for high-demand periods, which can be more cost-effective than committing to long-term slots.

2. **Cloud SQL cost management**

   a. **Instance sizing**: Regularly review the performance and capacity metrics to right size your instances, ensuring you are not paying for unused capacity.

   b. **On-demand vs. reserved pricing**: Evaluate the cost benefits of reserved instances, which can offer significant savings over on-demand pricing if you can commit to long-term usage.

   c. **Automated backup and maintenance windows**: Configure backups and maintenance to occur during off-peak hours to minimize the impact on performance (where costs could increase due to longer processing times).

3. **Google App Engine optimization**

   a. **Scaling settings**: Optimize the automatic scaling configuration by setting appropriate instance classes and tuning the number of instances based on demand to prevent over-provisioning.

   b. **Environment selection**: Choose the standard environment for applications with variable traffic and where instances can be started and stopped quickly to save costs, as opposed to the flexible environment which is suited for applications with consistent performance demands.

4. **Google Cloud functions cost control**

   a. **Execution time and memory allocation**: Monitor and adjust the function's memory allocation to fit its workload to avoid excess charges. Optimize the code to reduce execution time.

   b. **Trigger management**: Minimize invocations by optimizing the event triggers that start the functions, reducing unnecessary executions.

Broader GCP cost-optimization best practices

To optimize costs across the broader GCP, it is essential to leverage various pricing models, optimize data management, and gain visibility into your cloud usage. Implementing the right practices can significantly reduce expenses while maintaining the performance and scalability of your applications. Here are some key strategies for cost optimization in GCP:

- **Commitment-based discounts**:

  - **Committed use discounts (CUDs)**: Purchase CUDs for compute resources like CPUs and memory for a term of one or three years to enjoy lower prices compared to on-demand rates.
  - **Sustained use discounts (SUDs)**: Automatically get discounted rates for VMs that run for a significant portion of the billing month. This can be particularly beneficial for continuous operations without upfront commitment.

- **Data management**:
  - **Data transfer optimization**: Utilize Google's network and choose the correct locations for your data storage and compute resources to minimize data transfer costs, especially out of GCP (egress).
  - **Lifecycle policies in cloud storage**: Implement policies to move older data to Nearline, Coldline, or Archive storage classes based on the access patterns to reduce storage costs significantly.

- **Monitoring and visibility**:
  - **Google Cloud's operations suite (formerly Stackdriver)**: Utilize this suite for monitoring, logging, and diagnostics. Keeping an eye on performance metrics can help identify inefficient resource usage and unnecessary costs.
  - **Cost management tools**: Regular use of the GCP Pricing Calculator, Billing Reports, and Budget Alerts to forecast, track, and control costs.

- **Efficiency in use of APIs**:
  - **Optimizing API calls**: Reduce costs by optimizing the number of API calls. Cache results where possible and adjust the frequency of calls according to the necessity.

Container image management

Efficient management of container images is critical for reducing storage and bandwidth costs in Kubernetes environments. By optimizing image sizes and leveraging caching, you can significantly improve deployment speed and minimize resource usage. Here are some best practices for managing container images in GKE:

- **Optimize container image size**: Smaller container images take less storage space and download faster, reducing storage and bandwidth costs. Techniques like multi-stage builds and image layering can help minimize image size.
- **Implement container image caching**: Utilize container image registries with built-in caching mechanisms to store and reuse previously pulled images. This reduces network traffic and download costs when redeploying containers.

- **GKE container registry**: Leverage GKE Container Registry for storing and managing your container images within GCP. This eliminates egress charges when deploying images within the same region and simplifies image management.

Tools and techniques for monitoring and reducing costs

Now let us look at the tools and techniques to reduce monitoring costs:

- **Enable GKE usage metering**: Activate GKE usage metering to gain detailed insights into your GKE resource consumption and associated costs. This data allows you to identify areas for optimization and track cost trends over time.

  Monitoring and analyzing key metrics in GKE are crucial for identifying inefficiencies and optimizing costs. By tracking resource usage, network traffic, and node pool utilization, you can make informed decisions to improve resource allocation and reduce unnecessary expenses. The following are some important metrics to monitor:

GKE usage reporting metrics	Description
Resource consumption (CPU, memory, storage)	Identifies underutilized or overprovisioned resources.
Network traffic	Helps identify unexpected network egress charges.
Node pool utilization	Provides insights into node pool scaling efficiency.

Table 10.5: Key Metrics for GKE Usage Reporting

- **Utilize GCP cost management tools**: Explore tools like GCP billing and cost management to analyse your overall GCP spend, including GKE costs. These tools provide detailed breakdowns, cost allocation capabilities, and cost anomaly detection.
- **Set up cost alerts**: Configure cost alerts to notify you when GKE spending exceeds predefined thresholds. This enables proactive cost management and helps you prevent unexpected charges.
- **Cost allocation tags**: Utilize cost allocation tags to associate specific costs with different workloads, teams, or environments. This granular cost attribution helps identify cost ownership and optimize spending across different business units.
- **Forecasting and budgeting**: Leverage GCP cost management tools for cost forecasting and budgeting. These tools can predict future costs based on historical trends and help you set spending limits for your GKE clusters.

- **Recommender for GKE**: Explore the recommender for GKE, a machine learning powered service that recommends cost-saving actions based on your GKE cluster configuration and resource usage. This can identify potential optimization opportunities you might have missed.

Figure 10.8 shows a simple flowchart to visualize the process of monitoring and reducing costs. The flowchart starts with enable GKE usage metering and follows through steps like analysing resource consumption, identifying optimization opportunities, implementing cost-saving actions, and monitoring cost trends:

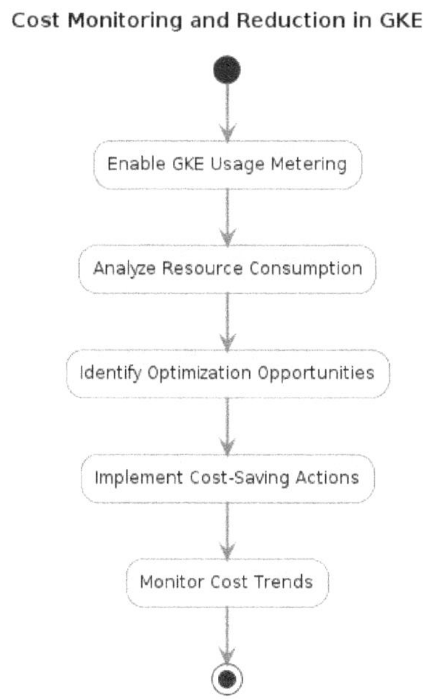

***Figure 10.8**: Process of cost monitoring and reduction*

This flowchart in *Figure 10.8* captures the essential steps:

1. **Enable GKE usage metering**:
    - **Process**: Activate usage metering in GKE to track resource usage data across the cluster.
    - **Importance**: Provides the necessary data foundation for analysing how resources are consumed, which is essential for cost management.
2. **Analyse resource consumption**:
    - **Process**: Examine the collected data to understand where and how resources are being used within the GKE cluster.
    - **Importance**: Critical for identifying high-cost areas and potential inefficiencies in resource usage.

3. **Identify optimization opportunities**:
   - **Process**: Based on the analysis, pinpoint opportunities where operations can be optimized to save costs, such as scaling down resources or switching to more cost-effective options.
   - **Importance**: Helps to systematically reduce unnecessary spending and optimize resource allocation.
4. **Implement cost-saving actions**:
   - **Process**: Take concrete actions based on identified opportunities to reduce expenses, such as adjusting resource allocations, turning off idle resources, or applying more cost-effective configurations.
   - **Importance**: Directly impacts the cost efficiency of the GKE operations, leading to potential savings.
5. **Monitor cost trends**:
   - **Process**: Continuously monitor the cost trends to assess the effectiveness of the implemented actions and adjust strategies as necessary.
   - **Importance**: Ensures sustained cost optimization and helps to adapt to changes in usage patterns or pricing models.

This flowchart outlines a cyclical process where after implementing cost-saving measures, continuous monitoring ensures that the strategies remain effective, and adjustments are made in response to new data or changing conditions.

Scenarios and solutions

Now let us look at few scenarios and their solutions along with examples:

- **Scenario**: Weekend/off-hour scaling: You have a workload that experiences significantly lower traffic during weekends or off-hours.

  Solution: Implement scheduled scaling with Kubernetes HPA or Cluster Autoscaler. Configure these tools to automatically scale down the number of Pods or nodes during low-traffic periods. This can significantly reduce compute costs associated with underutilized resources.

  Example: An e-commerce platform might see a surge in traffic during weekdays but minimal activity on weekends. By implementing scheduled scaling, they can reduce resource utilization and associated costs during off-peak hours.

- **Scenario**: Microservice refactoring: You have a monolithic application that can be broken down into smaller, independent microservices.

Solution: Refactor your application into microservices. This allows for independent scaling of each service based on its specific resource requirements. You can deploy resource-intensive services on more powerful machines while running less-demanding services on cost-effective machine types.

Example: A content management system might consist of separate services for user management, content creation, and content delivery. By decoupling these services, you can scale the content delivery service during peak traffic times without affecting the cost of the user management service.

- **Scenario**: Serverless for short-lived tasks: You have workloads that consist of short-lived tasks, such as image processing or data analysis jobs.

  Solution: Utilize Google Cloud functions, a serverless offering for running stateless functions. You only pay for the time your function executes, which can be significantly more cost-effective compared to running dedicated VMs for short-lived tasks.

  Example: A company might use cloud functions for processing customer feedback forms or triggering automated security scans. Since these tasks are short-lived and infrequent, serverless functions offer a cost-efficient solution.

- **Scenario**: Idle resource reclamation: You have long-running Pods that experience periods of inactivity.

  Solution: Implement liveness probes with Kubernetes to monitor Pod health. If a Pod remains inactive for a predefined period, the probe triggers a Pod restart. This helps ensure that only actively running Pods are consuming resources and minimizes wasted costs on idle resources.

  Example: A batch processing application might have Pods that remain inactive between processing jobs. By implementing liveness probes, you can ensure these Pods are restarted when needed without incurring unnecessary costs during idle periods.

- **Scenario**: Cost-effective logging and monitoring: Your GKE cluster generates a significant amount of log data that is stored in expensive storage classes.

  Solution: Implement log filtering and aggregation strategies to capture only relevant logs. Consider using cost-effective storage classes like cloud storage archive for long-term log storage. Additionally, explore tools like Stackdriver Logging with advanced filtering and retention policies to optimize log storage costs.

Example: An application might generate detailed debug logs during development. By filtering these logs during production deployments and storing them in cheaper storage classes, you can significantly reduce logging-related costs.

Conclusion

In the exploration of *Advanced Topics in GKE*, we have covered a wide spectrum of features and strategies that significantly enhance the management, deployment, and optimization of applications. From multi-cluster configurations to cost-efficient practices, GKE provides a robust platform that adapts to the complexities of modern software needs. Tools such as the VPA, Cluster Autoscaler, and advanced network policies not only streamline operations but also optimize both performance and costs. The integration of service meshes like Istio, expands capabilities further by offering sophisticated traffic management and enhanced security. Leveraging these advanced functionalities, you ensure that GKE environments are not only scalable and resilient but also aligned with the best practices of cloud computing. By embracing these technologies and strategies, organizations can expect to achieve higher efficiency, better resource management, and improved security, positioning themselves to thrive in an increasingly digital landscape.

Multiple choice questions

1. **Which GKE service is optimal for handling temporary external access to a service for development or testing purposes?**
   a. ClusterIP
   b. NodePort
   c. LoadBalancer
   d. ExternalName
2. **What feature should be implemented to manage and optimize resource provisioning and scaling automatically in GKE?**
   a. GKE Autopilot
   b. Vertical Pod Autoscaler
   c. Cluster Autoscaler
   d. Horizontal Pod Autoscaler
3. **Which component is essential for distributing Pods across different zones to enhance fault tolerance in GKE?**
   a. Node Affinity
   b. Pod Security Policies

c. Topology Spread Constraints
d. Taints and Tolerations.

4. **Which GKE feature provides detailed insights into resource consumption and assists in cost optimization?**
    a. GKE Usage Metering
    b. Network Traffic Monitoring
    c. Cloud Monitoring
    d. Resource Quotas

5. **What GKE capability ensures that only healthy Pods receive traffic and unhealthy ones are restarted or repaired?**
    a. Auto-scaling
    b. Readiness and Liveness Probes
    c. Health Checks
    d. Deployment strategies

Answer key

1.	b.
2.	a.
3.	c.
4.	a.
5.	b.

Index

D

H

I

K

www.ingramcontent.com/pod-product-compliance
Lightning Source LLC
LaVergne TN
LVHW080808011026
849160LV00015B/1564
* 9 7 8 9 3 6 5 8 9 7 1 3 5 *